Withdrawn

FOR THE
GOOD
OF THE
GAME

ROBERT EVANS
EDWARD BELLION

© 2000, 2002 Youth Sports Publishing Inc.

For questions or comments contact Youth Sports Publishing • 7349 Canoga Avenue, Canoga Park, CA 91303 • (800) 297-6386

ISBN 1-889424-08-0
Printed in the United States of America

TABLE OF CONTENTS

PREFACE

Why read this book?

We have long wanted to write a book about refereeing, if for no other reason than to put down on paper most of what we know, what we have learned from others, and what we have discovered for ourselves. It comes naturally to both of us, for we have spent our professional lives learning things about the world—its geology (RE); its biochemistry (EB)—and then putting what we have learned down in print for others to share. We have both enjoyed the satisfaction of publishing a lot of work that we did, but we admit that the satisfaction and enjoyment were largely our own. Neither of us was under any illusion that what we said in the pages of a scientific journal was going to change the world, improve someone's life or cause people to get excited. The reality is that we contributed knowledge that only the tiniest fraction of the population would ever know about.

But all the time that we were engaged in scientific research, we were also playing, coaching and refereeing soccer, the most popular sport in the world. Just as we observed and noted down geological features and biochemical phenomena, we observed and noted down events in soccer matches in many different countries. Just as we conducted research into geological interactions that changed the landscape, or into chemical interactions that affected microbial life, we also studied the interactions that affected the relationship between player and referee. We studied and researched methods to improve the way that a referee performed on the field, and we put those methods into practice in youth, amateur, professional and international soccer matches.

So now that we sit down to write a book about refereeing soccer, we are aware that this is not the same as writing about science. Some of our biochemical and geological work may change the way a few other scientists do things, but writing a book about refereeing soccer is different from writing about science. We are talking about an activity that engages thousands upon thousands of men and women every week in every country in the world. And that makes us realize that what we set down in these pages may give some enjoyment and satisfaction to many thousands of soccer enthusiasts in this country and elsewhere. The satisfaction and pleasure are still originally our own, but we know that if we do this well, we may be able to share the satisfaction and enjoyment with many others—far more people than those who got excited about our scientific research!

That's all well and good, but why should you—the reader, the referee—care? Or more to the point, why should you read this book, and what are you going to get out of it?

1. *You will share the experience of two referees with thousands of matches between them at all levels of the game—from youth games on the local park, to international matches between world-class teams in front of crowds in the many tens of thousands.*

2. *You will learn something new, not only about refereeing, but about the game itself, how it is played and what is important. No matter what games you referee every week, whether they be youth, amateur, professional or international matches, there is something here for you.*

3. *You will become acquainted with techniques of refereeing you have never heard about. Some we learned from others, many we devised ourselves, but no matter what their origin was, we used them whenever we stepped onto the field, and we proved their value.*

4. And finally, we hope that what you read here will change your attitude to the sport, cause you to think more deeply about what you do every week as you officiate, and ultimately make you a better and more satisfied referee. That is what the sport needs!

Robert Evans
Edward Bellion

About the Authors

Robert Evans, Ph.D.

Robert Evans grew up near Swansea in South Wales, and played soccer in the local youth and senior leagues. Graduating from the University of Nottingham with a degree in Geology, he emigrated to Canada to pursue his studies, earning a Master of Science degree at Dalhousie University in Halifax, Nova Scotia. It was in Nova Scotia that he first studied the Laws of the Game, and qualified as a referee while recuperating from a broken leg suffered while playing -- for the local brewery -- in the Nova Scotia league. Then followed a Ph.D. in Geology at the University of Kansas, where he was the player-coach of the university soccer team.

Bob (right) with his friend Kafka

He arrived in Texas in 1969 to work as a research geologist for Mobil, and was convinced that his soccer career was over. But within weeks he was invited to be player-coach of the eventual league champions. He was also only the fifth registered referee in the city, and soon started teaching others, including a likely young lad named Edward Bellion. But for one more season they played together on the eventual State Champions of Texas, but then Bob gave up playing and coaching to concentrate on the fine art of refereeing, encouraged by the appearance of the North American Soccer league and its obvious need for officials.

He worked in the NASL from 1972 until the demise of the league in 1985. Bob joined the International Panel in 1979, and refereed preliminary games in the World Cup and the Olympic Competition. Travelling overseas throughout Central America and three times to Asia for tournaments, he refereed teams from every confederation in FIFA. He retired early from the list to accept the position of National Director of Referee Instruction for the USSF in 1988. In 1992 he became the first American to be appointed a FIFA Referee Instructor. Currently he is a National Referee Instructor and National Referee Assessor.

Continued on next page

In 1996 he left Mobil, returned to school, completing the Science Communication program at U.C. Santa Cruz, and now freelances as a science writer from his home in northern California. In addition to his scientific papers in national and international journals, he has published articles in major popular magazines and websites, including Smithsonian, New Scientist, Exploratorium, WebMD and others. He is the author of "Manual for Linesmen" and "Teaching Offside" (with Tony Waiters), and dozens of articles on refereeing. Bob is the recipient of the Eddie Pearson Award, and the Bill Scofield Award of the United States Soccer Federation.

Married to the writer Jane Ellen Stevens, he has two daughters, Rhiannon, a flight attendant in Atlanta with Delta Airlines, and Siân, a surgeon in Merced, California.

Edward Bellion, Ph.D.

Edward Bellion was born and raised in Liverpool, England. He was educated in the local school system, after which he attended the University of Leeds where he received a B.Sc.(Hons) in Chemistry and a Ph.D. in Biochemistry. Following a research fellowship at the University of Minnesota, he accepted a faculty position in 1970 at the University of Texas at Arlington, where he is currently Professor of Biochemistry. His research interests lie in the biochemistry of growth of microorganisms in which he has authored over 30 scientific articles in national and international professional journals, and has lectured on his work at various International Scientific Symposia in Europe, Asia and North America.

Ed Bellion

His lifelong interest in soccer was ignited as a boy in Liverpool, a well-known soccer hotbed. He pursued his interest by playing and later coaching at the amateur level, and became a referee shortly after arriving in Texas. He was subsequently appointed to the North American Soccer League, first as linesman, and then as referee. His NASL career reached its zenith when he refereed the 1983 Soccer Bowl (NASL Championship game) in Vancouver between Tulsa and Toronto. He also refereed the US Open Cup Final and the American Soccer League Final.

He was a member of the International Panel of Referees of FIFA for ten years (1980-89). He refereed matches in World Cup and Olympic preliminary rounds and was selected for the 1983 World Youth Championships in Mexico, the 1984 Los Angeles Olympics as well as several other international tournaments in Europe, Asia and Latin America. He is a former USSF National Referee Instructor and has conducted numerous clinics for referees and referee instructors throughout the USA. A current USSF National Referee Assessor, he also holds a USSF coaching "C" badge.

He is married to Vickey, has three grown children (Rebecca, Sarah and Brandon) and has lived in Grapevine, Texas for the past 16 years.

ACKNOWLEDGEMENTS

Almost four hundred years ago, John Donne wrote a sentence that even today, we see over and over again. His words survive because they are so true: "No man is an island, entire of itself." We are both aware that we succeeded as referees because of the teachings, the patience, the observations of others who had paced the fields before us. It is our pleasure to acknowledge some of them.

Our introduction to the difference between amateur and professional soccer came from the words of the late Eddie Pearson, Director of Officials for the early years we spent in the NASL. He laid the foundation upon which our careers were built, but that foundation was strengthened by many of the referees in the league at that time: Paul Avis; Peter T. Johnson; Roger Schott; Toros Kibritjian; John Davies; Larry King; John DiSalvatore; all of whom shared their experience willingly, and gave us advice patiently. We benefitted too from the careful observations of assessors: Harry Baldwin; Don Byron; Pat Smith; Hans Struffenegger.

But we must mention that were it not for the intervention of several special individuals who maintained their faith in us after we had slipped from grace, we would not have had professional or international careers, nor would we have written this book. Don Byron, Roger Schott and Harry Baldwin fought on our behalf, Keith Walker made a wise decision, and Tom Webb endorsed it. We will always be grateful to them.

For several years when we were all refereeing in the NASL, our friend Manuel Ortiz, Sr. spent hours and hours talking with us about his matches and ours as we analysed incident after incident in a way that only those who shared the experience can do. We could not have wished for a more understanding and informed colleague to help us develop as officials, and we recommend to all referees -- as we have done in the book -- that they find someone similar to talk things over with throughout their careers.

Finally we give our thanks to all the referees and linesmen we worked with, and to the legion of coaches whose comments, both positive and negative, gave us food for thought that ultimately nourished us to become better officials. No man is an island, indeed.

1

A BOOK AS MENTOR

*I can easier teach twenty....than be one of the
twenty to follow mine own teaching.*

William Shakespeare,
Merchant of Venice

A tale of two errors.

We saw the following two incidents recently, and choose to describe them because they appear to us to be typical of the kind of refereeing errors that we see in game and after game. On any given weekend you will see the same sort of thing going on in fields all over this country, and, we dare say, in fields in many other countries. Now, if you are the kind of referee who carefully examines his work, and thinks about decisions you have made, you may well admit that you too have made these same mistakes. That is good, for it is the first step towards your improvement as a referee. We wish to state right at the start that *our*

> *"...our intention in this book is to guide you to a level of understanding and knowledge that will prevent you from making these errors."*

intention in this book is to guide you a level of understanding and knowledge that will prevent you making these errors again. We want this book to be your mentor throughout your progress as a soccer referee.

IN THIS CHAPTER:

- *Two errors to convince you that something is wrong*
- *Themes that run through this work*
- *This book can be your mentor....at all levels of the game*

1. The red card in a cup final.

For sixty minutes the teams had been battling for supremacy, but neither side had scored. The one player most likely to create a scoring chance was being snuffed out of the game by tight marking, which if it didn't succeed in stripping him of the ball, slowed him down enough that a nearby covering player would win it. Until the sixtieth minute it seemed as though a goal-less draw was inevitable.

Then one player went in for a tackle in a way that is perfectly described in the new wording of the laws: recklessly. He made contact with his opponent's legs, brought him to the ground hard, and then added insult to injury by making a comment and pushing him slightly as he was on the ground. Seeking to break loose from the man who had fouled him, the aggrieved opponent jumped up and swung his right arm behind him and in the direction of the other player. His hand made slight contact with the fouler, who reacted with all the theatrics of a man who had been punched by Muhammad Ali.

The referee responded in the way that 99% of all referees respond: he sent off the player who had swung his arm, and did nothing to the player who committed the foul. All right, you say, what's the purpose of this story? Justice was done; the retaliator was sent off. How was this an error on the referee's part?

The reaction of the players—and the spectators, many of whom were knowledgeable observers of the game—gave us a clue that not everyone agreed with the referee's decision. The team-mates of the player sent off were incensed at the decision. Not just because they were a man down, but because they had seen the whole incident and knew that justice, in fact, had *not* been done. In their analysis, the man who provoked the whole incident had got away with a crime, whereas the victim of that crime had himself been punished. Their reaction was immediate and understandable: for the remainder of the game, the man who committed the foul was subjected to rough justice that took the form of hard tackles and fouls every time he touched the ball. They were acting according to the code of the player; if the referee won't administer justice, we *will.*

This went on until the coach of the harassed fouler took him off to save him from further punishment, and to prevent the possibility of the referee taking action against him if *he* retaliated to the attention he was getting. But the story doesn't end there, for the following week the two teams played again. It doesn't take a genius to figure out what happened next. Yes! The original fouler came in for more "special treatment" at the hands (or feet) of his opponents, and the referee in that match had to issue six cautions to keep things under control. All because the first incident had not been handled justly, and the players knew it.

Later in the book we will deal with this kind of situation in more detail, but we can state now that there are several lessons to be learned from incidents like this. First, the referee must administer *justice,* not merely punishment. Second, the players have a sense of what is right and wrong, and referees would do well to **understand how players think.** Third, players give out information in many ways, and one of the skills you need as a referee is the ability **to notice what the players are saying,** even when they aren't uttering a word. You can't afford to ignore a good source of information.

2. The offside that wasn't.

The second error involves that old favorite—offside. After a corner-kick, a player ran back on the left wing, gathered the ball and passed it forward along the ground to a teammate (Figure 1-1). Note that another forward (Y) is in an offside position in the penalty-area perhaps thirty-five yards from the original pass, and twenty yards further downfield than the player (G) who took the pass. The recipient of the ball played it at first touch towards the goal-line, beating the nearby defender (D) who had come across to challenge him (Figure 1-2). Sprinting after the ball, the forward G reached it near the goal-line and pulled the ball back into the corner of the goal-

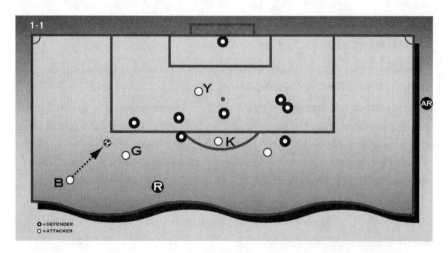

area for the forward Y to head across the goal. His teammate (K) ran in behind the covering defenders and scored (Figure 1-3). But hardly had the celebration begun, when the goal was cancelled....

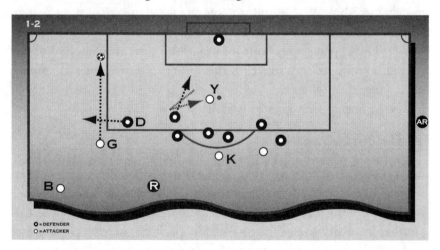

As the ball was first passed forward to G, the linesman had raised his flag because Y was in an offside position. The referee didn't see it. When play went on, and K scored off Y's headed pass, the linesman raised and waved his flag again because he thought that Y should be penalized for his original offside position as G played the ball forward. The referee came over for a discussion and called back a perfectly good goal.

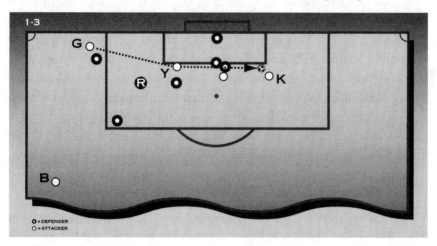

We devote a complete chapter to situations involving offside and not offside, but as we just did for the incident of retaliation, we can state that there are several important things about this offside call. First (except under very rare circumstances), as long as *a player keeps possession of the ball (as player G did), none of his team-mates in an offside position can be penalized* for interfering with play. Second, *linesmen must hesitate before flagging for offside* until they are sure that the ball is going to go to the player who was in an offside position, or until they are sure he is involved in the play. In this case, player Y was never involved when he was in an offside position, nor did he gain an advantage from that offside position. By the time he did become involved, play had passed him, he was behind the ball and could not be offside. Third, we must pay heed to FIFA's exhortation to encourage attacking play; *we must not cancel perfectly good goals unless we are certain that the offside player was actively involved.*

What are we to make of these two errors?

We look at these incidents from the perspective of more than ninety years between us of playing, coaching and refereeing. If you count the years when as little lads we went to watch the local professional club— Liverpool (EB); Swansea (RE)—play in the Football League in England and Wales, you can say we have about one hundred years of being steeped in the lore of this great game. As players we have been on the receiving end of decisions—like these two—we thought were unfair; as coaches we have been frustrated by them; as spectators we have yelled about them; and both of us as referees have made them, regretted them, and now hope to continue to teach others to avoid them. Unfortunately, these kinds of mistakes are all-too-common.

What we didn't say as we described the incidents is what matches they were from. These incidents involved clubs from the Premiership in England, possibly the toughest league in the world. The referees were members of a small group of fewer than twenty who referee those games, and one of the men was an international official. What that means to us is that there is something fundamentally wrong with the way we prepare referees, here and overseas. If the highest-ranking referees in a country with the toughest league in the world make mistakes that are not mistakes of inexperience, but of knowledge of the game, and attitude to the players in it, then we think it is fair to say that *something is wrong.*

What is wrong is that many, *many referees have been taught to make the very decisions that we have just condemned.* They have been taught the traditional ideas from fifty years past, in a game that is not anything like the one that the world played half-a-century ago. In these pages we will write more than once that *the game is changing, and we, the referees, must change with it.* In the case of the offside decision in the paragraphs above, the persistent adage "better a dodgy offside than a dodgy goal"—the mantra of too many referees—must be laid to rest.

We believe that if you read, understand and take to heart what is written in this book, you will begin to make some changes, that you will not make those same errors we have just described—or if you have been making them, you will make them no more. For this book is aimed at new referees, at experienced referees and even referees in professional leagues. There is something in these pages for everyone who officiates.

Be aware though, that this is not a book about the laws of the game. Only two laws—Law 11 and Law 12—are examined in detail. It is a volume about "what to do on the field". It is about *technique*. It contains advice that will help you referee more comfortably, more effectively, with far less conflict with players and coaches. The advice we hand out comes from our own experience at all levels of the game, from new ideas that we devised and tested, and from the teachings of many very good referees and instructors who taught us. Last but not least, we have learned from the mistakes of others we have watched, just as many referees may have learned from watching the mistakes that we made.

Themes that run through this book.

Number 1: Remembering whose game this is.

If your immediate reaction is to say that this is a statement of the obvious, we urge you to conduct a little experiment next time you are in a gathering of referees. Listen to the conversations, the telling of "war stories", the comments that referees make about their recent games. Count the number of times a referee talks about "...*my* game last week...", or says "...in *my* games, I..." Many referees talk as though they are the central figure in the match, that everything revolves around the person with the whistle. Count the number of times you hear a referee describe with great glee what he or she did to take care of a troublesome player: "care" as in "deal with", "punish", "control". So many of the conversations you hear at referee meetings revolve around an "us and them" attitude, that you have to wonder whether punishment and discipline applied to players are the sole reasons for officiating!

After you have finished counting those incidents, then try to record how many referees talk about what they did to protect a star player, or what techniques they used to ensure that an excitable player stayed in control and on the field. Listen to the rare descriptions of a game that went without incident, that ebbed and flowed back and forth, that brought enormous pleasure to players and spectators alike. Count the referees who describe the pleasure they had in refereeing great players, referees who talk about games only in positive terms, and you will find that they are in the minority among their colleagues. *There is a culture of confrontation in officiating, a culture that must change for the benefit of the sport.*

The game is never for the benefit of the referee. *In youth and amateur soccer the game is for the players*, for their enjoyment. The activities of the referee must ensure that the game is a pleasure for all the participants, that no one gets hurt, and that no single player or coach spoil the enjoyment of all the others. *In professional soccer, the game is for the enjoyment of the spectators*, and the activities of the referee should be designed to guarantee that the paying customers get their money's worth in watching players play, watching a game without unnecessary interruptions. And since the professional game is the livelihood of players (and coaches), the referee must make sure that the professionals are protected from those who might injure them. Let us say it again: Although we derive a lot of pleasure from officiating, *no game is solely for the benefit of the referee.*

Number 2: Preparation is an essential part of refereeing successfully.

By "preparation", we don't mean shining your shoes, or counting your whistles, or making sure you have a coin and a set of flags. Yes, you have to do all those things, and your uniform must be clean and your face should be scrubbed. But there is much more, for what we mean by preparation is the work you have to do that gives you as much knowledge about the match and the teams and the players as you can gather before the game starts. And once the match starts, you should be gathering more information that may be useful as the game goes on. Great referees are never caught by surprise.

No professional activity in any sphere of life can be conducted successfully without preparation. No lawyer goes into court without knowledge of what he or she is about to face, nor does a pilot start any flight without knowing the route, the weather, the potential hazards. Yet we are amazed time and time again to hear referees say something like: "I didn't know that one more caution would mean he was suspended," or "How was I to know that they had kicked the hell out of each other three weeks ago?" We devote an entire chapter to the subject of preparation, because it is a big failing of referees at all levels of the game. And, we are happy to know that twenty years after we (and others) routinely prepared in the way that we advocate in this book, the Major League Soccer administration—after years of rejecting the concept, as did some North American Soccer League administrators before them—is recommending that its officials do the same thing.

Number 3: Do the least that is necessary to control a situation.

After all our years in the sport, we have concluded that it is easy to control a soccer match. All you have to do is flash some cards early in the proceedings, then dump a few trouble-makers, and everything will be peaceful and quiet from then on. But that is not good refereeing, because it *ignores the responsibility you have for trying to keep all the players on the field from start to finish*. And that is a sometimes difficult art.

It involves knowing when you have to be tough and when you can be sensitive and understanding. It means knowing what is the least you have to do to manage things. Is it a lecture, a public dressing-down of a player? Or is it merely a stern look or a shake of the head? Can you manage things with a wisecrack, or does the situation demand the formality of a caution? But whatever it is, **you must do no more than is required.** We examine this in the chapters on game control. In our days as players and coaches, we both experienced and witnessed black-shirted dictatorships. We believe passionately that the game does not need heavy-handed referees, although we recognize that there are a lot of them about! We hope this book will change them.

Number 4: Good refereeing is a combination of empathy and strength.

On more than one occasion we have had to wonder whether the referees we were watching actually *liked* what they were doing. They seemed to be quarreling with the players constantly. They never smiled. Anything that a player did was open to the suspicion that it was some form of trickery designed to cheat the opposition and fool the officials. Did those referees—and there are many of that ilk—have any *empathy* for the people who were playing the game?

We would go so far as to say that if you don't *have* that empathy, if you don't *enjoy* watching enthusiastic youths play the game, if you can't appreciate the skill of senior amateur players, and how they suffer when they are brutalized by less skilful opponents, then perhaps you should take up another activity on weekends. When you, the referee, can understand all the emotions that pour out of the players in this great sport—the excitement of scoring, the joy that comes with triumph, the frustration at injustice, the pain of injury or humiliation, the anger, sorrow, and abject misery that accompany last-minute defeats, and the pride that drives an effort that may be hopeless—then, and only then, will you become a referee that the players are glad to see walk onto *their* field. ***Let your empathy show, and the players will welcome you week after week.***

But with that empathy for the players, there comes a responsibility to the game itself. The referee is on the field, quite simply, to see that the game is played fairly, more-or-less in accordance with the laws of the sport, and to ensure that cheating does not decide the result of the match. And that means that you have to be able to make tough decisions against players for whom you may have a great deal of empathy. But whether you like the player or not, you have to be able to penalize him or take disciplinary action against him if the need arises for the sake of the game. You must ***develop the hardened will to do what is right***, irrespective of whether the decision will excite controversy, irrespective of whether it is politic to take stern action. Home or away, you have to be able to give the penalty-kick when the defender fouls the forward on the eighteen-yard line, even if the week before you saw a senior referee "diplomatically" move the ball outside the area, or worse, give an indirect free kick.

How to use this book.

Although we have put the chapters in what we believe to be a logical order, it is not necessary for a reader to go through the work chapter-by-chapter from start to finish. Instead we suggest that you use this book as a continual reference, looking at different chapters on different occasions as your need dictates. Keep it handy and refer to it often, particularly when a problem or question comes up that we might address. We do not expect anyone to read straight through the book in one or two sittings as you might do with a gripping novel; nor do we expect you to remember everything that is written here. As a matter of fact, you may need to read some of the individual chapters more than once before our ideas become clear. We hope we reassure you by saying that when we were learning, it sometimes took us several seasons to fully understand! Nothing will make us happier than if over time this book will become well-worn and dog-eared, a much-used source of both inspiration and perspiration.

Final words of introduction.

We intend this book to be your mentor, to provide you with guidance in dealing with problems on the field, or situations you may never have seen. We also hope it will introduce you to some new techniques that will improve your effectiveness as a referee. Certainly they worked for us, at whatever level we were refereeing! And if you apply them correctly and wisely, we know they will work for you also. Our ultimate goal, and our ultimate satisfaction is to know that we may affect the thinking of some referees and to make them more comfortable and more accurate in what they do.

And now, to the accompaniment of a fanfare of trumpets, we state our philosophy:

> *We believe that well-trained and courageous referees are essential custodians of the integrity of the game.*

If you agree with us, then read on. This is a book for you!

2

SETTING THE TONE
FOR THE GAME

*Next to enjoying ourselves, the next greatest pleasure consists
in preventing others from enjoying themselves, or,
more generally, in the acquisition of power.*

Bertrand Russell,
British philosopher

The youth and amateur game.

1. My name means "power" and I'm in charge.

It was Sunday afternoon at Samuell-Grand Park in Dallas, Texas.
Two teams of players ran about, kicking balls around, warming up
for the three o'clock match in the Dallas Soccer Association Senior
League, Division I. Spectators—perhaps a couple of hundred—sat
on the bleachers or stood on the touchlines. Some wandered across
the street to get another beer, others surreptitiously passed a bottle
of wine around, pouring the contents into paper cups that hid the
contents from any park
police who might happen by.
Children yelled and
screamed, their mothers
fussing over them. And if
you wandered by this park,
you would hear the chatter
of many languages filling
your ears, for this was the
festive and friendly
atmosphere of every Sunday

IN THIS CHAPTER:

- *In amateur soccer, the referee's task is to ensure the pleasure of the players*
- *The referee as colleague, not enemy*
- *What to say and what not to say before a match*
- *In professional soccer, the referee has a responsibility to the spectators as well as to the players*

in the season, with immigrant and native players coming out for an afternoon's pleasure. It was a scene repeated in a hundred cities in dozens of states all across the country every weekend.

Soon a small figure strode out towards the center circle, blowing his whistle to get the attention of the players. Impatient now with their lackadaisical response to his first imperious blast, he blew again, adding some shouts to various players to get over to where he stood. Finally a couple of men strolled over, one in green-and-white, the other in the dark blue of Scotland, and a conversation of sorts started.

"What's up, ref? Ya need a couple of linesmen?"

"Yes, I do. Get them over here so I can instruct them. And call your players, I want to talk to them and inspect the boots."

"Sure, ref. Hey, lads, come over 'ere. The bloke wants a word."

More players wandered over, chatting and laughing, thoroughly enjoying the prospect of a good match on a nice afternoon, and the thought of a few beers and hamburgers afterwards. Then things began to get serious.

"Alright, gentlemen, please be quiet and listen. My name is Kraft, and I'm the referee today. You can call me 'ref' or 'Mr. Kraft', OK? During the match, I want only the captain to talk to me. Is that understood? And I will listen only if you speak in English. Now, here is what I expect of you. You must retire ten yards at every free kick or else I'll book the player who doesn't get back. And anyone who questions what I am doing will also get booked. Is that clear? I had a lot of dissent last week, and I'm not going to take it today. I'm not paid to take a lot of crap from players, so keep your opinions to yourselves and we'll get along fine! Now, line up in two rows, and kneel down so that I can inspect the studs on your boots."

The referee put both his hands behind his back, strutting back and forth while waiting for the players to comply with his instructions. By now the joking and laughing among the players had stopped, replaced by muttering.

"What's going on with this guy?"

"Who does he think he is?"

"Well, I'm not kneeling down for any bloody referee..."

After a lot of argument between the referee and the players, some of whom removed their boots and held them up defiantly in the official's face, everyone assumed their position for the start of play, and the game got under way in an atmosphere of conflict.

2. My name means "fair" and I'm here to enjoy myself.

A few miles away at Fair Oaks park in that same city, two under-18 teams warmed up for their three o'clock kick-off. A few minutes before the hour, the referee and his two young linesmen walked out to the middle of the field, where they stood for a few moments chatting. A few of the players from both teams noticed them and called the captains.

"Hey, Chris, John, we're ready to go!"

The captains of the teams came over, and the referee held out his hand.

"Hi! I'm Fred Ehrlich, and these are my two linesmen, Jack Justice and Megan Right. Oh, hello, Chris! It's nice to see you again. A couple of weeks ago, wasn't it?"

Turning to the other captain, he said the same sort of thing and introduced the linesmen again. Then he looked at both captains and said:

"Didn't you guys play each other three or four weeks ago? Three-three, wasn't it? And I heard it was a great game! Well, when I got this assignment I was hoping we would have a game just like that one. Anyway, it's a beautiful day for a game of soccer, so you guys enjoy yourselves, OK? And if you want something explaining, just ask. I'll be glad to help you. OK, Chris, you're the visitor, so call it in the air."

Then as the players changed ends for the kick-off, the referee wandered about among the players, having a word here, shaking a hand there. He was looking at the boots of all the players, noting the brand name of the shoes they were wearing. The ground was hard, and all of them were wearing molded soles with short studs. Then he noticed a player with a small cast on his arm, so he casually strolled over to him and asked him how it got hurt.

"I broke a bone in my wrist falling off a trampoline."

"You'd better stick to soccer, then! How's it feeling now? Getting better?"

"Yeah, ref, another couple of weeks, and it'll be out of the cast."

"Good. You're John, right? Can I feel the cast?"

The player held out his arm, and the referee ran his hand along the padding over the cast.

"Well, you be careful, John. I wouldn't want you to hurt yourself more. And no backflips if you score, OK?"

"Oh, sure, ref! I'm pretty careful with it."

The linesmen were checking the nets, and both of them were tying up some loose parts. While that was going on, the referee walked over to the coach of one of the teams and introduced himself. He knew of him from watching him play in the senior league over a couple of years. After the exchange of names, he said:

"Listen, Dick, I'm going to let these fellers play as much as I can, but if you think I'm letting it get a bit loose, let me know and I'll tighten things up for the players, OK? And also if you think I'm calling it too tight. By the way, there's been a bit of bother with substitutions lately, so the league wants us to clean it up. Could you help me with that? I'm going to ask that you make sure the sub stays off until the player has left the field. Great! Have a good game."

That done, the referee looked around, saw the opposing coach talking to some players in the middle of the field, and walked to him. He then had essentially the same conversation as he had just had with the other coach, patted him on the shoulder and went to the center circle as everybody lined up for the kick-off. By this time, the linesmen had taken up their positions on the touchline, their flags were unfurled, and so with a short peep of the whistle, the referee started the match.

Who is the game for?

Any discerning reader can see the difference in attitude between these two referees, and any reader who has played the game will have experienced both of them. In a few paragraphs further on, we analyze what was wrong and what was right with these two referees, and draw some conclusions about how *the referee can create a pleasant atmosphere* for the players in all the games he or she referees. But first, let us consider the underlying purpose of youth and amateur soccer, or youth and amateur sport generally.

By most general definitions, a sport is a recreational activity indulged in for exercise or pleasure—*pleasure* being the operative word. Introduce competition into the definition, and the pleasure will include winning and trying to win, even though you know that victory is not always possible. But in amateur sport, although winning is important to the competitors, it is not the only purpose of participating, for if it were, the number of amateur athletes would diminish rapidly! No, there is great *pleasure in merely playing*.

Now when we put a coach and a referee into this equation of sport-for-pleasure, things become a little more complicated. The coach is supposed to train the players, to teach them how to play the game, and to organize their various talents into a scheme that will produce victory. Unfortunately, however, many—if not most—coaches are seeking *vicarious* pleasure from producing winning teams, as though they were playing in the games themselves. The victories becomes *their* victories, not the players'.

The referee is needed in the game, not as a trainer or an educator, but because it is a competition, with certain rules to follow, rules that players break simply because they are trying to win. Making sure that the contest is played according to the laws of the game, that neither team gains unfairly by cheating or by bullying—these are important functions of any official. *But they are not the only ones.* Equally important is the task of ensuring that the *players derive pleasure from the experience of playing.* But in their zeal to be in control, to show that they have the power over the players, too many referees forget this important function. They forget *that they are there to provide a service to the players.* And because so many referees forget that they are there to provide a service, we chose to start this chapter with the comment by Bertrand Russell, that there is pleasure (for some referees) in the acquisition of power.

The two referees on a Dallas Sunday.

Mr. Kraft:

From the moment he walked onto the field, his one concern was to display his authority. He wanted the players to come to him *immediately.* He wanted to *instruct* the volunteer linesmen, he wanted to talk to *all* the players. He told them that only the captain was to talk to him, and then *only in English.* Imagine how a new immigrant would feel upon hearing that from a referee in the country whose history is one of welcoming immigrants. And why can't a player talk to the referee? Is the official an Emperor-God, separate from normal mortals?

Then our good Mr. Kraft gave the players a lecture about the laws of the game and misconduct, as though they don't know anything about the game. And like the parent who says to a child going out to play: "Now, be good!" this referee *assumed* that the players were going to get out of line. Worse yet, the terms he used—"…a lot of crap from players…" and "…keep your opinions to yourself…" are aggressive and inflammatory. What a way to start a relationship!

Finally, he piled indignity upon insult by having the players *kneel* in front of him. What a symbol of power and subservience the referee sought from the players, and how right some of them were to refuse to submit!

Mr. Ehrlich:

This man knew what his role in the game should be. From the outset he was personable and friendly to everyone he met, especially to those he had met before. He was informal, using first-names, and remembering them from a previous match. He made it clear that he was on the field to enjoy himself, to share a pleasant experience with the young players. He chose his words carefully: "…if you want something…just ask…" and "I'll be glad to help you."

He showed that he knew something about the teams; he knew of their match against each other recently. The players weren't mere names and numbers to him; he was interested in what they had done, and expressed pleasure about it. And he made it clear that this business of refereeing was something he looked forward to and enjoyed.

Notice the way that he did the boot inspection: casually, unobtrusively, by wandering around among the players. Knowing the major brand-names by their symbols and flashes on the footwear, he knew that they would conform to the laws (the major manufacturers always clear their products through FIFA), and since this was a day for molded soles, not screw-in studs, he knew that he did not have to inspect every single shoe. No, he took care of his responsibilities without interfering with the players' warm-up and their socializing before the kick-off.

Then the cast on the player's arm. Because of treatment they may have received from referees who are sticklers for the letter of the laws, some players get a little defensive about wearing a cast, worrying about how the official might react. In this case the referee was gentle, kindly and thoughtful, but nevertheless he did what he was supposed to do: inspect the cast for safety. And he topped it off with a little humor to make the player comfortable.

With the coaches, he adopted a cooperative approach, *asking for their assistance*, not only with something that they were responsible for managing (substitutions), but also with something that belonged exclusively to the referee (what to call and what not to call). He offered to tighten things up "...*for the players*..." He knew that most people respond positively to requests for assistance, and by inviting the coaches to help him, he was trying to ensure that there would be complete cooperation between coach and referee throughout the game, cooperation for the sake of the players. The referee and coach are colleagues, not enemies, and they are colleagues for the benefit of the game and players.

What to say and do, and what not to say and do before the match:

1. Never make threats.

There should be no "If you do this, then I'm going to do such-and-such..." The players know what is allowed and what is not allowed, and in the case where they are so young that they do not have much idea about the laws, what good does it do to give them a lecture? Threats do nothing except create unpleasantness. And with the little kids, it is the coach's job to teach them, not yours. Don't waste time trying to do it.

LETTING THEM KNOW WHO'S BOSS.....
(A TRUE STORY)

When the players saw who the referee was going to be, they were more than a little upset, because they had seen him in their under-16 match the week before, and to say the least, things had not gone well. The three captains of their team came to the center circle at the beginning of the proceedings, but one of them could not hide his displeasure. He stood to one side and stared at the referee during the toss of the coin and throughout the referee's big speech, which went on and on about what was going to happen, and what the players shouldn't do, and so forth.

All six or seven of the captains from both teams fidgeted back and forth while the referee droned on and on. Suddenly the referee noticed the one player scowling at him in disgust, and stared back at him. For a boy of sixteen, this was a test of burgeoning manhood, and so he put his hands on his hips and continue to fix the referee with his withering gaze. He won the battle, but lost the war, because after a short while, the referee averted his eyes, pulled out a yellow card, cautioned the player for "ungentle-manly conduct", and later wrote in the report that it was for "...a go-to-Hell look..."!

2. Don't spell out your expectations of the players.

They know what is required of them; they've played the game before. Imagine how you would feel if one of the captains said to you before the kick-off: "Right, ref, here's what we want from you. We expect you to deal firmly with any bugger who starts kicking, and to book anyone who holds up one of our free-kicks. And when we start a fast breakaway, we want you to be right there with us to see everything that's going on, all right? And one more thing: if there's a foul by a defender on the eighteen yard line, I don't want you to chicken out and give an indirect free-kick, or pull the ball outside the penalty-area. That cheat last week screwed us! We're paying you forty bucks for this game, and we expect you to earn it, OK?"

We are sure that you would be surprised and a little distressed at someone (especially a player) telling you so aggressively what to do, when you feel confident that you already know what to do. *Well, believe it or not, the players feel the same way.*

3. Let the players know that refereeing is a pleasure for you.

Smile. Be friendly. Look as though you are enjoying yourself, and if you are *not* enjoying yourself, give up refereeing.

4. Show an interest in the players.

Before the match, learn something about the teams. Find out the names of the captains and coaches, and use them when you introduce yourself. This should be part of your preparation for each match (see Chapter 3).

The professional game.

Amateur games are sport and recreation; professional games are business and entertainment. The referee must therefore approach the professional game differently from the way he looks at a youth or amateur match. And note also that this applies to college games where admission is charged, for those athletes are supported (paid) by the college, just as the professionals are paid by the team they play for.

Professional soccer is also a multi-million dollar business venture. Soon will come the day when a single match between two top clubs like Liverpool and Manchester United may earn tens of millions of dollars in pay-per-view from around the world. Yes, a single match! In the section above, we stressed that the referee should focus his attention on providing a pleasant experience *for the players.* In professional games, although consideration of the players is important—especially the protecting of them from foul play and injury—consideration of the spectators' enjoyment, the investments of the shareholders in the teams, and the huge sums of money paid by the electronic media to broadcast the games to additional millions must not be overlooked. The referee has a definite role to play in the business and the entertainment. He himself is *not* an entertainer, and never should be, but he *does* ensure that the stars are allowed to entertain the public.

The referee in the eyes of the players.

The players and coaches are professionals working at their livelihood, and all around the world, many of them resent the fact that referees are not full-time professionals themselves. They may be scornful of these "amateurs" coming out on weekends to mess up the game for the *real* professionals. Since we are aware of that attitude even before going into a game, what can we do to improve our image in their eyes, to give them some reassurance that this week, they will be refereed by a pro?

Be as professional as possible—look as though you know what you are doing!

Come with us now to a professional match, and see how our deportment shows that we know what we are doing. We'll give you warnings and comments periodically, dressed in **[parentheses like these].**

Two hours before the game, we show up at the stadium for our first contact with representatives of the clubs. We present an impeccable appearance in our blazers and slacks (or equivalent for our female colleagues), shirt and tie. **[At this moment, there could be a crew filming "puff pieces" for showing during the televised match.]** We are well groomed, and our shoes are clean. Head held high, we stride through the entrance and find our way to the locker-room. **[You could encounter anyone from either of the clubs, and you can be sure that they will notice any sign of lack of confidence.]**

Almost immediately, after a few pleasantries among ourselves, we walk out to inspect the pitch, and now Beware! **[The first piece of work we do, so let's get it right!]** It is at this point that we will first come under scrutiny. We have to check everything, but we don't have to march about, striding out the measurements, looking like some goose-stepping militarists intent upon finding flaws. We simply stroll around and on the pitch and casually take note of the markings, nets, flags etc. We know that if we stand on the goal-line six yards outside the post, the edge of the goal-areas will line up with the edge of the center-circle, showing that the field is properly squared off. Over the years we have calibrated our normal walking pace with the formal (and too obvious) strides of one yard, so that even when we appear to be casual, we are actually taking fairly accurate measurements. If all is well, we will seek out the groundskeeper, who will probably be watching from some vantage point, and compliment him on the condition and markings of the pitch. And if we find an item that needs to be corrected, [**careful now…!**] we will *ask* for assistance. No orders, no instructions, just a simple request, without criticism, will be enough to get the problem resolved. The "Can you help us to make this better?" approach gets more results than does the "You must do this!" plan. You will be more welcome the next time you go there, and you might even be able to suggest mowing the grass in rows at right angles to the touchline, so that the lie of the grass will make it easier for the assistant referee to stay aligned with offside.

Once back inside the referee will be faced with many situations in which his mettle will be tested. He must be sure to deal with them in a smooth, well-organized fashion and firmly, so as not to appear weak and a pushover, easily manipulated. It is at this time that coaches may attempt to test the referee, and to set up the psychological contest that might continue into the real game. The referee has a lot to deal with: approval of the match balls [**inspect them all**]; checking on jersey colors [**for those occasions when there is a quick deflection into touch, don't forget the socks**]; inspection of players' shoes [**don't just look; feel the studs**]; paperwork such as team line-ups and substitution cards [**read everything completely and carefully**]. Each one of these events provides an opportunity for the creative coach or club manager to find out what kind of a person you are, or to upset you, to distract you from the real job on the field.

IF YOU CAN'T RAISE THE GOALS,
LOWER THE PITCH!

We were assigned to a CONCACAF region World Cup elimination match in Haiti. During the inspection of the facilities, which takes place the day before the match in such competitions, we noticed that the cross-bars on both goals were too low, only 7 feet 3 inches above the ground. Using our best high school French we pointed this out to the officials of the Haitian FA and asked them for their help in solving the problem for FIFA. Then there followed much animated discussion among themselves in French and Creole about how to correct the problem. Some wanted to insert a new section into the posts, some suggested new goals entirely, and probably several other ideas were thrown into the mix also. The obvious one of raising the goals was not possible because they had been firmly fixed into the ground with a large base of cement. We stood to one side observing all this, more than a little amused.

Then someone barked out some commands, and several dozen groundstaff and assistants sprung to action with shovels and wheelbarrows. We were amazed to find that they had decided that if they couldn't raise the goals, they would lower the ground in the vicinity of the goals, and remove all the excess material! Apparently, the problem came about because they were in the habit of spreading sand in the goalmouths as part of the maintenance procedures, and over the years this had built up so much that it had the effect of lowering the height of the goals. We left them to it, as it clearly was going to take several hours to remove all the excess sand. When we returned the following day, everything was in order. The goals were eight feet high, suitable for the World Cup match. We had asked for their help, and they gave it. They actually thanked us for pointing out the error, as they had not realized the cumulative effects of the sanding process.

The purpose of the psychological contest is to disrupt your concentration so that they can take advantage of you during the game. Also, a confrontation over some minor matter before the game may lead you to subconsciously allow certain things in their favor during play, so that in your mind they will not then be able to claim that the disagreement caused you to be biased against them. [**You find that the use of subtle manipulation is hard to believe?**] Consider the following examples.

John Sewell, the coach of St. Louis in the NASL, came into the dressing-room with his teamsheet and substitution cards to get them signed by a referee (RE) he had never seen before in a league match. The official looked over the papers as Sewell stood close by, smiling affably. On the sheet seven subs were listed, two more than was legal [**this is a big deal**]. You know, and we know, and Sewell knew that he had included too many names, but the question is: Why? Well, it is possible that the referee might not notice [**that's why we say to read everything carefully**] and would simply sign the sheet. That being the case, Sewell would have an advantage and could choose from seven rather than five substitutes. Furthermore, the coach would know that the referee was either incompetent [**not knowing the regulations**], unobservant [**then what is he going to miss in the match?**], or too intimidated early in his career to do something about it [**in which case the coach might have other tricks to pull out of his sleeve**]. But in this case the referee pointed out the error, refusing to sign the teamsheet until it was amended or replaced. But then Sewell [**not giving up so easily on a chance to manipulate a referee**] applied another test—he told the referee to simply cross out two of the names! [**This was a trap.**] Aware of the game being played, and calling the coach's bluff, the referee took out his pen and (out loud) pretended that he was going to cross out the names of the two best players among the substitutes [**the game was up!**] Foiled, John Sewell quickly took back the teamsheet, left the dressing room and, smiling affably once again, returned shortly afterwards with a correct version.

In another case, a visiting coach complained to the referee (EB) about the markings and said the halfway line was not in the center, thereby making one half of the pitch longer than the other, and providing a possible disadvantage to one of the teams, namely his. But the referee had already done his pitch inspection, knew that there was no error, and guessed a con game was going on [**the purpose: to raise doubts in the referee's mind, and to make him do the inspection over.**] Wise to the game going on, the referee simply suggested that a coach of his obvious talents should be able to tell his team how to play on such a pitch and could turn the error to his advantage. Now playing a game of his own, the referee then *promised not to tell the other team about the coach's amazing discovery!*

THE REAL STAR AND A REAL REFEREE

While on international duty, one of us (EB) had a notable confrontation with a famous coach. The story illustrates how the referee *must* know all the regulations, must have the *confidence* to enforce them, and must not retreat in the company of the famous, however admirable they may be.

The Uruguayan international defender Jose Santamaria had a distinguished playing career with Real Madrid during its heyday in the 1950's and '60's. He had become the head coach of the Spanish national team, playing some friendly matches on a goodwill tour of Mexico prior to the 1982 World Cup to be held in Spain. He came to the locker room to ask if all of his reserve players could sit on the bench, even if they were not suited up to play. The referee told him no, as it was strictly against international rules, and if that were not enough, several FIFA dignitaries were present at the match, and they would be sure to notice.

A loud and animated argument then broke out in Spanish. Santamaria challenged the decision by arguing with the two linesmen from Paraguay and Argentina, and with the Mexican fourth official, who, unlike his colleagues from South America, was fluently bilingual. The referee took no part in the uproar, and could follow only portions of the "discussion". After several minutes of this, however, the referee stood up, and with the aid of translation, simply told the coach that although he remembered and admired him as a great player, the rules were there to be followed, the decision had been made and would not be changed. He then requested that Santamaria honor this as the gentleman the referee knew him to be, and preserve his respect in the eyes of the officials.

Santamaria had found out what he wished to learn: the referee knew his business, and would not hesitate to do his job. The coach immediately apologized, thanked everyone, and left.

We have heard complaints about the size of the goals, which would adversely affect one team because they always shoot for the top corners of the goal [**and always hit them, right?**] We have been told that the other team has a bad disciplinary record and need to be stopped by a tough referee [**here's an opportunity to turn the tables, if your records show that both teams are about equal in yellow cards and red cards**]. These stratagems are all designed to disrupt the referee's concentration and confidence, to raise that little demon—Self-doubt—nothing more. The referee should be prepared for, and not taken in by these games. You should instead simply deal with each issue in a calm, firm and dignified manner, with a touch of humor if you can, just to let the coach know that you know what is going on. The mental toughness that enables the referee to remain unshaken comes from having confidence in his own abilities and knowledge [**make sure _you have_ that knowledge!**], and in having the composure to handle these issues without getting flustered, angry or confrontational. Once you lose that composure, you lose the mental game that is played before the real game. The coach will gain the psychological upper hand.

No matter how you may feel about a particular coach or manager, he should always be treated with respect, but without familiarity. He should be addressed as "Mr. Newman" (or whoever) no matter how well you know him. Many of them will have been former players, some with distinguished careers. Others will have been coaches for many years, probably in the league before you were, and they have all earned and are entitled to some degree of respect in the game. Respect the player and the man, but don't be over-awed or starstruck in their presence [**and never ask for an autograph!**].

All too soon the time comes to leave the friendly confines of the locker room and to enter the field, where the real work will be done. But before you leave, you need to make sure that you look the part of the professional you are: clean, pressed shirt and shorts, badge on straight, shoes clean and polished, laces in good order, hair (if you still have any left) neatly combed. You have a few words with your assistants, expressing your confidence in them, then walk outside with a confident demeanor [**even though the teams by now** have a sense that you know what you are about, they will still be watching], towards the field entrance, to take your place in the line up of participants. Now is a good time to exchange pleasantries with the players; not extensive chats but a just few words of greeting and best wishes.

"YOU ARE IN MEXICO NOW!"

With our friend and colleague Angelo Bratsis, we travelled to Monterrey to officiate a match between Mexico and Argentina shortly before the World Cup in Mexico in 1986. Both teams were going to the finals with high expectations of success; justified expectations, as it turned out, for Argentina won the World Cup that year, and Mexico reached the quarter-finals, their best-ever showing. The stadium was full and noisy, the spectators fuelled by more beer than had ever been sold for any match in this place. The anticipation of a good match created great excitement.

As the players and officials were about to enter the field, the referee (EB) noticed that there was a color conflict with the Mexican goalkeeper's shirt. Just as the referee asked the 'keeper to change it, a voice—in very good English— spoke from near the back of the line of players, "You are in Mexico now, remember!" Curious to see who said this, the referee took advantage of a short delay to casually stroll towards the sound of the voice, and there recognized a Mexican player, Javier Aguirre, who had played for Los Angeles in the NASL, in different games that all three of us had refereed. As players from both sides looked on to see what would happen now, Aguirre looked a little apprehensive, but the referee simply smiled and replied, "Yes, it is a pleasure to be here, and to see you again, Javier." Aguirre smiled back, the other players relaxed, and were no problems throughout a hard-fought match that ended 1-1 after a splendid soccer spectacle.

As in the amateur game, the occasion of the coin toss is a good opportunity to show your personality and attitude [**no threatening speeches!**] The coin toss is no place for the referee to give instructions

DID THE REFEREES BEST GEORGE?

In the professional league, with players from all over the world, we always tried to use a coin that was familiar to the captain of the visiting team, who usually makes the call. A little research and a little trouble was all it took to ensure that a pleasant chat would take place between referee and player. The captain would ask about the coin (from his own country) and a short conversation would take place, reducing the tension between player and official. We found that the few remarks exchanged about the captain's home made things easier later in the match when things got tough.

This caused a humorous incident when within a week or two of each other, we both refereed games in which the captain was George Best, a world-class player but a bit of a handful sometimes. We both used an obsolete English coin known as a threepenny bit, which we knew he would recognize. This 12-sided brass coin is unique and instantly recognizable to anyone of our generation. In the first match, George had had a few words with the first of us (RE) about some decision or other. He was unhappy because his team was on a losing streak, and he wasn't scoring. In the second game, refereed by EB, Best was again unhappy and complaining. "Referee," he said, "you screwed us a fortnight ago, and now you are screwing us again today." "But I didn't referee you two weeks ago," came the perplexed reply. "Don't try that one on me," said George, "I'd know that damned threepenny bit anywhere!" So much for being recognized personally by players.

to professional players. They don't want them, won't pay any attention anyway, and generally resent listening to them. All you need to say are simple words of encouragement to have a good game and good luck. Then wait for them to get organized, clear the practice balls from the pitch, check with your linesmen and blow the whistle to start the game.

By doing this, you set the stage for a game to be played, in which the players view you also as a professional, there to do a competent job to the best of your ability without being too overbearing. They know that since you are a referee, you almost certainly were not good enough as a player to become a professional, and therefore are in someway inferior to them, as far as understanding of the game is concerned. Nevertheless, the referee can influence the way the players think about him by exhibiting a professionalism that cannot be denied.

One area that will immediately indicate your degree of professionalism is your fitness. As discussed in detail in Chapter 16, if you are not fit enough to keep up and be in the correct positions, the players will be justified in believing that you don't know what you are doing. But if you are sharp, well positioned and clearly fit, that lets the players know that at least you have been putting in the effort to get in good condition, and they can relate directly to that. This then will give them extra confidence in your decision-making ability.

Professional games must start on time. Nothing upsets spectators more than a delay. They have paid their money to see the match, they been waiting for quite some time, hours in some cases, for the game to start. Furthermore, many have been eagerly anticipating this match for several days, and for many it is the high point of their week. A delay is not acceptable. In an amateur game a few minutes delay doesn't really amount to much, (although the referee should never be the cause of it), but it is significant in a professional game, and especially when there is live television coverage.

Respect the players' time in the moments before the action starts. Almost all players are nervous, for a lot rides on every game. Not simply the result of the match, but money in bonuses for the players. Attendance may depend upon the home team winning. Near the end of the season, one goal may be the difference between entering the play-offs or trying again next year. Younger players or less-experienced players are often more-than-nervous. They may be scared: of the pressure, the opinions of their peers, the attitude of the coach, the reaction of the crowd, their first experience playing against a top-class opponent. They don't need a referee intruding into their thoughts and their space in these tense moments. Your demeanor, your professionalism will reassure them that they are in good hands. You have set the right atmosphere with everything you did before the game. *Your skill before the game will allow them to show theirs when the whistle blows.*

THAT DIDN'T LAST LONG...!

In the late seventies the NASL management, following the lead of the Football League in England, decided to clamp down on misconduct, gamesmanship (the polite word for cheating), encroachment, dissent and thuggery. Each club was given a list of what action would be taken by the referee in the event of this or that misconduct, and the referee was required to go into both dressing-rooms before the kick-off to make sure that the players knew what was going to happen. In the meeting, the referee would make a speech, listing the behaviors and the punishments. One of them was the deliberate handball to break up a dangerous attack. It would be a yellow card at first occurrence.

The players were horrified. A yellow card for some of their favorite activities? The league was destroying cherished traditions of the professional game. The players were not happy, but they had no choice: comply or suffer the consequences. Early in the season in Philadelphia, one of the senior referees went into the dressing-rooms, gave the speech, and then started the match. In the first few minutes of the game, the visitors attacked, a midfield player chipping a beautiful ball over the two Philadelphia center-backs and into the path of a winger flying by his defender on the left. The captain, one of the central defenders, had no choice. He jumped up, pulled the ball down with his hand to eliminate the danger, and waited for the yellow card that was surely to come as a result of the new "get tough" policy. The referee blew his whistle, ran to the site of the free kick, but said nothing and did nothing to the defender. Throughout the stadium there was a momentary hush as the players prepared for the kick. In that moment of quiet, the captain's voice could be heard clearly: "Well, that policy didn't last long, did it?"

The lesson? Never make a threat you don't mean to carry out. Better yet, don't make any threats at all!

Of course, it is now well accepted that players should and will be cautioned for deliberate handball, and in the case of handling that prevents a goal being scored, the player must be sent off.

3

PREPARATION FOR THE GAME

It is through the regulations we impose upon ourselves that we are happy; in a word, through freely accepted discipline, whether in soccer or in the study of science.

Alain
French philosopher

Disciplined professionals prepare for everything.

A lawyer enters the courtroom knowing as much as he can about the case, the client, the judge, the person he represents, and the likely tactics of his opponent. He enters the courtroom *prepared.* A competent lawyer could not imagine proceeding with a case without **having all the information he could gather**, for to proceed without it would invite failure and humiliation.

Before she steps into the cockpit, a pilot checks her airplane, makes a call to get the weather on the route of the flight, calculates the take-off and landing distance for her destination, assesses the amount of fuel that she will use, and plans her route and alternate airfields in case she is diverted. She takes to the air prepared. A pilot would not dream of taking off without *having all the information she could gather* about what she was going to face in flight, for to proceed without it would invite serious danger.

IN THIS CHAPTER:

- *All professionals prepare for their task*
- *Examples of how it pays off and helps your control*
- *Learning all you can about the teams and the players*

The same attitude—gathering all the necessary information ahead of time—is characteristic of every profession and of every activity requiring knowledge and skill. Every profession, that is, except one: soccer refereeing. For reasons we do not understand, *most referees, at all levels of the game, imagine that they can just step onto the field and referee.* They believe that they do not need any more information than the names of the teams. We do not agree, and in the pages that follow, we plan to convince you, and show you how it will help your refereeing. Elsewhere in the book we describe incident after incident that could have been avoided if the referee had been prepared. So if this chapter doesn't convince you, keep reading; there's more to come on this subject!

Examples of where knowledge can help the referee:

A corner-kick: Was there handball, and did the ball go in?

The score was 1-1, and only a few minutes of play remained. In desperation a defender, under heavy challenge, played the ball across his goal-line for a corner on the left. The referee had followed play and was close to the top corner of the penalty-area. As the defenders got themselves organized, the attacking number 8 retrieved the ball as his teammate number 7 ran across the penalty-area, apparently to take the kick. As the number 8 placed the ball, he kicked it short to his teammate, who quickly turned and played a beautiful inswinging cross to the near post. A crowd of players went up for the ball, there was a great shout from the attackers (Handball!), the ball bounced and bobbled towards the goal line in the face of the goal, and then was hooked away by a defender. There was no signal from the assistant referee, whose view was obstructed by the crowd of players.

As the referee turned to follow play upfield for the counter-attack, he was chased by three forwards shouting at him about the handball and the possible goal. The shouting continued, and the referee had no choice but to stop play to deal with the chorus. He explained that he had seen no handball in the crowd of players, and since he had received no signal from his assistant, he believed that the ball had not gone in the goal. Eventually, before the fuss died down, two of the attackers were booked, and one, who had committed the unpardonable sin of accusing the referee's mother of grossly immoral conduct, was ordered off the field.

All this could have been avoided if the referee had done his homework before the game. This team often used the number 7 to take or be involved in corner-kicks on the left. Since he was a right-footed player, the ball was inevitably going to swing into the goalmouth. The referee should have known this, and as soon as he saw the number 7 crossing over to the left side of the field, he should have sprinted down to the goal-line close to the post, to be in the best position for what was almost surely coming next. Had he been close to the action, close to the supposed (or real) infraction, he could have made a credible decision about both the supposed infringement or the goal or no-goal. And in all probability, there would have been no huge outburst of dissent and abusive language from the disappointed attackers.

Later in this chapter, we will tell you how the referee could have had the information he needed.

Control using a caution from a previous match?

It was the semi-final of the cup competition, and the game was tough. The star forward from one of the teams was having trouble breaking through the last line of defenders, and as the game progressed, he became more and more frustrated. Not for the first time that season, he started questioning the skills of the referee: a comment here, a snide remark behind his back there, a loud laugh after his opponents were awarded a free-kick.

At a break in the action, the observant spectator might have seen the referee sauntering over to the dissenting player, and ever-so-casually pass a remark as he walked by him. The player's face registered surprise and shock that all could see, but from that moment on, he spoke not a single word to the official. At the end of the match, that same player walked to the referee and shook his hand. The referee smiled the beatific smile of one sure of his place in Heaven, and returned the player's thanks.

At the end of the game, one of the assistant referees, himself the subject of this player's derision several weeks before, expressed his admiration for the referee's ability to handle the notorious orator.

"What did you say to the number 9 that caused him to shut up?" he asked.

"Ah!" said the referee, "I reminded him that he already had two cautions in this competition, and that a third would mean that he couldn't play in the cup final two weeks from now. I simply asked him if he wanted to be responsible for his team playing the cup final without their top goal-scorer. I didn't have to wait for an answer. I knew what it would be!"

"But how did you know all that?" exclaimed the assistant referee.

"Well," said the referee, "I once read a book by two former FIFA Referees and they recommended getting a lot of information before the game. I took their advice, tried it out in various matches, and there you are. As you can see, it worked!" (Now read the sidebar and contrast our imaginary scene with a real one from a big match in England.)

The magical moving ball no more!

The free-kick was twenty yards from the goal-line, at the top edge of the penalty-area on the right. The referee moved the wall back ten yards, and started back-pedaling to a position off to the left. As he was moving and blowing his whistle for the restart, there came a great shout of anger from the left side of the penalty-area. Most referees would instinctively and quickly turn to look, to satisfy themselves that there was nothing serious that needed attention, and then turn back to watch the ball and the kick. But not this referee! He kept his eye on the kicker and saw him, with his foot, gently roll the ball eighteen inches to his right, giving himself an extra few inches of space beyond the end of the wall that the defenders had constructed.

HE DOESN'T KEEP STATISTICS, BUT HE SHOULD!

In Chapter 17, we describe an incident that occurred in a match played between Liverpool and Manchester United. Controversy erupted over the the usual sort of thing: a debatable penalty awarded to the home team (Liverpool), and a player from the away team sent off for two cautions, the second one for kicking the ball away to delay a restart. But it was more than that, because of the consequences of the decisions.

The sending off in the league match meant that the player would not be able to play in the Cup Final, which Manchester United had already reached. We won't argue with the correctness of the decision, because, although for "only" a technical offence, we are instructed to caution a player guilty of deliberately delaying the restart. But we should, and do ask whether the second caution could have been prevented, *if the referee had known about the potential suspension from the upcoming cup final.*

Reports in the press tell us that the referee had no idea that a sending off would result in the player missing the Final. One of his colleagues came to his defence by saying "I'm not some football saddo* who keeps 100,000 statistics. We deal with what's in front of us at the time." Well, yes, and what was in front of the referee was free information he could have used.

While issuing the first caution, he might have said something to the effect that another yellow card in this match would mean the player would miss the Cup Final, and you don't want that to happen, do you? So don't do anything silly. It might not have worked, but the referee could not even try it if he didn't know the player's disciplinary record. We believe that he *should* have known!

* "saddo" is derogatory British slang for "a pathetic person, a loser, a bit of a geek or nerd".

Without a moment's hesitation, the referee gave a loud blast on his whistle, walked over to the surprised taker of the kick, and issued him a caution for ungentlemanly conduct. At half-time, one of the assistant referees commented on the incident, asking how the referee had seen the player move the ball, when everyone's attention was diverted to the place where the shout had come from. The referee smiled and said:

"I learned from some of the other referees in the league that this is a ploy that this player uses every now and then. They plan to create a diversion, then the kicker moves the ball and takes the kick when no one is looking. By moving the ball about eighteen inches, he can curve it around the edge of the wall and score. I knew it might happen so I did not move when the players shouted. I kept my eye on the ball and caught the bugger in the act!"

How was I supposed to know?

From the kick-off, the referee watched as the ball was played out to the right wing, where a forward was in full flight. As the player hared downfield, the referee started trotting across the center circle. Very quickly the ball was swung over into the middle of the defence about sixteen yards from the goal-line. By this time the referee had crossed the center circle and turned to look where the ball was going to land. All he saw was a central defender heading the ball clear while two forwards, one a tall target player, stood with their arms upraised in protest as a loud shout came from the touchline: "Referee, have they stopped calling obstruction now?"

Time and again throughout the match, the bench personnel shouted about obstruction, the central forward appealed to the referee and ugly exchanges of opinion took place. By the end of the game, the atmosphere was so unpleasant that the referee deliberately walked away from the players and waited on the field until all the participants had dispersed. The following conversation then took place between referee and assistants.

"You two were on the line near that coach. What the heck was he on about?"

"He said that one of the defenders was deliberately running in front of his central striker to slow him down as he went in for crosses. In the last game, the bloke scored twice, and so they had this plan to obstruct him before the ball got near him."

"God, they expect us to see everything! How am I supposed to see something that is going to happen so far away from the ball? How was I supposed to know what they were going to do?"

How indeed! A little research would have given the referee the knowledge that the forward was an extremely effective player in the air, that he often dominated opposition defenders, and that he was the linchpin of the attack. With that knowledge he should have changed his pattern of movement and observation to make sure that he saw what was happening to the forward as he penetrated without the ball into the center of the defence. In other words, with information that was freely available, he could have ensured fair play, would have stopped all the trouble before it started, thereby controlling the game without acrimony. A little knowledge is a valuable thing!

What information you need, and how you gather it.

1. The league or the competition:

In addition to the leagues rules and regulations, or the rules of competition for the cup— which you get in the mail or in the pre-season meeting—you also need the standings at the time you do the game. What will a win or a defeat mean to each team? For example, a team is low in the table, losing by 4-0 near the end of the game. In most matches, this score means that the game is over, and at certain free-kicks near the goal, you can afford to relax a little, and not be insistent on the players retreating ten yards immediately. But if you know that the losing team can avoid relegation to the lower division by getting one more point, and you know that there is a bonus point for each goal, then the free-kick takes on a different and more important meaning! (See the chapter on free-kicks, and how *they are not all the same!*)

Most of this information is freely available from the league office, so make it your habit a few days before a game to check with the staff and get all the data you need.

2. The teams and their tactics:

The importance of understanding the tactics of teams is covered in some detail in a later Chapter 13, with many more examples than we give here. Suffice it to say that in order for you to be in the right place at the right time, in order for you not to get in the way of players and their movement, *you have to know how they play.* Before the game, can you answer these questions? What do they do at free-kicks near goal? Do they have any trick maneuvers at throw-ins? Do they favor a slow build-up with a succession of short passes? Do they break out of defence with a long ball to a target man near the halfway line? Do they overlap their fullbacks (into the area on the wings that you might want to use)? Who is their leading goalscorer?

When the ball changes possession to a team with a slow build-up, you can afford to wait for the ball to pass you on the way upfield. Simply follow play downfield by staying behind the player with the ball. That way you can see a lot of players in front of you and watch for any impeding of the attackers who are off the ball. But with the long-ball tactic, it is to your advantage to be able to be close to where the ball is going to land. When you see the clearing defender in possession, you should take off early, looking over your shoulder and then ahead of you to where the target man operates.

You get this information by watching the teams (and taking notes), and by asking referees who have seen them play. If you haven't seen either of the teams, then a few days before a game call up some other referees and ask them. If they don't know, or can't tell you, then call up some coaches. However you do it, gather and think about the information, then make some plans accordingly. In professional leagues, get hold of videotapes of matches involving both teams, analyze what they are doing, or discuss the teams with another referee of your experience.

For more examples of this approach to a game, read the chapter on tactics and movement [13].

3. The players and coaches:

Speaking not as referees, but as players and coaches, we can say without hesitation that talented players are the intended targets of unfair play. This applies to all levels of the game, not merely the professional and international scene, where players such as Pele, Cruyff, and Maradona were sometimes brutally treated. An experienced coach in youth play will teach his players to contain an star opponent by unfair means. In the teams we played on together, we schemed to neutralize opponents we knew to be a danger to us, and we admit that the way we did it was not always honorable (see sidebar).

Knowing this reality of the game helped us when we refereed, for we reasoned that if we did that sort of thing, then so did most other coaches. This meant that we had to learn to anticipate what an unscrupulous coach might do, and we had to learn about the players in any league in which we refereed. In professional leagues, read the newspapers, watch the television reports, or look at games. In local youth and amateur leagues, you learn by watching games and by talking to other referees. Coaches can also be a source of information, but most of them won't willingly admit to the planning of unfair play!

CONFESSION (RE): WE NOBBLED A PRO!

The following true story illustrates the benefits of preparation, and how an unprepared referee can be caught completely unawares, much to the detriment of the game.

In the early years of the NASL and the local team, the Dallas Tornado, I was player-coach of the Dallas Rangers, the top team in the amateur league. Ron Newman, the coach of the Tornado, approached the league and asked if his players could play in the league throughout the winter season to keep reasonably fit and in touch with the ball. To keep things fair, the league agreed to the arrangement that no more than one of Ron's players could play on any single team.

One of the players was Pepe Dill, an amazingly fast forward from Bermuda. We knew he could outrun any of our players, so what could we do to stop him? We came up with a plan that was both ruthless and effective…. Whenever we watched Pepe play for the Tornado, Alex Holmes (our team captain) and I had noticed that he didn't like to get hit hard. After being clattered, he would give the ball away quickly, rather than suffer another hard challenge. That knowledge gave us our plan….

On the day of the game, we saw that he was lined up on the right wing. We gave our fastest player, who happened to be our left fullback, the task of clobbering Pepe as hard as he could and as soon as possible in the match. After several attempts, it was clear that our fullback didn't have the heart to do what we wanted, so shortly afterwards, when the ball was next given out to the right wing, our centerback and captain, Alex, covered across at full speed. Without hesitating a single step, he went in for the challenge on Pepe at full speed, sliding the ball into touch and hitting the forward at the same time with hips, thighs and shins. Pepe went up in the air and came down to earth a tangle of arms and legs. It was one of the most ferocious tackles I had ever seen in the amateur game, and it did the trick. We gave away a free-kick, but Pepe, unwilling to come near Alex again, retreated into midfield where he simply popped the ball around whenever anyone came near him. As a result he became ineffective. The referee, because he was unprepared and not paying attention to the words that were being exchanged by our defenders and the faint-hearted fullback, was completely unaware of what had gone on, and we won the game easily.

There was a sequel fifteen years later, when I travelled as National Director of Referee Instruction to teach in Bermuda. I asked about Pepe Dill, who was a national sports hero, and found out where he lived. I went to see him and we had a nice chat about the Dallas Tornado and his time in the NASL. As I was getting ready to leave I mentioned the year when the pros played in the amateur league. Pepe's face became animated. "You know, man," he said "I never wanted to play in that league again! Some of the tackling there, man, it was brutal, brutal! A player could get hurt."

"Oh! You're right, Pepe," I replied with a slight smile, "we had to put up with that tackling every week. The referees weren't prepared to give us any protection…"

But there is another source of information, and this is the warm-up that takes place before a game.

As the players start moving about the field before the kick-off, take a few moments to watch them. Look at their skills: Who seems to have a delicate touch on the ball? Who knocks the ball without effort thirty yards right to the foot of another player? Are players dropping the ball into the middle of the penalty-area, where the goalkeeper is plucking each one out of the air with ease? Does the coach seem to be spending a lot of time with one particular player, talking things over, pointing here and there, planning strategy? These are key players. Imagine now that you are the opposing coach or captain, and ask yourself what you would do to neutralize those players. The answers you get will tell you what you may have to look out for right from the start of the game.

Gather information about the so-called "hard men", the "destroyers", "enforcers" or whatever they are called. These are the players who announce their presence on the field with a ferocious tackle early in the game, a solid crunch on a dangerous opponent. Know who they are so that when you see that first unfair challenge, you are not caught by surprise (see sidebar overleaf).

Learn whatever you can about the coach of each team. Is he or she a shouter? Does he put pressure on a referee throughout a match, hoping thereby to get a favorable decision at a critical time? Is he the sort of individual you can reason with, or—can you imagine this?— who will cooperate with you for the good of the game? You need to know ahead of time so that you can choose the most appropriate response when the pressure or misconduct starts. Your immediate response, carefully thought out ahead of time, will stop things escalating.

"CHANCE FAVORS THE PREPARED MIND"

The teams in the 1983 NASL Soccer Bowl (refereed by EB) were not what the league officials wanted. Instead of being played between two of the glamour clubs, such as the Cosmos, the Vancouver Whitecaps, or the Seattle Sounders, which would have guaranteed a full house and a large TV audience, it was contested between two of the lesser lights of the League, Tulsa Roughnecks and Toronto Blizzard. Both were well-coached teams comprised of solid journeyman players but with no superstars save for the aging Italian Roberto Bettega playing for Toronto. Both teams were underdogs who had battled their way through the playoffs by sheer will to reach the final match.

Tulsa owed much of their success to the goalscoring of Njego Pesa, a short and stocky player who possessed a very powerful shot, but who was otherwise unimpressive. It was clear that in order to beat Tulsa, Toronto had to prevent Pesa from scoring. How was he going to be stopped? In the heart of Toronto's defence was a tough-tackling Scot, Derek (Jock) Spalding. He had spent several seasons with Chicago, but had recently joined Toronto to bolster their defence. He was the kind of defender coaches love to have on their squads, but was quite often a handful for referees to deal with. Both of us had dealt with him previously, and knew his style. Furthermore, he had collected two cautions in the previous play-off matches. It was clear that he would be going up directly against Pesa, with the mandate to neutralize him.

There are several ways this can be accomplished; one way is to mark tightly, kicking the ball away as it comes near, together with perhaps foul or two or three to put him off his game. The other way is by a really hard tackle early on to slow him down, and to destroy his concentration by making him worry about another tackle of the same kind. Many defenders think that a referee will not caution or send a player off in the first few minutes of a match, and especially in a cup final, so that is the time to do the dirty work. As a boy, I had remembered what happened to Liverpool's most dangerous player Billy Liddell, in their F.A. Cup Final against Arsenal. He was fouled out of the game with impunity by a well-known tough Arsenal defender.

It did not take long to find out what would happen in this match! In the 53rd second of the game Pesa prepared to receive a pass about 35 yards out from goal, but he was suddenly felled by a heavy tackle from behind from—surprise, surprise!—none other than Derek Spalding! Without hesitation, the referee cautioned him, delivering a message that was evidently received loud and clear by all of the other players. There was not another really bad foul for the rest of the match, only one other player was cautioned and that was late in the 2nd half for dissent (regarding an offside decision).

What would have happened had Spalding not been cautioned? The game could have deteriorated, as Tulsa also had enforcers in their defence who might have felt that they could do the same. We will never know, but Pesa was allowed to play his game (in fact another defender became his marker, presumably to avoid the possibility of Spalding being sent off) and at the other end of the field the Toronto forwards were also allowed to play without being fouled. Tulsa won the match 2-0. In an ironic act of justice, the first goal was scored by Pesa, directly from a free kick given after Spalding fouled him just outside the penalty area, and Pesa was chosen as the MVP by the members of the press.

The rest of your preparation.

Before every match, you have other things you need in order to be ready. They make a simple list:

1. Uniform, clean and pressed, referee for the use of.

2. Shoes, clean and shiny, with wings on their heels.

3. Whistles, two, each with different pitch (so you don't disturb the match on the adjacent field, where the referee has the same whistle as you—and vice versa).

4. Notebook, for keeping your memoirs during play.

5. Pencils or pens, one in your pocket and one tucked in your socktop for a fast draw.

6. Colored flags—never a white one—for your forgetful assistant referees.

7. Two yellow cards, one easy of access (fast draw to defuse an explosive situation), the other out of the way in your shirt pocket.

8. Red card, safely out of sight and buttoned away, (shorts back pocket is the best place) to give you time to think before using it.

9. Change for a dollar.

10. Our best wishes!

NOTES

4

THE ART OF
REFEREEING

De minimis non curat lex.
(The law takes no account of trifles.)

Principle of the legal profession

The new referee.

The aspiring referee of today begins to learn about the business of officiating by attending a basic training course, taught—we trust—by a qualified instructor with some experience gathered on the field. Our neophyte hears about all the laws, from the markings on the field to the pressure in the ball, from the scoring of a goal to the ball being out of play. He (or she) is shown how to start the game and how to stop it. He learns what is permissible between the players, what has to be punished, and what the punishment must be. And if he is especially fortunate, he will have an instructor who has played the game and can physically demonstrate various kinds of legal and illegal contact when players are challenging for the ball. The student will be introduced to the mysteries of offside, and will be advised about when to take disciplinary action against players who are not obedient to the laws. All this instruction has to take place before we allow the

IN THIS CHAPTER:

- *What is not taught about refereeing—the art*
- *The law that defines refereeing but is no longer a law*
- *How to make any game a thing of beauty*
- *Stuff you shouldn't penalize*

new referee onto the field, for of all the participants in this game of ours, the person with the whistle certainly must be familiar with the laws that govern it. The policeman must know when the law is being broken.

Then will come the day when our shiny new referee steps onto the field, whistle in hand, head filled with the laws of the game, to start his first attempt at controlling a match. He will run about, blowing the whistle here and there, giving a free-kick for this and that, and (we hope) in between doing his duty, he will enjoy himself. And if all goes well, at the end of the game he will walk off the field with a feeling of satisfaction that he had done a good job. He had been introduced to the art of refereeing. Or had he?

Actually, no, for it is a sad fact for the preservation and health of this beautiful game, that the *real* art of refereeing is rarely taught in basic training courses. **For the *real* art of refereeing is as much about *not blowing* the whistle to stop the game, as it is about blowing it**. We are taught what to punish, but not what to ignore. We are exhorted to keep things under control, but are not taught how to do that without stopping the game. Read on, and you will see our attempt to define the art of refereeing, justify it in the laws of the game, and give you some examples of its application in all kinds of matches from the kids to the international pros.

Our attitude to the game.

From the days when we first became involved in this game—from some time back in the fifties—as spectators and players, then as coaches and referees, we absorbed a particular *attitude* to the sport, a *fundamental attitude* that is defined in a short paragraph of 64 words in the old version of Laws of the Game. In our youth we didn't know it was a law; we learned about it only from hearing others mention it, especially to express outrage when its principles were violated.

Taken by our fanatic dads and neighbors to the terraces of football grounds in Liverpool and Swansea and elsewhere in Britain, we heard about it from the crowds of spectators around us complaining that the referee was "…choking the life out of the bloody game!" When we went with other lads to our favorite piece of (mostly) flat ground to play on Saturday morning, we heard about it from the older boys who first bumped us over and then told us to shut up complaining, because "I hardly touched ya, sissy!" Later on we learned that many times when we were fouled in a *proper* match—when we wore boots, and all the players on the team had shirts of more-or-less the same color—the bloke who hit us could be left behind if we just took the knock and kept going. As coaches we encouraged the players in our charge to keep playing, and in their training we arranged exercises that taught them how to "..ride a challenge.." and to position themselves so as to change a foul that was meant to *stop* them, into something positive *for* them. We showed them how to take a throw-in or a corner or a free-kick quickly, taking advantage of their opponents' instinctive relaxation when the ball went out of play.

All this playing and coaching experience, and all those years on cold and damp terraces in the middle of a British winter served us well when we became referees and actually looked at the Laws of the Game for the first time. There in black-and-white on page 14 of the Football Association's "Referee's Chart" was the paragraph we understood thoroughly but had never seen: *International Board Decision number 8 of Law 5 – Referees*. It is the paragraph that told us how to referee. It is the paragraph that defines a good official, one *who understands what the game is all about, and what the referee's role is.*

Let's take a look at this law-that-no-longer-exists, figure out what it means, and at the same time make an appeal to FIFA and all its members to find some way to make sure that every referee in the world is taught it and reminded of it.

Law 5, International Board Decision 8

The words:

> The Laws of the Game are intended to provide that games should be played with as little interference as possible, and in this view it is the duty of Referees to penalize only deliberate breaches of the Law. Constant whistling for trifling and doubtful breaches produces bad feeling and loss of temper on the part of players and spoils the pleasure of the spectators.

That's it! Believe us, that's all there is to it: the essence of refereeing in two sentences.

The analysis:

Notice the phrase on the second line: "...as little interference as possible..." The implication of this phrase is that *some referees actually interfere with the game.*

Read on a little further and you come across another gem: "...penalize only deliberate breaches of the Law." The implication of this phrase is that many times the *laws are broken* by players, but *unintentionally.* (Take note: This is of major importance in youth soccer.)

Next we come to "Constant whistling for trifling and doubtful breaches..." The implication of this phrase is that sometimes referees penalize *infractions that are unimportant or even questionable.*

Why are we concerned about these items? Because the next line describes the consequences of all this whistling: It "...produces bad feeling and loss of temper..." among the players. The implication of this phrase is that *something the referee does can upset the players he is supposed to control.*

Finally, there is one more important phrase. All this whistling "...spoils the pleasure of the spectators." The implication of this last one is that in a match with an audience (especially fans who have paid to watch), *the referee must take into account the pleasure of the spectators.*

The 64 words of I.B.D. 8 boil down to this:

The framers of the Laws of the Game have long believed that:

1. Some referees interfere with the game;

2. Sometimes laws are broken unintentionally;

3. Some infractions are unimportant or even doubtful;

4. Some referees can upset the players;

5. The referee must take into account the spectators' pleasure.

When we say "long believed", we mean it. In 1906—yes!—the author of "The Book of Football", published in England, wrote:

> *We have referees who are temperamentally unable to disregard the printed word—others (all too few) who read between the lines and recognize that the first object should be to ensure the game being played honestly, fairly and in a truly sporting spirit.*

Today, as yesterday, we have too many referees who are obsessed with the letter of the law, who want to call every infraction they see, who believe that stopping the game is the way to keep it under control. What can we do about them? First, we believe we must educate them from day one of their exposure to refereeing. The basic training course must have a session explaining the principles numbered 1 through 5 in the section above. Second, we must teach them to recognize clues that they are choking the game—clues, incidentally, that many players may give the referee. Third (and we are going to do this right now), we must describe examples of unintentional, trifling, doubtful infractions that the referee would do best to ignore. And fourth—well, buy them a copy of this book!

Trifling and doubtful breaches of the law.

At a throw-in:

The match was in Dallas, but it could have been anywhere in the country, for on any given Saturday in the season there are thousands of incidents similar to the one we witnessed. The ball went over the touch-line for a throw-in. Three or four of the players—from the same team of under-8s—scrambled after the ball so as to get to it first and have the privilege of throwing it back into play. The coach eventually picked one of them—presumably his throw-in specialist—and the kid stood where the referee indicated and prepared to throw. Although the ball was a size 5 and larger than the player's head, the young boy hauled it back and threw it into play. But the effort of getting this large awkward object over his head and then into flight caused the little lad to jump a wee bit as he let go of the ball. The assistant referee on the touch-line raised his flag, the referee blew his whistle and gave the throw-in to the other team. Now the throw-in specialist from that team picked up the ball and went to the line.

He did a little better, for only *one* of his feet left the ground. Nevertheless both the eagle-eyed assistant referee and the vigilant referee saw the heinous crime, and by flag and whistle respectively, indicated another throw-in. It took four throws for the officials to be satisfied that the law was not being broken, four throws during which every player on the field save one was standing around doing nothing.

Was this an infraction? Yes. Was it a deliberate one? No. Was it trifling? Yes, especially since two of the throws went straight to an opponent of the thrower! Was the referee interfering with the game?

Yes. Should this crime have been punished? Absolutely not. All that the referee had to do was to say to the player after the throw: "Try and keep your feet on the ground when you throw the ball in, OK?" Or if there was a break in the action, he might take the opportunity to walk over to the coach, tell him what he saw, and ask for his help in solving the problem. This was supposed to be a soccer match, not a throw-in practice.

At the same level of play, you frequently see a player taking a throw-in before he looks at the referee to see where the correct position is. He may have been only four or five yards away from the right spot, but the referee gave the throw to the opponents. Does this "deliberate breach" of the law harm the game in any way? No, and it is best left unpunished.

At a free-kick:

If there is a free-kick for a team *in its own half of the field,* well away from the halfway line, does the referee have to be pernickety about making sure that the ball is placed exactly on the point of the infraction? Will it make any difference to the game if the ball is kicked from a few yards away to the left, right, or even forward? The answer is no, of course, in which case why should any referee waste time enforcing the letter of the law, which says that the free kick shall be taken "…from the place where the infringement occurred"? And similarly, if the team tries to get the game going quickly after the foul, by taking a short, quick free kick almost anywhere on the field, what harm is done if it was a few yards out of place?

Referees are encouraged all the time to punish the encroachment at free kicks, and well they should be. But if the game is essentially over, the result a certainty, with no bonus points at stake, then the official does not need to be in a hurry to get all the defenders back, nor does he need to use the threat of a caution. The enforcement has no meaning other than to satisfy the letter of the law. This is discussed at greater length and in more detail in Chapter 7.

A MIX-UP WITH MARADONA

A big crowd came to Giant's Stadium in New Jersey to see the great Maradona show his skills for Barcelona in a Transatlantic Cup game in the days of the old NASL. Determined to ensure that the spectators got their money's worth by seeing the Argentinian display his incredible skills, the referee (RE) was especially aware of his responsibility to protect the player from cynical fouls designed to keep him out of the play.

Immediately after the kick-off, the opponents came after Maradona. As soon as he got the ball, a defender would challenge him and make illegal contact of one sort or another—a push here, a thigh across his legs there, contact with man and ball at the same moment and designed to take him down. The referee saw all this and, unwavering in his plan to protect the player, started calling the fouls. At the first one, Maradona put the ball down and looked at the referee with a slightly puzzled expression. At the second, he again looked at the official, staring into his eyes. At the third incident a few minutes later, the player stopped, turned to the referee and with his arms out from his sides with palms up, he shrugged at him. He was obviously puzzled by what was going on, and by this time, so was the referee!

At the next foul on Maradona, the referee hesitated a split second and then saw that the Argentinian shook off the challenge and continued playing. He had been clearly fouled, but kept on playing and was not upset in the slightest. Then it became clear: Maradona was so used to being fouled a lot that he had his own way of dealing with it. A foul that would have brought down a lesser player did not disturb him. Short and stocky, he could take a push that would have taken another player off-balance. He did not want those fouls called! So the referee adjusted his measure of what was trifling or doubtful for this one particular player. He was not going to interfere with how this marvelously gifted player wanted to play.

At an offside situation:

In Chapter 9 on offside, we describe a situation where there has clearly been an infringement of the law, but because the ball is going to run through to the goalkeeper, who will be able to collect it quite safely, the referee can allow play to proceed. Similarly a defender may be able to gather the ball without experiencing pressure from the attacker who committed the offside infringement, and then boot it upfield. Again the referee does need to stop play.

Both of these infringements are real, but trifling in the meaning of I.B.D. 8, and should be ignored. Refer to Chapter 9 for details and drawings, as well as for the case where a shot at goal misses as an offside attacker interferes with the goalkeeper, but should not be penalized.

At penalty kicks:

There is not a referee alive who has not watched a penalty kick and seen the goalkeeper move prematurely. That is, before the kick was taken. And there is not a referee alive who has not seen this and other infringements of Law 14 *in matches he has refereed*, but has not called for a retake of the kick. Recognizing that most referees do not have the fortitude to take the heat that comes from ordering a second penalty kick, FIFA changed the law to allow a certain amount of movement on the line by the goalkeeper. But still the officials do not call more serious infractions, as we saw in the 1999 Women's World Cup final, when the United States goalkeeper charged a couple of yards off the line to make the crucial save that gave the cup to the host country.

Are we to assume that every infringement of this law is considered to be a trifling breach and therefore should be ignored? Our answer is an unequivocal "No!" and during our active days we both earned reputations for being hard-nosed when Law 14 was broken (see in this chapter the sidebar on Chicago versus Montreal). In Chapter 7 we describe all free kicks—including penalty kicks—in detail, but we can summarize our attitude thus:

If the goalkeeper breaks the law and saves the shot, the kick <u>must</u> be taken again,

If the goalkeeper breaks the law but his movement has no effect upon the kicker, whose shot goes over the bar or past the post, you can treat this as a trifling breach of the law, as do 99.9% of all referees in the world.

With encroachment by attackers or defenders or both, ask yourself if their early movement into the penalty-area has an effect. Did they gain anything from it? If they did, then penalize; if they did not, then don't.

THE REFEREE WAS RIGHT
BUT THE REFEREE WAS WRONG

In the history of the North American Soccer League, only two matches were terminated (abandoned) before the 90 minutes were up. One was for a major punch-up that the referee and linesmen were helpless to stop, and the other was over the retaking of a penalty kick. Here's what happened in the latter case, with RE in the middle.

The awarding of the penalty was beautiful. A Chicago forward made a diagonal run from left to right into the penalty area, heading for the far post as the winger on the left brought the ball down. The Montreal defenders were at sixes and sevens, and one of them, seeing the danger from the forward penetrating into the middle, grabbed him and pulled him down. The referee, wise to the behavior of defenders away from the ball, was also on the left, but looking into the penalty area and not following the movement of the man with the ball, who was under no threat of a challenge. He saw the foul in the area, blew his whistle, and without having to endure much fuss from any of the defenders, gave a penalty kick.

[Now a little history. The referee was on the international FIFA panel of referees for the U.S. and had received, as did all his colleagues, a letter from FIFA stressing that Law 14—every provision—was to be enforced, and that National Associations must take action against any referee who did not follow the law. Those were tough words and this referee took them to heart. Like most FIFA referees, he was ambitious, and certainly did not want to ruin a career as an international referee over such a thing as a penalty kick. So he was prepared to "Damn the torpedoes! Full speed ahead" with Law 14. He did not know that by giving the penalty kick in Chicago, he was about to be tested...]

The players lined up for the kick. The referee took his customary position off to the left, about six yards off the goal line and eight yards outside the post. The kicker ran to the ball, the goalkeeper moved a little early, the ball was shot over the bar, and the referee blew his whistle and said: "Take it again!" The

Continued next page

defenders were a trifle upset, and expressed a few words of disagreement to the referee, at the same time as some of their colleagues on the bench stood up with their coach and also shouted a few words that were not encouragement for a sound decision.

Sticking by his guns in the face of these verbal torpedoes, the referee got everyone settled down, though not happy, and blew his whistle for the retake. The kicker ran to the ball, the goalkeeper moved a little early, the ball was shot over the bar, and the referee blew his whistle and again said: "Take it again!" At that the coach became incensed and shouted for his players to leave the field, no doubt for a tactical discussion. No amount of persuasion by the referee was able to convince them to return, and so the match was abandoned, leaving both teams and the spectators very unhappy.

The sequel was also unpleasant, for the owner of the Chicago team, a charming man named Lee Stern, went into the dressing-room of the officials, and after airing his deep knowledge of the game in the first few seconds, subjected the referee to a ten-minute abusive harangue. Finally he asked what the decision was, and when told that the match had been abandoned (a word he had never heard before in this context), he became apoplectic, shouting at the referee: "Abandoned? Abandoned? You are the one who should have been abandoned! You should have been abandoned at birth!" (And to think that if that had happened, you wouldn't be reading this book.....)

All this, because the referee, at the insistence of FIFA, followed the letter of the law, and insisted on punishing what is obviously a trifling breach. He wouldn't do it today, and neither should you.

Fouls:

The descriptions of fouls in Law 12 do not require that the referee penalize every one that he or she sees. This sport of ours *is* a sport of physical contact, and the line separating what is legal or acceptable, from what is illegal or unacceptable is a fine one. Without wishing to write a major discourse on the subject, we can suggest that you consider the following case.

The new law says that if a player commits one of six *offences carelessly, recklessly or by using excessive force*, the referee shall award a direct free kick. One of the offences is pushing. So, let us picture the ball sent across the face of the goal after a corner kick. The goalkeeper went up for the ball, but just as he was about to catch it, a forward very gently gave him a little push in the small of his back, causing the goalkeeper to miss the ball. The push wasn't careless; it was deliberate and calculated. It wasn't reckless; it was planned. The attacker didn't use excessive force; it was a gentle, but perfectly timed use of one hand. *According to the letter of the law, it wasn't a foul!* But was it unfair? Yes. Did it have an effect upon the opponent? Most certainly! Should it be penalized? Of course it should.

Based upon this kind of analysis, showing that it may be impossible to *define* what is unfair, we need an easier way for all referees to make decisions about what fouls to call and what not to call. And, well, yes, you guessed it! We have one...

When you see a foul—a push, trip, kick, or any of the ones mentioned in Law 12—ask yourself one question: Does it have an effect upon the opponent or the play? If it does, you should give a free kick; if it does not, you can allow play to go on.

What you will have done is decide what is trifling or doubtful, and what is not. In other words, you will have done what the old IBD 8 exhorts you to do. You will have done what the framers of the laws wanted every referee to do. You will have done what the game needs.

An example may clarify this point. Everyone involved in the game will agree that trying to kick a ball that is up around an opponent's head is dangerous. According to the laws, a player who does that should be penalized by an indirect free kick. In fact, most players who see a boot coming in the direction of their head will pull back from trying to head the ball. In other words, their actions will have been *affected* by the other player's dangerous act. Give a free kick (assuming there is no advantage situation). But if the player *was not deterred* by the boot in the air, and he succeeded in heading the ball away, then the infraction by the player playing dangerously was insignificant—trifling, doubtful—and need not be penalized.

But now there comes a very important point that all referees must take to heart:

A foul that is significant at one level of play may be trifling or doubtful at another. The referee must adjust his decision-making to suit the level of play of the teams, or even of the individual players.

That philosophy can be illustrated by the story of the encounter that one of us (RE) had with Maradona, the great Argentinian midfielder, when he was playing for Barcelona (see sidebar, p. 62). You must be able to judge what the players can accept, or do accept in the way of physical contact, and adjust your decisions accordingly. Aha! You say, but how do we *know* what they can accept? We know, because the players will tell us, in obvious and in subtle ways.

How the players will tell you:

The most obvious attempt at assistance is the frustrated cry of a player: "For God's sake, referee. Let us *play!*" or "Ref, you don't have to call *every little thing!*" They don't want the game stopped, and they are telling you so. In that case, make some adjustments.

When you see a foul, take a look at the player who was fouled. Is his balance disturbed? Does he lose control of the ball? Does his face grimace in pain? These are signs that the foul had some significance, and unless there is a clear advantage, it should be called. But if the player just keeps on going, shrugging off the unfair challenge, then let him play. You can still quietly say something to the player who committed the foul, and you might even run by the player who was fouled and ask him if he is OK, thus letting him know (in the devious, subtle way that referees have) that you saw the foul. He will be reassured, and he might even give out more information that you can use. "Thanks, ref, but I can handle it," or "Yeah, but if he keeps on after me, I'm going to get him!" This latter is a warning to you that the fouled player is not endlessly tolerant of the illegal attentions of his opponent. Pay attention! Human words and human faces are very expressive, and they give out all kinds of information to the referee.

Coaches, too, give out information that you may be calling things too tightly or too loosely. In youth games with teams you don't know, you might even suggest to the coach that he tell you at a suitable opportunity if he thinks you are choking the game, or not protecting the players enough. We guarantee that he will be appreciative (not to mentioned surprised!) of your cooperative attitude. Building a relationship with a coach for the protection and enjoyment of the players is always a good thing for the game.

"Advantage" or "trifling and doubtful"?

When a referee sees an infringement of the laws, he may choose not to stop play, for one of two reasons:

1. He is applying the advantage clause
2. He considers the incident to be a trifling or doubtful breach of the law

So what? you may ask. All that matters is that he let play go on, right? Well, no, because there is an important difference between those two apparently similar decisions.

In the first case—advantage—if things don't work out quite to his liking, the referee can still stop play and give a free-kick as punishment for the original infraction. In the second case, he can not. In the first case, the referee has a few seconds to consider the matter. In the second case, he has only a split second to make up his mind. And bear in mind what we write in Chapter 8 on advantage, that there are only a few situations of true advantage during any game. You cannot use the change in the advantage law as an excuse for delaying blowing the whistle in situations where advantage *does not* apply. In simpler words:

Don't use the new wording as an cop-out for indecision!

Final words:

We have watched soccer for a hundred years between us; we played the game as kids and as men. Pressed into coaching in communities where the game was new, we passed on to others what we had learned. We played together for a few years, and then expressed our passion for the game as referees, rising through the ranks to become FIFA referees and to walk on the same international fields together. *And in all those years and all those games, we have held close the idea that the game is meant to be freely played, that it should be interrupted only when absolutely necessary.*

The fine art of refereeing is the art of knowing when to stop the game and when to let it go. It is the art of being able to recognize what is significant and what is not; what the players can accept and what they find intolerable. This art of refereeing is embodied in the International Board Decision number 8 of the Law 5. Though it no longer appears in the Laws of the Game, it is the cardinal rule that will be fundamental to the sport for as long as anyone plays it.

Our last words of advice on this subject take the form of a metaphor that some instructors have used: that of driving a team of horses. If the driver holds the reins too tightly, the team will not run as fast, whereas if he holds the reins too loosely, the horses may pull them out of his hands and cause him to lose control. Hence the driver must correctly gauge how tight or loose to hold the reins to obtain the desired effect. So it is with the referee and his application of the now non-existent but still important International Board Decision number 8 of Law 5.

NOTES

FOULS AND MISCONDUCT

*It is necessary only for the good man to
do nothing for evil to triumph.*

Edmund Burke

Physical contact: What is allowed?

When you learn a little about the origin and early development of the game of football, the notion nowadays of it being played without mayhem comes as a source of wonderment. For the original game was intended to be rough and hard, or even worse. In the early nineteenth century, according to one historian, when "...the exercise becomes exceedingly violent the players kick each others' shins without the least ceremony..." Even as late as the eighteen-sixties hacking, tripping and elbowing were permitted, and when the first meetings were held to regularize the rules, one group left the discussions in a huff when they learned that there was talk of banning hacking, the act of "kicking an opponent below the knee!"

In more organized versions of the sport—as it was conceived in the early and middle nineteenth century on the playing fields of exclusive schools in England—the rules still allowed vigorous contact.

IN THIS CHAPTER:

- *Fair and unfair physical contact*
- *Other unfair play*
- *Indirect free-kick offences*
- *Misconduct and other really serious stuff—the yellow and red cards*

Part of the philosophy of those private schools was the idea that young men should be able to stand up for themselves, to accept and administer rough physical play as part of the growing-up process. In other words they should learn to "dish it out and take it". To the teachers with that philosophy, a "manly" sport without physical contact was useless. Well into the nineteen-seventies, goalkeepers could legally be charged shoulder-to-shoulder with sufficient force to propel them and the ball into the goal. Even though the sport of soccer has changed in the hundred-and-thirty years since the first standardized set of rules was established, it is still a game in which physical contact is allowed and expected between the players. It is not, and never has been, a game for milksops.

How do you regulate such a contact sport so as to prevent injury to the participants? Look at any collection of prints and paintings of the game before the middle of the nineteenth century, and you will see players reeling about holding their heads, others hopping here and there rubbing their shins. It was a rough game, and we are glad to say that *some* of that kind of violence has gone. In the modern game—faster, more skillful, more tactically varied than ever before—the fundamental question still remains, however: What physical contact *should* and *should not* be allowed? Strange as it may seem, the answer to that question comes not from the letter of the laws, not from administrators and referees, but from the actions of the players themselves, as we have described in Chapter 4.

But first we *will* talk about parts of the actual laws, for they *do* form a basis for some decision-making by the referee. We should warn the reader that this chapter and the one that follows are not intended to teach you all the details in the laws. You can pick up a copy of the laws and study it for those details. We deal here with what we consider to be the important information *behind* the laws and their history, our purpose being to give you a perspective that you don't get in most classes and referee meetings. Understanding is the backbone of sound decision-making.

The laws about physical contact.

For as long as we have been in this game, the laws have said that there were some things you were not allowed to do to an opponent. The old version of Law 12 stated that a player who *intentionally* committed certain acts was to be penalized. Although as players we were completely unaware of the wording of that law—any laws, for that matter!—we knew what those forbidden acts were: kicking an opponent, tripping him, jumping at him, hitting him, pushing him, charging him too hard, holding him, and finally the weird one: charging him from behind unless he was obstructing. All those acts are what you might call man-to-man contact to establish physical superiority over your opponent so that you can win the ball in a challenge. We never thought about the word "intentionally", because every thing we did was intentional. We went in to get the ball, and if our opponent pushed us off, or held us away, or tripped us and so on, we knew we had been cheated. And when we did the same to our opponents, even though in our heart of hearts we knew it was an unfortunate accident—nothing more!—we expected the referee to blow his whistle. Believe it or not, players know these things.

But that word "intentionally" did cause some problems in officiating because there were referees who used it as a device for *not penalizing*, even when the illegal contact was clear. The excuses were various: "It was an accident"; "The grass was wet and he slid too far when he tackled." or "I know he's not a mean player, and he wouldn't do something like that deliberately." Worse yet were the excuses for an infringement by a defender in his own penalty-area: "I didn't feel it in my heart that he meant to trip him." In other words, he didn't think it was *intentional.* That's a referee's roundabout way of admitting that he didn't have the courage to give a penalty-kick. And the reality is that sometimes there truly was *accidental* contact between players, with no intent to clobber, clatter, kick-the-hell-out-of, maim or otherwise hurt the opponent. Two players came into contact because their paths through the universe happened to cross at that moment. We knew in our hearts, however, that the referee still had to call it. Players know these things.

In the new wording of the laws, the problem with the word "intentionally" was solved. Simply take the word out! Describe every one of the naughty things that players do to each other and make them all illegal, however they happen. So the framers of the laws introduced new terms to describe unfair challenges: *careless, reckless, excessive force.* That should solve the problem, they thought, for now it is clear. Well, almost, but not quite!

The challenge on wet grass, the slide tackle that brings down an opponent, even though there is no intent to foul, *that* is penalized for being *careless.* The player committing the foul should have known better. The inexperienced defender who jumps in the air, turns his back and then collides with an opponent attempting to play a high ball is guilty of committing a foul because his action is *reckless.* He was, as the dictionary says, devoid of caution, heedless of danger. His recklessness is penalized, and his inexperience is not an excuse. But now in order to emphasize how the referee must look beyond the letter of the laws, let's look again at the little push mentioned in Chapter 4, the slight jab of the hand at the right moment, the most unhurtful touch you could imagine. Should it be penalized, and where in the laws can you justify it?

For this discussion we are indebted to Ken Aston, for many years a top-class referee, member of FIFA's Referee Committee, subsequently a member of the International Board that considers the laws of the game. A more knowledgeable and entertaining instructor you could not wish to meet. Let us imagine, Ken says, a crowd of players at a corner-kick. The ball comes swinging over into the crowd, several members of which go up for a header. As the central defender is about to head the ball, an opposing forward moves his hand into the small of his opponent's back. With just a little push, he distracts the defender and moves him out of the best position to head the ball away. It was not *careless*, for on the contrary, it was a calculated, deliberate act. It was not *reckless*, for he was indeed acting with caution, so as not to draw attention to the foul. Nor was it done *with excessive force*, but with only enough to achieve his purpose: destroy the defender's header. So according to the letter of the new laws, this was not a foul. But we know it *was*. It was an intentional push-in-the-back designed to give the criminal an unfair advantage. Players know these things, and so should we—the referees—by learning from the players, regardless of what the law says.

Let's summarize this discussion so far. The old laws weren't quite adequate to describe properly the unfair physical contact that takes place between players and their opponents. However, the players knew what they weren't supposed to do and what shouldn't be done to them. The new laws, written in the last few years, are also not quite adequate to describe some aspects of unfair physical contact. However, ask a player and he will tell you what's fair and what is not. So where does this leave the referees?

Strictly speaking, ***most physical contact between players is illegal,*** whether it is described by the new laws, or was described in the old laws. Any kick, trip, jump, charge, push, hold or strike, any tackle where the player makes contact with the opponent before making contact with the ball, is illegal. But the question remains: ***What should and should not be allowed?*** As we said earlier in the chapter: The answer to that question comes from the actions of the players themselves. ***What should be allowed is what the players will tolerate; their actions will show you what they can accept.***

The chapter that follows this one gives you our experience at trying to decide what players are doing to each other and why. It will help you to anticipate potential foul play, and we trust, be more valuable to you than would a mere recitation of Law 12.

Other unfair play.

Of the direct free-kick offences, two bear some discussion, one because it is new, and the other because it is very old and consistently penalized incorrectly. Spitting is new, handball very old.

Spitting.

On June 15th, 1968, the International Board adopted a decision to write the act of spitting into the laws, requiring that the referee send the player off the field. It did not matter whether the spitting was directed at a player, an official or anyone else; it was violent conduct and the offender had to go. The truth was that this behavior had been increasing and some referees seemed powerless to do anything about it, because until then the law said nothing about expectoration (the fancy word for spit), but simply said that a player guilty of "violent conduct" should be expelled. Without a definition of violent conduct in all its forms, the hapless referee didn't know what to do.

We can state unequivocally that *you must send off any player who spits at an opponent, a teammate, a match official or a spectator.* The new law mentions only "spitting at an opponent", but no matter. The practice of spitting at anyone is unacceptable in soccer or any other sport and must not be tolerated. Now, a word or two of caution....

Make sure that you are punishing *"spitting at"* and not *"spitting"*. The former is rare, whereas the latter occurs frequently during the average match, as players clear saliva or phlegm from their mouths, or expel excess water they may have drunk. However offensive the act of spitting may be to you personally, you cannot rewrite the law and use it to send off a player whose innocent behavior you don't happen to like. You must be sure that the offending player *spat deliberately at another individual, not merely onto the ground near him.*

Handball.

It was over the issue of handling the ball that two different versions of football developed. In the early games, some sets of rules allowed a player to knock the ball down with his hand or arm, but not to carry it or throw it forward. Then an over-enthusiastic young man named William Webb Ellis picked up the ball during a match at his school—Rugby—and ran with it. "Rugby Football" was born, and shortly after that, handling the ball in any way was banned in the other football—our football, "Association Football", or soccer, as it came to be known. Rugby, as though unable to decide what it wanted to be, evolved into a variety of forms: Australian Rules Football, Gaelic Football, Rugby League Football, Rugby Union Football and ultimately, American and Canadian Football. All those corrupt versions of the original game involve some form of chucking the ball about with your hands, but the delightful game of soccer retained its simple purity. It is a game to be played with the feet, the body and (especially for referees) the head.

The law states quite simply that a player should be penalized if he "handles the ball deliberately." The law once included the phrase "carries, strikes or propels the ball with his hand or arm" , but most people involved in the game don't need to have all that spelled out. We understand that no part of the arm below the shoulder can be used, *so our problem is simply to learn how to recognize deliberate handling, as opposed to accidental handling. Accidental handling is never penalized!*

From our observations of officiating in youth soccer, we estimate that twice as many "handballs" are penalized as should be. Many inexperienced referees are over-zealous, but if you then add the problem that parents and spectators unfamiliar with the game shout every time the ball touches a hand or arm, the tendency for the official is a compulsion to blow his whistle in response. This only makes matters worse, because the lack of knowledge by the spectators is then reinforced by the action of someone who is in their eyes a (presumably) trained referee. He's got a badge and a uniform; he must know what he's doing. On top of that, the players, hearing all the appeals when they make hand or arm contact with the ball, react as though they are guilty of touching something sacred, a holy relic. In such a case, it takes a great deal of strength and conviction for an inexperienced referee to be deaf to hundreds of voices baying in unison, and to ignore the horrified expression of a player who acts as though guilty of a cardinal sin. What they need is knowledge and an understanding of clear methods of determining whether a player "handles the ball deliberately". We are about to describe those methods, so stay with us.

The most evident handball is where the player reaches out to touch or control the ball, or moves his hand to intercept it and change its path. Examples might include: the defender who reaches up to knock a ball down that was going over his head; the player who while trying to deal with an awkwardly-bouncing ball, flicks out his hand to put the ball in front of him; and the *really* obvious ones, like stopping a shot going into the goal, or using a hand to stop a pass that might produce a scoring chance. These latter two are punished very severely in the latest versions of the laws, and are therefore becoming less common.

All these examples are covered in the first part of that familiar old refereeing question: *"Was it hand to ball, or was it ball to hand?"* You will still hear that question at training clinics and courses, and the answer supposedly will tell the new or inexperienced referee what to do. In many cases it will help you make a decision, and some of those decisions will be correct. But in an equal number of cases it will be wrong! Here's why...

In the cases we described, the player *does deliberately* move his hand towards the ball in an effort to touch it or move it. There is no doubt he moved "hand to ball", as the old saying goes. If he succeeds in touching the ball with his hand, he should be penalized (assuming there is no advantage, or that the infraction is not trifling). But many times a player as part of a natural running or jumping motion *appears* to move his hand towards the ball. There may have been no *intentional* touching of the ball with the hand, yet still he will get penalized—incorrectly, we should add.

And then there are cases where the hand doesn't move, and yet the handball is nevertheless *intentional*. Think about a wall at a free kick near goal. The kicker plays the ball hard towards the goal, aiming to curve the ball around the end of the wall. The player at the end of the wall has his hands down to his side, but sees that the ball is going to hit the arm on the outside of the wall. He leaves the arm in that position even though he knows the ball will strike it. He has time to move it, but chooses not to, and as a result, blocks the shot on goal. If we stick by the old saw "ball to hand", the player has committed no infraction. And that is why this old piece of refereeing wisdom—like so many of them—is useful *up to a point*. Because it does not cover every situation, it should be used with care.

So in the case of supposed handball, ask yourself these questions:

1. Did the player move his hand with the purpose of touching (handling) the ball?

If the answer is "yes", then you have witnessed an infringement of the laws, and you may penalize. If there is no advantage situation, or if the player gains some benefit from his handling, then give a free kick to his opponents.

If the answer is "no", then allow play to proceed.

If the answer is "I can't decide", then look for something else to help you make the decision. If the handled ball goes straight to an opponent, then you don't have to decide. You can just allow play to go on unabated.

2. Did the player have time to move his hand out of the way, but chose instead to leave it where it was?

If the answer is yes, then you have witnessed an infringement of the laws, and you may choose to penalize.

If the answer is "no", because you can see that (for example) a shot was taken so close to the defender that he couldn't possible have had time to get out of its way, then there is no breach of the law, and no matter how many people shout about it, you must let play go on.

3. Was the movement of the hand or arm an instinctive act of protection for the face, the groin or (in the case of young female players) the breast?

Young players especially deserve the benefit of the doubt in these cases. Their instinct is to protect vulnerable parts of their body, especially ones that hurt when struck hard. Older players learn to turn their head quickly, or deflect a ball with their shoulder, rather than take a hit in a place that would be painful.

4. Was there some other factor that could have caused the contact between the ball and the hand or arm?

On a lot of fields in youth soccer, the surface is not as smooth as we would like, and as a result the ball pops up unpredictably. When in such cases the ball makes contact with a young arm, could it have been the playing surface and not the action of the player that created the "handball"? We describe one such case in the sidebar.

One final point of great importance: In the case of accidental contact between the ball and the hand or arm, even if the ball drops to the benefit of the player who made contact with it, you must not penalize. Where there is no infraction, no infraction must be called!

WHY WOULD THE PLAYER HANDLE THE BALL?

During an invitational tournament in Dallas, Texas in the fall of the year, when the fields are as hard as a rock, and have only a straw-colored mat of vegetation that passes as grass, two under-16 teams of skillful boys were going at each other with great enthusiasm. The ball was thumped out of one defence, deep into the opponents' half, bouncing down into the penalty-area. The last defender chased back for it and tried to bring it under control off to one side of his own penalty-area. He was not under pressure, because there was no opponent within thirty yards of him. On the rough surface the ball popped up after a bounce, struck him on the arm and dropped in front of him. The whistle blew, and the referee—from forty yards away—awarded a penalty-kick.

On too many occasions for us to remember, we have advised referees who get into trouble frequently during games, to try to put themselves in the position of the player. It is a way of trying to understand why a player acts or behaves the way he does, why he gets hot or why he chases after an opponent for no apparent reason. Thinking like a player can be a useful tool for a referee.

In this case, let's pretend we are the player penalized for handball. We know no opponent is nearby, which means we have a lot of time to get the ball under control, to pass it back to the goalkeeper, or to thump it back upfield. **We have no need to handle the ball in order to accomplish what we are trying to do, especially so in our own penalty-area.** Handling the ball in an open space where everyone can see you would be the ultimate act of stupidity. What good can possibly come of it? Despite all that, and without thinking (and that is the real problem here) the referee saw the hand and ball come together, and chose to award a penalty-kick. A moment's reflection, as we recommend in item number 4 above, would have told the referee that this was a classic case of accidental handling brought about because of a rough playing-surface.

Indirect free-kick offences.

Goalkeepers:

Five of the indirect free-kick offences involve illegal activity by the goalkeeper. All of them were written into the laws because goalkeepers and their coaches had found ways to slow the game down, to waste time, to cheat their opponents of opportunities to attack and possibly score. Believe it or not, but it was once possible for a 'keeper to hold onto the ball for a long time, provided that he bounced it as he moved about the penalty-area. In the days when goalkeepers could be charged shoulder-to-shoulder, this led to some dramatic confrontations between frustrated forwards and the man who was causing their frustration. We are not going to go into the history of the way that the laws about the goalkeeper have changed, but we have to emphasize certain points about why the laws were changed. As we say throughout this book, we believe it is important to understand the purpose of laws in order to apply them correctly.

The five offences have to do with delay, with negative play that sends the ball backwards instead of forwards, with tactics whose only purpose is to use up valuable playing time. Without these laws, *the one player on the team who can hold the ball in his hands [and who is at the same time immune from a challenge by an opponent] could stop the game.* Under the new laws, the goalkeeper cannot hold the ball for more than six seconds, cannot release the ball and pick it up again, cannot handle the ball thrown to him from a teammate taking a throw-in, and cannot handle the ball after a teammate has deliberately kicked it to him. All that seems straightforward enough, but now let's temper some of those regulations with a little prudence, a little wisdom.

If the framers of the laws wanted you to use a stopwatch to measure the time the goalkeeper had the ball, they would have specified that you do so, or they would have you count off the time publicly. But no, they believe that six seconds is probably enough time for the goalkeeper to catch the ball, look around the field for an open teammate, and then get rid of the ball. And as long as the goalkeeper appears to be following the spirit and purpose of the law, he should not be penalized for using up 6.3 seconds with the ball in his hands! If you begin to have suspicions that he may be deliberately abusing his privilege, a little word to the wise is all that is necessary. "It took you more than six seconds to get rid of the ball a few moments ago. Speed it up a little, OK?" Or you might even impose a little pressure on the 'keeper by using one of his teammates for your purposes. Tell the central defender that you are a little concerned about the amount of time the goalkeeper is holding the ball, and that you may have to give a free-kick if he doesn't speed up releasing the ball. We guarantee that the defenders will take care of it, for they know the chaos that reigns during an indirect free-kick near their own goal area! They'll convince the goalkeeper to speed things up.

One of the remaining offences—handling the ball received directly from a throw-in by a teammate—needs no further comment than to say that if the goalkeeper does handle it, you give an indirect free-kick. You have no choice. But the other two "handling offences" *do* require a few more words of explanation or caution.

We have seen referees get into trouble when they zealously enforce the letter of the law that says the goalkeeper shall be penalized if he "…touches the ball again with his hands after it has been released from his possession and has not touched any other player." *If you read the words without understanding the purpose, the spirit, the intent __behind__ the words, you would blow your whistle when a goalkeeper simply bounces the ball and catches it again.* That would be wrong. When he bounces the ball, is he delaying the game? Is he using negative tactics to take away an opponent's opportunity? Is he abusing his handling privilege? The answer to all three questions is "No!" and so you must not penalize him for technically breaking the letter of the law.

But when he rolls the ball onto the ground and follows it to pick it up, he has abused his privilege, because his opponents, knowing that they cannot challenge him when he has the ball in his hands, usually back away to mark other players. Once the opponents back away, the goalkeeper would be rolling the ball knowing that no one was going to tackle him for it, and could gain both distance and time. The instant a player came to challenge him, he could pick it up safely. The framers of the laws want to prevent goalkeepers from using such a device to slow the game down.

The final infraction by the goalkeeper is the act of touching a ball with his hands after a teammate has **deliberately kicked** the ball to him. Both the highlighted words are important. "kicked", because players are allowed to *head* the ball back, or *deflect it off another part of their body*, like their chest when the ball is bouncing high; "deliberately" because the 'keeper is allowed to pick up a ball that flies of the foot of a defender desperately trying to clear the ball. And note also that nowhere does it say "...kicked *back to*..." the goalkeeper. The pass could be forward or sideways. The whole idea here is that the laws do not allow a defender to get himself out of trouble by passing the ball to a player who has handling privileges and is immune to a challenge. We want the goalkeeper to play the ball with his feet and be subject to the same challenges as any other player on the field. For then play will go on, the attack will continue, and *that* is what the laws intend.

Other offences:

The law that tells you to penalize a player who **plays in a dangerous manner** does not mean what it says! After such a provocative statement, we hear thousands of our readers saying: "Huh? The wording seems so clear. What are these guys talking about?" Consider these examples:

1. In order to block the ball, the goalkeeper dives at the feet of a forward who is in the act of delivering a powerful shot towards the goal.

2. A ball is delivered low to the front post, where a forward dives headlong a couple of feet above the ground, flicking the ball into the net and colliding with the post as he scores.

3. The ball curls into the goalmouth, where a defender, unaware of the presence of a teammate, leaps up and clears the ball upfield and away with a bicycle kick that almost takes his teammate's nose off.

4. A defender close to and facing his own goal is trying to hook the ball away, but as he does so, a teammate comes in from the side and plays the ball down with his studs right in front of his teammate's reproductive equipment.

5. From a corner-kick, the ball curls in to the goal close to the near post, and the nearest defender rushes forward to head the ball away inches from the woodwork. A collision with the upright is inevitable.

In all these examples, the individual *plays in a dangerous manner*, but must not be penalized. Why not? Because although the acts are dangerous, they have had no effect upon their opponents. They are not intrinsically unfair, and since a principal purpose of the laws is to prevent and punish *unfair* play, these dangerous plays must be allowed as part of a game that is not without danger to the participants. Soccer is not, and never has been, a game for milksops.

A WAYWARD INSTRUCTOR

A few years ago, we had the sad situation of a senior instructor from Canada going about preaching that dangerous play should be called even when a player endangered a teammate. We are sure that the instructor's motives were based upon wishing to protect young players, but it was not his right to change one hundred years of experience and tradition that work well. Even sadder is the fact that he continued to preach that idea after a member of the international board of FIFA had (very tactfully) corrected his wayward thinking!

WE SAY AGAIN: UNDERSTANDING IS THE KEY TO SOUND DECISION-MAKING.

You must not penalize a player who plays dangerously in the vicinity of only his teammates.

What the law doesn't say is that there are two elements to penalizing dangerous play. The first is that the act must be inherently dangerous, and the second is that it must have an effect upon the opponent. In this philosophy, a player who reaches up and plays the ball with his foot right in the face of an opponent would be penalized if the opponent pulled back from trying to head it. A forward who dives or bends down to head a ball would be penalized if a nearby defender, intent on kicking the same ball, pulled his foot back to avoid removing his opponent's nose. The fundamental point is this: *A dangerous act should be penalized only when it produces an unfair situation.*

A player who *impedes the progress of an opponent* shall be punished by the award of an indirect free-kick to his opponents. Here again, what the law *doesn't* say is as important as what it *does* say. Once upon a time, this infraction was called "obstruction", and we are glad that the old term has gone. We have spent many, many hours trying to explain legal and illegal obstruction to beginners, and no matter what we tried, some people couldn't get their head around the idea that the same term—obstruction—could mean two different things, one of which was permissible, but the other illegal. Let's try an explanation of the new wording.

If a player puts himself in front of an opponent in order to prevent or slow down his progress to the ball, he should be penalized. If in his attempt to impede the other player, he makes contact with the opponent, he could be penalized with a direct free-kick for charging an opponent. But if he merely gets in the opponent's way, and the opponent *runs into him*, only an indirect free-kick should be given. But there is an important rider to that instruction....

A player is allowed to place himself between an opponent and the ball when he himself is within playing distance of the ball. What is playing distance? It is being close enough to the ball that you can reach out with your foot and play it at any time. So if a ball is running out of play, a player who shields the ball from an opponent is committing no infraction when in doing so he remains within playing distance. Similarly, a defender is not breaking the law when he shields the ball rolling through for the goalkeeper to pick up, provided that the defender is always within playing distance of it. Even if the player moves from side-to-side to keep the opponent away, he commits no infraction *as long as he remains within playing distance of the ball.*

With the laws now stressing that the actions of the goalkeeper should not cause delay, it would be unfair if anything were allowed by the opponents that would prevent the 'keeper from putting the ball back into play rapidly. Hence the law that states a player shall be penalized by an indirect free-kick if he *prevents the goalkeeper from releasing the ball from his hands.* The key word is "prevents". Someone standing in front of the goalkeeper does not prevent him from releasing the ball; the 'keeper could easily throw it or move slightly to one side and punt it. Someone running alongside the goalkeeper getting ready to punt the ball does not prevent him from releasing it. Inexperienced and over-zealous referees imagine that they are protecting the goalkeeper by calling both those infractions we have described, but in fact they are defeating the purpose of the recent law changes! They are contributing to slowing the game down. Don't become one of the co-conspirators against the progressive changes. If the goalkeeper succeeds in getting rid of the ball, the likelihood is that no forward committed an infringement of this law.

The final indirect free-kick infringement is a technical matter specifying that after the referee decides to take action after any of the cautionable offences, he will start play with an indirect free-kick *if the guilty player did not commit one of the direct or indirect free-kick offences we have been talking about.*

The serious stuff that leads to yellow and red cards.

Most of these offences are covered in our chapters on game control, free-kicks and so on, so we are not going to deal with them here. We can say, however, that many cautionable offences are within the discretion of the referee; he can caution or not, depending on the circumstances. The letter of *the law gives you permission to caution a player, and does not say that you have to show the yellow card at every occurrence.* We will remind you of the principle that *the referee should do the least that is necessary to control the situation.*

Those words notwithstanding, there are some acts for which the laws insist that the referee issue a caution. Many of them you will probably never see—a player changing places with the goalkeeper without notifying the referee; a player ordered to leave the field to fix his equipment, and who returns without permission; a player distracting or impeding an opponent taking a throw-in; some infringements of Law 3 (number of players); entering or leaving the field without permission—but others are more common. The act of faking an injury or a foul in order to deceive the referee is now considered so serious that an automatic caution is decreed, and a player must be cautioned if he attempts to defeat the purpose of the law that does not allow a deliberate kick-to-the-goalkeeper, either from a free-kick or a pass. Flipping the ball into the air to head it back or play it back with the chest or thigh is considered to be unfair trickery.

Among the offences for which a player may be sent off the field are several in which the referee does not have any discretion; he *must* send the player off. The two most obvious ones are the fouls that players commit to deny a goal-scoring opportunity or to prevent a goal. They are spelled out in the new laws and nicely illustrated by colorful perspective drawings. We can't add much to what is printed, except to say that referees who do not do what the new laws require are doing a grave disservice to the game, at whatever level they are refereeing. Remember our dictum that *well-trained and courageous referees are the custodians of the integrity of the game.* You can't protect the game by being cowardly!

6

RECOGNITION OF FOULS: OTHER INFORMATION TO USE

Tackling is better than sex...

Paul Ince,
England midfielder.

Introduction:

The Laws of the Game tell us what is not allowed, but they don't elaborate, and what we told you about in the previous chapter

> "*...if you can't win by fair means, you are going to try to win by foul.*"

and elsewhere was meant to emphasize that what is illegal and what is punished are not always the same. The infringements you call vary from game to game, from competition to competition, they differ from country to country, and are not the same in the amateur game as in the professional.

Each time you take a step up the ladder that leads to the top games, you have to learn what is acceptable and what is not. To help you with what is acceptable, and with what happens on the field, we are going to provide the elaboration that the laws omit.

IN THIS CHAPTER:

- *The laws tell little of the story*
- *Where on the field do the battles occur?*
- *Players cheat to compensate for weaknesses*
- *Fouls by and around the goalkeeper*
- *Creating a foul to gain a free kick*
- *How to nail an opponent and disguise it*
- *Fouls you can hardly see*
- *A foul that doesn't exist*

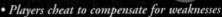

The real stories in the game.

A soccer match is played between two teams, but the contest actually consists of a series of little battles going on all over the pitch, battles between individual players. In any game you will see personal contests between, for example, the central defender and the opposing central striker. On each flank, you will have to adjudicate the touchline battles—four of them—between the wingers and the outside defenders. In midfield, the players that control each team are in constant opposition to each other. In all of these little battles, one player is trying to best one opponent: the forwards are trying to beat the defenders, and the defenders are trying to stop the forwards. These may be contests of skill, but they may also be battles where *physical* superiority is at stake.

Because there will be fouls committed by both participants in these individual battles throughout the match, the well-prepared referee will look for such confrontations early in the game, and be ready to deal with them when they occur. When one of the participants is fouled, he may be looking to return the compliment sometime later in the game—even if the first foul is punished. If you do not insert your presence into such contests as soon as you see them start, you will be heading for a steady loss of control. To both players, you make it clear that you realize what is going on, and that you will be on top of things. But now let's look at some of these individual contests and see if we can *anticipate* the fouls that will occur.

Players cheat to compensate for weaknesses.

The heading of this section may seem to some readers to be a harsh analysis of players' behavior, but based upon our own experience as players and referees, we won't retract it. All we ask you to do is to put yourself in the position of a player in the contests we are about to describe, and then ask yourself what *you* would do. Let's start with the central defender-central striker contest for high balls.

In theory, this will be a contest between physical equals. The winner of the ball delivered into the heart of the defence will be the one who can jump highest, or who can time his leap perfectly so as to be at his maximum elevation off the ground as the ball arrives. In a game without fouls, sometimes the defender will win, sometimes the attacker. But now imagine that you are the striker and you are playing against a central defender who is six-foot-four. He will win the ball every time it is delivered to you in the air, so what are you going to do?

A saint will say: "It is the will of the gods. You have to accept it." A canny coach will say: "We have to find a way around that tree in the middle of the defence. Keep the ball on the ground." But if you don't know a saint, and if your coach is sleeping, and if your midfielders won't change their service to you, what are you going to do? *If you can't win by fair means, you are going to try to win by foul.* (Unless, of course, *you are* a saint, in which case, don't read any further.)

You have to try to keep the defender away from the place where the ball is going to fall to him at the maximum height of his leap. And you have to try to be in a position where *you* can reach the ball after you have kept *him* away from it. You do this by backing into the defender, with your back against his front, and you maintain contact with him as the ball falls. At the last instant, you step forward to head the ball. In the words of the law, *you push your opponent backwards.*

The only way a referee will see this (very common) foul is to anticipate it (by understanding what is going on) and to be looking where the ball is going to come down. You are looking at that place before the ball arrives, so that you can see the action between the two players. The central defender (if he is smart) will try to show to the referee that he is being fouled, and may appear to leap up, but with the forward pressing back, the defender will appear to go over the back of the forward. Many an inexperienced referee has been fooled by this and given a free kick to the forward. (In Chapter 12, read the sidebar

"How a striker gets pregnant" to see how one referee used humor to deal with a forward backing into a defender.)

Now let's reverse roles. You are an average-sized defender, and you are playing against a taller, slender striker who can leap single buildings with...... He will win every ball. *If you can't win by fair means, you are going to try to win by foul.* Here are some of the things you can do; they are what you as referee must be aware of and watch for:

1. You can keep the forward away from the optimum place for getting the ball at the height of his leap. You do this be stepping up as the ball is played into the middle, holding your position in contact with the forward, and then at the last second stepping back to take the ball in the air yourself. In other words, you *impede the progress* of your opponent.

2. You can wait until the ball comes, and as you jump with the forward, you give him a little *push in the back* to take him off his leap, so that you can win the ball.

3. You can jump with him, but as you do so, you have one arm straight out in front of your shoulder and extending over your opponent's. This has the effect of keeping his head below the level of yours, allowing you to win the ball. You *hold him* down slightly.

The only way a referee will see these (very common) fouls is to anticipate them (by understanding what the players are doing) and to be looking at where the ball is going to come down.

Now transfer yourself to one of the four corners of the field, where winger and flanking defender encounter each other. In the good old days when we first started watching soccer, fullbacks were stocky, strong and hard. Wingers, on the other hand, were slight, speedy and delicate. The first thing a fullback tried to do was to kick the winger up in the air so as to discourage him from attempting to come close again. In other words, intimidate him. In the modern game, the role of the flanking defender has changed. He is less a tackler than an interceptor of passes, and he has to be fast in his own right, to assist in attacking by overlapping outside the forwards. But what if he knows he is not as fast as the forward he is supposed to mark? What can he do? (For one solution, see the sidebar on Pepe Dill in Chapter 3).

He can certainly try the intimidation of old. But he can also be more subtle, and less obvious to the inexperienced referee. By marking his opponent closely—within less than a yard's distance—he can actually be in contact with him as the attacker may start a run at a ball played forward for him. All he has to do is hold his position for an instant, and then take off after the ball himself. By giving himself a slight start on a faster opponent, he can win the race for the ball. *The referee will not see this slight but significant act of holding unless he is looking ahead of the ball as it is passed, anticipating where it is going to be played.*

The forward who is not as fast as his defender also has to gain an illegal edge. He can do this by maintaining contact with the close-marking defender, his back to the defender's front. As the ball comes to them, the forward leans backwards into his opponent and turns him away from the path of the ball. Then he steps forward, and goes after the ball, knowing that he has the defender beaten. Once again, *the referee will not see this foul unless he is looking ahead of the ball, and unless he has anticipated what can happen between two players of differing physical abilities.* Their abilities he knows from seeing them in other games, by learning from other referees, and by watching the two players early on in the contest. (See Chapter 3 - Preparation.)

Fouls by and around the goalkeeper.

A basic point to be emphasized is that outfield players committing one of ten offences described in Law 12, give away free kicks (occasionally a penalty), but a goalkeeper committing one of those ten gives away a penalty most of the time, because he spends the entire life of the game in his own penalty-area. Goalkeepers know this, and coaches know it.

For that reason, it is unusual for goalkeepers to do the sort of things that get outfield players in trouble. Goalkeepers are not entirely innocent—as we shall see—but they are less likely to commit fouls than are the other players.

Another point referees have to understand is that goalkeepers generally dominate the air close to the goal. If a cross is too close, it is gobbled up by most goalkeepers, simply because they can get higher into the air than forwards can. Arms add almost two feet onto the maximum height any player can reach, and if the 'keeper times his leap correctly to get the ball at maximum height, no forward in the world can beat him to the ball. Goalkeepers know this, and so do forwards and coaches, which brings us back to the fundamental dictum of play: *If you can't win by fair means, you are going to try to win by foul.* To avoid losing every cross to the goalkeeper, the forwards have to commit fouls.

The simplest way of preventing a goalkeeper from reaching the ball at the best height is to impede his progress to the ball. One forward reads where the ball is coming down, another reads where the goalkeeper is going to go. The first one goes for the ball, and his teammate jumps with the goalkeeper, disturbing the defender's leap just enough to allow the ball to fall to another attacker. How does the referee recognize this?

Remember that unless the goalkeeper is unusually small, his hands or fist will be able to reach higher than the head of any forward. That being the case, why does any forward jump with the goalkeeper in the place where the 'keeper is going to win? He does it to impede the goalkeeper, to put him off his leap, to disturb him just enough that he may drop the ball, or miss it completely. It is a reasonable assumption for any referee that if a forward collides with a goalkeeper going for a ball in the air, the attacker is acting recklessly or unfairly.

But what about the supposedly innocent custodians of the goal? What fouls do they commit? In the last few years, we have seen an increase in attempts by goalkeepers to intimidate the onrushing forwards in cases where there is a 50-50 chase for a ball going through the defence. Normally a goalkeeper will have to dive at the feet of the forwards to smother the ball. What we are seeing lately are goalkeepers who lead with their feet as they go down for the ball. Their footwear, studs showing, are up off the ground as the 'keeper's body smothers the ball. Make no mistake, *if a goalkeeper makes contact with a forward in this manner, he has committed a foul — his action was reckless, potentially injurious, and a clear violation of Law 12.*

We have a suspicion that this kind of action is being taught. It was not too many years ago that there was horror in the refereeing world here because we learned that coaches were teaching goalkeepers to have one foot up and forward as they gather a ball being chased by an attacker. The explanation from goalkeepers and their coaches is that the foot is for "protection". Make no mistake—this action is against the law. At the very least, it is dangerous play if the forward is unfairly put off or affected by the sight of the foot—studs gleaming—coming at his chest; at worst, it will be a penalty-kick of the goalkeeper's momentum carries him feet-first into the forward's body. *No player is allowed to protect himself by endangering or injuring an opponent.*

Creating a foul to gain a free kick.

In the last few years, soccer shoes and soccer balls have been so improved that many an average player is able to kick a dead ball and make it "bend" in flight. A skilful player can make the ball bend six feet or more—horizontally or vertically—in a distance of twenty yards, with the ball travelling at more than fifty miles an hour! A free kick near goal is now a tremendous scoring opportunity, and many players specialize in taking these kicks, training themselves to hit the ball over or outside the defensive wall into the top corners of the goal. But this exciting development in equipment and skill also has a sinister companion: a new way of cheating.

Attacking players will deliberately seek to get themselves fouled just outside the penalty-area, in order that their free-kick specialist will have a goal-scoring opportunity. In games we have either refereed or watched, we have seen three techniques that produce a free-kick, and all of them were intended to deceive referees. Karl-Heinz Granitza of the Chicago Sting in the NASL mastered the art of one of them, and the second and third were brought to perfection by Haji of Romania and Stoitchkov of Bulgaria.

Here's the way they worked.

Method One: The forward in possession of the ball is moving across the top of, and a yard or two outside the penalty-area. Close on his heels is the pursuing defender. As the forward senses the defender right behind him, he slows down slightly. The effect is predictable: the defender cannot slow down at the same moment, and consequently runs into the back of the forward, who falls down from the impact. This was Granitza's masterpiece. Ninety-nine percent of people watching such an incident would give a free kick to the attacker. After all, *there was actual contact, and the forward was knocked to the ground.* But the contact was initiated by the attacker, and while slowing down, *if he was no longer in playing distance of the ball, he would be guilty of impeding the defender.* An indirect free kick should be awarded to the defender. Yes, the defender!

Method Two: The attacker in possession of the ball is being challenged by a defender, who may be coming up alongside. As the defender draws close, the forward turns his back slightly to the defender, apparently shielding the ball, but as soon as there is even a hint of contact, the attacker falls down. Everyone sees the apparent contact, and since the forward was in possession, assumes that he has been fouled, even though the "contact" was initiated by the attacker. He was seeking to be fouled, and the referee obliges him with a free kick. Timing here is important, because *a player is allowed to shield the ball by turning his back* to his opponent. But players don't wait until the last second before shielding the ball; they do it early on in possession so as to keep the opponent away. The artful mischief of Haji and Stoitchkov, turning at the last second in the guise of protecting the ball, was the ability to change a legitimate maneuver into cheating.

Method Three: A defender challenges an attacker just outside the penalty-area. He runs alongside to tackle from the goalward side of the ball, and, timing his challenge perfectly, knocks the ball away with his outstretched leg. The attacker however, keeps moving forward, runs into the defender's leg, and falls like the last of the Giant Redwoods. The audience sees the outstretched leg, sees the contact, sees the result and agrees with the referee—deceived once more—who gives a free kick. Timing is important once again. If the forward allows the ball to be exposed for the challenge too early, the defender will simply knock it away cleanly. By waiting a little longer and by not turning to protect the ball, the forward *invites the tackle from the defender*, and then uses his opponent's leg as the device to get a free kick. A player who does this kind of thing more than once in a game must be cautioned. That will put a stop to it!

[As an aside, let us explain why players do this, for there is more to it than just cheating. These players use their knowledge of too many referees who hesitate to give a penalty kick for a foul that is near the top of, but inside the area. Such officials will refrain from blowing the whistle. Players who have experienced this officiating weakness will seek to exploit it by simulating a foul outside the area, knowing that many referees will not hesitate to make the "safe" call. We study the players, and believe us, they study the referees!]

How to nail an opponent and disguise it.

We feel a little uncomfortable about describing these fouls, because to our minds they represent the malevolent side of what is—by any standards—a great sport. Despite the beauty of this game, competition among professionals and top-class amateurs can be hard and brutal, and no matter how often or how strongly we may say we don't like the nasty side of the game, its existence does provide employment for hundreds of thousands of referees. So we describe these offences here, not to teach players how to nail an opponent, but to show referees an unpleasant reality they have to learn to recognize and punish.

These fouls have one purpose only: to hurt an opponent, to injure him or to incapacitate him—in other words, to take him out of the game. The most cold-blooded individual in the sport can't excuse this violence—and violence is what it should be called. But too many great players have been the object of brutality, too many have been injured in the name of competition. Pélé was removed from the World Cup in 1966 by a ferocious, foul challenge in midfield. Maradona's ankle was broken deliberately when he played in Spain. The illustration (Figure 6-1) shows the ankle of Kenny

The ankle of Kenny Dalglish of Liverpool as it was struck by an opponent's foot, studs first.

Dalglish of Liverpool as it was struck by an opponent's foot, studs first. We could describe many, many others...

In order to disguise a terrible foul, the player who commits it must be accurate, fast and have perfect timing. If he can also use his opponent's own momentum to increase the severity of the contact, so much the better. One you may have heard of is known among the players as "...going over the top." Here's how it's done....

An attacker is in full flight chasing after a ball rolling in front of him, as a defender comes across to challenge. An instant after the forward reaches the ball to touch it forward, his opponent slides in with leg outstretched, appearing to try to block the ball. At almost exactly the moment the forward touches the ball, the defender's leading foot comes slightly off the ground, passes over or rolls over the top of the ball and goes—studs first—into his opponent's ankle. Done well, and timed perfectly, a foul such as this can look like a terrible accident, a mere mistake in timing, which—if followed by an act of contrition by the perpetrator—can and does fool most referees. Done well, and timed perfectly, a foul such as this can break a player's ankle.

Variations on "going over the top" are committed by simply leaving a leg in front of the ball when say, a defender is attempting a big clearance. The ball gets thumped away, but in following through, the kicker's foot encounters the judiciously-placed studs of the supposedly innocent opponent. Or, approaching from the side of an opponent in possession of the ball, an unscrupulous player intent upon injury may stab downwards with the foot nearest his opponent, and just as he is about to release the ball. The effect can be devastating, for the forward swing of the player passing the ball, and the downward motion of the fouler's leg meet at the top of the ankle of the player who will shortly limp off the field, unable to play.

These acts of brutality can look so accidental that they deceive referees and spectators alike. But nowadays, under the new wording of Law 12, all these acts can be penalized even by inexperienced referees who don't know what they have seen, for "accidental" or not, at the very least the fouls are reckless. However, if you believe us when we say that intentional harm is a feature of this game of ours, *these are fouls with no purpose but injury, and the player committing one deserves no punishment less than sending-off.*

Fouls you can hardly see.

In the previous chapter we described a foul done by a little push-in-the-back, a foul so delicately done that it cannot be fitted into the new wording of Law 12. There are others that are as hard to see, but just as effective. One that comes to mind is also a push, perfected by many a good player, and by one of the greatest: Pélé; and the other is a handball, demonstrated perfectly by another great player, Maradona.

Both of these players were so skilful with the ball, and so adept at shifting their weight to left or right, that they could dribble freely around most opponents. A player up against Pélé, for example, knew that if he were not to be beaten by the Brazilian genius, he had to stop him turning with the ball when he received it. This meant he had to mark him so closely as to be sharing his shirt. Pélé knew this, too, and expected it in every match. It never troubled him, though, because he had found a way to defeat the close marking by illegally pushing off his opponent. Most referees did not detect the foul; perhaps—Pélé had become such an icon of fair play—because they couldn't imagine he would play unfairly, and thus did not penalize him.

What Pélé did as the pass came to him, was trap the ball and then bend forward slightly, as though bracing for contact from behind. But since the defender was already close up against Pélé's back, the effect of bending was to push the marker back a short way. Then Pélé straightened up quickly with (now) half-a-yard of space between himself and his opponent. That was more than enough space for him to quickly spin around and dribble past the hapless defender. Pélé had thus effectively pushed his opponent away, even though there has never been a definition in the Laws of a "push with the buttocks". When you first see it, you can't believe it's a foul, but once you gauge the effect of it upon the opponent, the infringement becomes clear.

In order to compensate for his lack of height, Maradona perfected another skill, this one with his fist. The goal he scored against England in the World Cup in Mexico was played and played again for all the world and every referee to see. "The Hand of God" reached up and played the ball over the head of a world-class goalkeeper six inches taller than the Argentinian. If you haven't seen this kind of play, it can be difficult to see. But reason should have made the referee suspicious that a short forward could not beat a tall goalkeeper in the air! Besides, Maradona had done this kind of thing before, and part of the referee's preparation…..well, we've said how important that aspect of your game is!

Other fouls that are hard to see, or difficult to assess as being worth calling, involve other uses of players' hands and arms. Is an outstretched arm for balance, or is it to hold off or hold back an opponent? When players' arms are intertwined in a challenge for the ball, is either player placed at a disadvantage? When a player arrives slightly late for a tackle and grazes his opponent's leg or ankle with his foot, was it reckless, or was it an accident of the speed at which the game is played?

We don't have definitive descriptions or guidance for matters such as these, except to say that our experience has taught us that in many, many situations, the players will let you know what is acceptable and what is not. You will hear repeated expressions of annoyance at what an opponent is doing, or you'll get a look of disgust in your direction after someone nipped at an ankle, or sometimes there'll be a direct appeal: "Jesus, ref, that feller's got more arms than an octopus! Are you goin' to let him play like that?" Those clues will tell you it is time to step in, penalize the foul and speak to the player who is committing what you may have thought were minor infractions. As we say elsewhere in this book, sometimes it is the players who decide what should be called.

A foul that doesn't exist.

Years after this particular event, we still shake our heads in amusement and a certain amount of sympathy when we talk about it, for we have to admit that the assignment was a tough one. Referee a pre-season game between an NASL club (Tampa Bay) and a visiting team from the Soviet Union, and do it in front of the critical eyes of seventy of your colleagues from the officiating staff of the league, every one of whom probably thought he could do the job better than you! And when the game was over, every one of the seventy critics, and the man-in-the-middle—if they were paying attention—should have learned something important about what a professional soccer player can do to a referee who does not have his wits about him.

On the field for Tampa was Rodney Marsh, a brilliantly talented midfielder/forward, former England player, and a very funny guy notorious for bringing his humor into a game at the expense of his opponents and sometimes the referee (see the sidebar on Marsh in Chapter 17 on emotions and ego). Rodney attacked in the inside-right position and ran into his opponents' penalty area with the ball at his feet. The defender was on his left—that is important!—close alongside him. The two players got a few yards into the area and then the most amazing thing happened. If you blinked, you wouldn't have seen it, and if you were the referee, you would swear that the defender had clipped Rodney's feet and brought him down.

The whistle blew and the referee pointed to the spot as Rodney got up off the grass. Some of the defenders protested, but the Soviet players, being as disciplined as they were before the fall of the Iron Curtain, didn't make much of a protest. What the defenders saw—and we saw because we didn't blink—was the most skilful simulation of a foul we have ever seen. This was not your common or garden variety of dive, with arms flailing upwards, and legs bent backwards, a dive so blatant that even beginning referees can recognize it. No, this one by Rodney Marsh was an act of great beauty. As he was running at full speed, he flicked his right foot behind his left ankle and brought himself down! He simply collapsed to the turf with none of the histrionics of lesser players who simulate fouls. Because it looked so natural, because it had none of the stuff of the typical dive, it completely fooled this particular referee, partially screened by the defender alongside Marsh. Without hesitation, he gave the penalty.

The lesson for everyone? *Professional players can be professional at everything connected with the game: the skills, the temperament, the manipulation of the referee and the artfulness in cheating.* And for the sting in the tail regarding this incident involving Marsh, take a look at what we reveal about him in Chapter 18.

Information from players.

After certain fouls, actions by other players may tell the referee what they think abut the incident. Whom do they blame? If you did not see the incident, or if you are uncertain of its severity, you can get important information this way. Sometimes there may be complaints about a certain player and fouls he is committing. If this happens, do not aggravate the complainer by telling him to be quiet or by giving some other offhand remark. Simply ask: "Who? Their number six, is it? Leave him to me. I'll take care of him." Of course, you do not have to do anything different. But when number six does commit his next foul, as you penalize him, you send a knowing glance to the original complaining player. In this way, he thinks you have listened to his complaint, and is usually placated.

NOTES

7

FREE KICKS

*"When more and more teams become adept at scoring from free-kicks,
the game will take a turn for the better, since teams will be punished...
for foul play. We should all encourage referees to use
their most stringent endeavours to hasten that day."*

Charles Hughes,
Assistant Director of Coaching,
The Football Association, 1973.

The meaning of "free"

Look in any dictionary of the English language and you will find
dozens of the meanings for the word "free". Buried among them
is the one that applies to free kicks in this sport of ours: *unimpeded.*
Quite simply, one team is punished for foul or illegal play, and their
opponents are given compensation in the form of *an unimpeded kick
at the ball, in any direction, for any distance, without interference in
any way by their opponents or by the referee.*

That underlined phrase is as important as the rest of the
definition, and we will use it as a justification for much of what we
write in this chapter, for
we see too many instances
where the referee is
responsible for denying a
team the compensation
they are supposed to get
after illegal play by their
opponents. A couple of
examples will convince you.

IN THIS CHAPTER:

- *The meaning of "free"*
- *Basic legal requirements at
  a free kick*
- *Not all free kicks should be administered
  the same way*
- *What you <u>must</u> know to handle a free
  kick wisely*
- *Special cases: the quick free kick; the
  late free kick*

The first comes from the World Cup finals in the U.S. in 1994. The match was Argentina against Nigeria in Dallas. A Nigerian defender cuts down an Argentinian attacker with a foul that is worthy of a caution, and this is clearly what the referee intends to administer. But before he has called the player, an Argentinian attacker sees an opportunity for an advantageous quick free kick. The ball is dead, and the player kicks it quickly to an open teammate. Within seconds, an attack develops and the ball ends up in the goal. Charlie Hughes would have loved it! This was the perfect punishment he advocates in the epigraph of this chapter, for the bad foul committed by the Nigerian defender. The referee, however, called it back to caution the defender.

This was an obvious injustice compounded by the fact that he picked out and cautioned the wrong player! But that error aside, the referee should have seen the potential benefit of the quick free kick and allowed play to go on. He could always caution the defender when next the ball went out of play. It comes down to this: *the referee interfered with the perfect execution of a free kick by the team that had been harmed.* (We will add, in accordance with one of the themes running through this book, that the referee was ill-prepared. Argentina had come into the tournament intent on playing quick free kicks whenever they could. They had clearly decided upon this as a strategy, had practiced them, and performed them in previous matches. All the referees should have been aware of this, and been ready to act accordingly. They should have been expecting one at every opportunity.)

The second example comes from a western region youth tournament in California. A free kick just outside the penalty area produced a wall of defenders. All the players waited for the formalities to be taken care of as the referee got the defenders back ten yards. Two forwards stood over the ball. The linesman went down to the goal line, and the referee took a position in line with the wall of defenders. He blew his whistle, one forward stepped up to the ball, tapping it sideways as one defender broke from the wall and rushed in. The second forward took the pass and without hesitation, curled the ball around the end of the wall into the goal. But the whistle blew as the ball bulged the net. Goal? No! The referee, waving his yellow card, ran up to the defender to caution him for encroachment, and then ordered the free kick retaken. *The referee interfered with the perfect execution of a free kick by the team that had been harmed.*

It is one of our purposes here to show you some techniques for avoiding interfering with a free kick.

Basic legal requirements at a free kick.

We are not going to deal with the obvious requirements clearly described in the laws—direct or indirect, position of the ball at a free kick in the penalty-area or goal-area, stationary ball, playing the ball a second time, goal scored or not, signal for "indirect", ball in play, infringements and sanctions—but will concentrate on the important ones that affect your conduct when you have awarded a free-kick. As far as the meaning and intent of the word "free" is concerned, there is only one important legal stipulation in Law 13 – Free Kicks: "*all opponents are at least ten yards from the ball until it is in play, unless they are on their own goal line between the goalposts.*" And if they are not, "*the kick is retaken.*"

But there are two others that are important, these from Law 5 – The Referee. One is the advantage clause, to which we devote the entire next chapter, and the other is the requirement that the referee restart the match after it has been stopped. Since the referee is the one person responsible for restarting the match, this requirement implies that he should give some kind of signal that the game shall go on. More on that in a moment. In the meantime, here's an indispensable principle:

The combination of the ten-yard rule with the advantage clause gives the referee all the power he needs to ensure that every free kick is truly "free".

Let's look at a few hypothetical cases, but start with a point of understanding:

The team that broke the law has no rights at free kicks except the right not to be distracted by something the referee does. Conversely, and most important, the team that takes the free kick has all the rights necessary to ensure that they are compensated for being wronged.

CASE 1:

The wall is lined up ten yards from the ball, but after the referee has stepped away, the players start creeping forward. The referee signals, the ball is kicked across the face of the goal and headed into the net.

Analysis: The ten-yard law was violated, but the maligned team benefits from allowing play to go on. A good advantage, and the goal stands.

CASE 2:

The wall lines up ten yards from the ball, but starts to creep forward before the signal is given for the restart. The ball is kicked but strikes one of the encroaching players.

Analysis: The ten-yard rule was violated; there is no advantage so the kick must be retaken.

CASE 3:

The wall lines up reluctantly ten yards from the ball. Before the signal is given, one of the defenders breaks from the wall and blocks the kick.

Analysis: The ten-yard rule was violated, and the defender willfully broke the law. The defender should be cautioned, and the kick retaken.

CASE 4:

The referee blows for a free kick, and the fouled player falls near the ball. Lying on the ground he stops it with his hand, but before he can play it, a defender runs in and stands with his foot on the ball.

Analysis: The ten-yard rule was violated, and an excellent opportunity for a quick free kick was taken away. The defender must be cautioned.

CASE 5:

The referee blows for a free kick, and the fouled player falls near the ball, with a defender close by. Lying on the ground, the fouled player swings his leg and plays the ball to a teammate a few yards away. An attack starts, catching the defenders by surprise.

Analysis: A perfect quick free kick! The ten-yard law was violated but the situation gives the maligned team an opportunity to take a great advantage. Play on!

[As an aside, we should mention that there is the idea going about that a player lying on the ground cannot play the ball. This is nonsense, especially when you consider a case like the one we have just described. Where there is real danger, say in the case of a youth player on the ground trying to play the ball when surrounded by the swinging legs of his teammates and opponents, the referee should stop play and give a dropped ball.]

CASE 6:

A defender commits a foul and after the whistle, walks back slowly away from the ball. The fouled player stands up and quickly plays the ball to a nearby teammate, but the ball strikes the retreating defender, who by this time is only five yards from the ball.

Analysis: The ten-yard rule has been violated, and the law requires that the kick be retaken. By allowing the ball to be played even though there is a defender fewer than ten yards from the ball, the referee is applying the advantage clause, and since the advantage doesn't materialize, he can and should penalize the original infraction, that of being less than ten yards from the ball. The kick must be retaken. The encroaching defender need not be cautioned if the referee judges that he was not willfully impeding the free kick.

In cases like this, you will find referees who insist that since the attacker voluntarily played the ball, he doesn't have the right to have another try after he misplayed the ball. "He can't have two bites at the apple. He should have waited for the player to get back," they say. Those referees (and the instructors who teach that philosophy) are wrong on two counts: their sense of justice is skewed in favor of the team that committed the foul; and they forget that the advantage clause *allows* "two bites at the apple" to ensure that justice be done. The first bite comes when the referee plays on (advantage), and the second bite comes when the referee gives a free kick because the apple didn't taste good (advantage didn't work out).

You will grasp the intent of these examples if you remember the dictum:

The team that broke the law has no rights at free kicks except the right not to be distracted by something the referee does. Conversely, and most important, the team that takes the free kick has all the rights necessary to ensure that they are compensated for being wronged.

Not all free kicks should be administered the same way.

What we mean by this is that there will be times when you don't need to be over-zealous in insisting upon ten yards at a free kick, nor do you need to caution players who deliberately take their time in retreating ten yards. At first glance, this may seem like a provocative statement, perhaps even contradicting what we have said in the section above. How can we argue that all the rights belong to the aggrieved, and then suggest that the referee does not have to enforce the ten-yard rule at every free kick? Stay with us, brothers and sisters, and we'll show you...

CASE 1:

You are the final few minutes of a rough game, and the result is a foregone conclusion. One team is leading 3-0, attacking once again, when a defender, tired of the beating he and his teammates are taking, brings down a forward a yard outside the penalty-area. The other defenders—moaning and groaning about how unfair the referee is—gather round about a yard or two from the ball, and are intent upon delaying the free kick for as long as they can. Before you decide what you should do in a situation like this, ask yourself some questions.

The defenders are cheating by delaying the free kick, but who suffers because of their behavior? Answer: they do, because time is running out, diminishing their chances of scoring a goal to redeem themselves.

With tempers getting a bit ragged at the end of this match, will it benefit your control of the game to have the action stop for a minute or two? Answer: yes, and no one will suffer for it.

If you caution a defender for delaying this free kick, what will you gain from it? Answer: nothing, and you might even be pouring gasoline on a smoldering fire.

This is one free kick that you can take your time about. Yes, you can tell the defenders to get back, and you can go ten yards and show them where to stand, but you don't need to rush, you don't need to pull out a card. Relax, be patient, and let the time wind down. Once the defenders are back approximately ten yards, signal for play to proceed.

CASE 2:

But what if the score was 2-1 in favor of the attacking team that had just been fouled, we hear someone say, would that make a difference?

In such a case, you can use the time and the score to help your administration of the situation. The defenders who are delaying are only one goal down, and as you start to move them back ten yards, you can ostentatiously announce—holding up your watch as you do so—that there is only a little time left, and that by delaying there are losing their opportunity to score an equalizing goal. We guarantee they will move back in a hurry!

CASE 3:

Early in a scoreless game you blow your whistle for a free kick a few yards outside the penalty-area. Players mill about, and it becomes clear that there is going to be no quick free kick. In fact, an attacking player says something like: "Make sure we get ten yards on this one, ref!"

Since there is no great rush to get things going again, you do not have to be ever-so-strict about defenders being reluctant to get back. You can make sure that they will respect the ten yards once you have got them back, but they cannot be accused of delaying something that everyone knows is already delayed, and what's more, is OK about it. So get them back the required distance, but don't waste energy fighting with them about something that bothers no one.

Towards the end of that same game, with the score still 0-0, deliberate delay takes on a different purpose, and you may have to resort to a caution to enforce the law.

CASE 4:

In the last game of the season and the final minute of a game, you give a free kick outside the penalty-area to a team that is well beaten. The score is 4-0, but the losing team needs one goal—which will give them one more point in the standings—to avoid being relegated to a lower division. The situation should make you aware that this free kick is every bit as important as any free kick you have ever given, so the law must be enforced strictly.

A defender who deliberately delays the kick should be cautioned, and you should be very strict about guaranteeing that the attackers get the ten yards. They deserve and need an unimpeded free kick to try and save their season.

CASE 5:

In the final few minutes of a game, one team is winning 3-1 when you award them a dangerous free-kick twenty yards out. It would seem that this is similar to CASE 1, in which we recommended that you could be patient with the defenders and use a bit of time to help you to keep things under control. But things are a little different here....

The match is the second in a home-and-away series, but the defending team here won the first leg 2-0. In effect then, the score is tied 3-3, *but* (and this is important) in many competitions, when the score is tied, away goals count double. In the case we have just described, the team conceding the free kick will win the game by that rule, if the second game stays as it is. In other words, the defenders have to prevent their opponents from scoring, and they will do every thing can to make sure the score stays at 3-1.

You have to make sure at this free kick that the attackers, even though they are ahead 3-1, get another chance to score. Enforce the ten yards and brook no delay beyond what is inevitable.

These cases allow us to segue nicely into the section that follows.

What you <u>must</u> know to handle a free kick wisely.

At free kicks near the goal, with such opportunities for scoring, especially with the free-kick specialists roaming the soccer world nowadays, the referee must be aware of all the significant elements at the free kick:

1. Will this one goal change the result of the game or the series?

2. Where are the teams in the league standings?

3. Is time a factor?

4. What are the rules in the event of a tie?

5. Who will be hurt by delay?

6. Can I use this moment to help keep things under control?

7. If I have to caution a player in the wall, does any one of the likely candidates already have a yellow card? (In which case, pick someone else.)

8. Am I being insistent upon the letter of the law because I don't like the players' defiance? (See Chapter 17 dealing with ego and emotions.)

Several of these items require that you have information ahead of time; in other words, that you have come to the match fully prepared with all you need to officiate properly. Read Chapter 3 again!

Special cases: the quick free kick; the late free kick.

In our opinion, the quick free kick is a marvelous stratagem for defeating your opponent. A planned pause in the game becomes no pause. Players who relax at the sound of the whistle are caught off-guard, and an attack that was supposed to be interrupted proceeds in full flight, much to the surprise and chagrin of the players who attempted the interruption. *All referees should do everything in their power to ensure that teams have every opportunity to take quick free kicks.*

Once you know that a team favors them, let the players know by your demeanor that you will allow them. Shout "Play on!" immediately after blowing the whistle for a foul, and remember that if it doesn't work out because a defender illegally interrupts the kick, you can always give it again. There is no better support for Charlie Hughes' appeal than a well-taken quick free kick perceptively encouraged by a knowledgeable referee. And it is so good for the game!

Consider one last free-kick situation, and then we'll move on to other subjects. Imagine it is the eighty-ninth minute of the game, with the score 2-1 in favor of the defenders at this free-kick, 26 yards from the goal-line and about 18 or 19 yards wide from the near post (Figure 7-1). It is the last chance for the attackers to equalize, and so

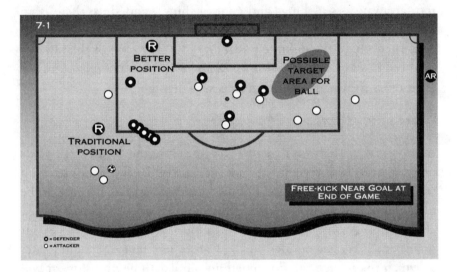

they bring everyone forward. With the ball this close to the goal, five defenders pack the wall to shut off as much of the goal as possible. Five of the attackers are closely marked, but that leaves three or possibly four attacking players free from attention. What are the possibilities?

The attacking team might have two players—one right-footed, the other left-footed—on the ball. This they might do to produce some uncertainty in the defenders' mind: Which way is the ball going to go? A right-footed player could curve the ball over and around the wall into the top corner near the far post. A left-footed player could chip the ball over the wall, pulling it away from the goalkeeper for the onrushing forwards. The right-footed player could be deceptive, and instead of shooting, could curve the ball over the wall into the space on the right, behind the defenders, too far for the goalkeeper, but dropping it into the "no man's land" as shown. Whatever decision the attackers make, there will clearly be a crowd of players in the penalty-area and close to the goal.

The referee in the normal position, monitoring the wall, will be too far away to see things and control things, and since there is an obvious possibility of offside, the linesman is best left to judge that. Because we have the definite possibility of a shot, one of the officials ought to be close to the goal-line. Who better than the referee, in the position as shown? For more details, see Chapter 14.

Some Final Points.

In the game of rugby, if defenders do not retire the required 10 yards before a free-kick (in rugby it's called a penalty) is taken, the attacking team gets to advance the point of the kick by 10 yards. Because of the many problems associated with getting players back 10 yards in soccer, and because many referees either cannot or will not enforce this provision, FIFA has decided to allow an experiment in certain games in which the referee can do something similar. The punishment will also be applied if the defending team indulges in other cheating such as kicking the ball away, and showing dissent at the decision. It will be extremely interesting to see the changes in tactics that this will bring about. It will certainly make the referee's job easier, but could also contribute to further problems.

Some players who have high skill levels actually prefer to have a defensive wall closer than 10 yards to the ball. This is to allow more room behind the wall for the ball to dip and swerve, and so hit its target. The alert referee will also be ready for such situations if and when they occur, and not rigidly require the 10 yards.

Summary points:

- *All the rights belong to the aggrieved party*
- *Advantage and the ten-yard rule give you all the power to make sure that justice prevails at free kicks*
- *Not all free kicks need to be enforced the same way*
- *Learn when to be tough on enforcement of the law, and know when to be patient*
- *Encourage the taking of quick free kicks is that is what the players want*
- *Prepare yourself with essential information for every game*
- *The last free kick in the match may be the most important one*

NOTES

USE AND MISUSE
OF ADVANTAGE

*Each of us can, by ploy or gambit,
most naturally gain the advantage.*

Stephen Potter,
British Writer

Referees' problems with "advantage."

Remember the opening match of the 1990 World Cup? A perennial world power—Argentina—played one of the upstarts from the African continent—Cameroon. In the first few minutes of the game, the Argentinian forward Caniggia, who possessed a sprinter's pace, set off on a high-speed run with the ball down the right side. He was tackled weakly and fouled by a Cameroonian defender, but was able to shake off the challenge and keep going. Advantage! Said the referee. Within seconds Caniggia was fouled again by another defender, but after staggering a couple of steps he recovered to continue chasing the ball. Advantage again! This was too much for a third defender, no doubt amazed and disgusted that Caniggia had been

IN THIS CHAPTER:

- *Examples of difficulties with the new law and the old*
- *Everything that affects the use of advantage:*
  - *Location*
  - *Skill and sophistication of the players*
  - *How serious is the foul?*
  - *Delayed caution*
- *How to apply it—technique*
- *Which laws does it affect?*
- *Examples of successful use of advantage*

clobbered twice and yet still ran on towards the goal. Determined to stop him, he body-checked the Argentinian at high speed and with such force that Caniggia was knocked into the air, after a short flight through which, he fell heavily to the ground. This time referee blew the whistle and sent off the third defender, no doubt for Cameroon's multiple crimes against Argentinian humanity.

In an F.A. Cup Final in England, Peter Beardsley of Liverpool was illegally impeded as he dribbled his way into his opponents' penalty area. Skilled player that he is, however, Beardsley shook off his opponent and put the ball into the net, unfortunately just as the referee blew the whistle for the foul. As we will show you later in this chapter, the referee could have saved the situation with a clever bit of subterfuge, but in this game, the advantage was gone, nothing came of the resulting free kick, and Liverpool eventually lost the game.

Our third example comes from an amateur USSF Over-30 Cup match, in which a very experienced referee was attempting to keep the game flowing by not stopping play for slight infractions when the fouled player or his team kept possession of the ball. One of the contestants—George Ley—had regained his amateur status after a career as a professional player for the Dallas Tornado in the NASL. The referee believed that by keeping the game flowing he was helping the players, but after about 25 minutes Ley commented—very politely—"I understand what you are doing, ref, but please realize that these players don't have the ability to benefit from keeping possession, and we would rather have the free kick!"

If you read the advantage clause in the "Powers and Duties" section of Law 5, and then examine the three examples described above, you might be a little perplexed. Advantage applied too often, says one; not applied when it should have been, says the second; and don't apply it for us, says a player in the third! We all know that it's not easy being a referee, creating all these problems for the players from a law that is supposed to be for their benefit, but can we ever be right? In the next few pages, we will attempt to help by providing guidance for referees in interpreting and applying the simple but problematical **advantage clause**.

New law and old.

In the recent revision of the Laws of the Game, Law 5 states: "The Referee...allows play to continue when the team against which an offence has been committed will benefit from such an advantage and penalizes the original offence if the anticipated advantage does not ensue at that time"

In theory, this should greatly simplify the job of the referee, because it allows the official two chances to make the best decision for the player: He can let play go on, but if doesn't produce an advantage for the player who was fouled, the referee can still blow the whistle and give a free-kick. But referees cannot live by theory alone, so let's take a look at the reason for this clause, what it really means, and how best we can use it.

For as long as this game has been around, participants have known that there are times during every match when blowing the whistle for a foul is positively detrimental to the team that is going to get the free kick. The old wording of the Law actually stated that the referee should not penalize where "...by doing so, he would be giving an advantage *to the offending team*" (italics ours)

Over the years this clause has been analyzed many ways. In one interpretation, the referee *gave* the advantage to the team in possession, and whose player had been fouled. Another interpretation was that the referee allowed a team fouled against to *keep* its advantage. Both of these interpretations considered only the team or player that had been fouled.

The opposite view, and more in line with the Law, was not to give the team that had fouled any advantage. No matter how you look at the situation, it is clear that what is intended here is that a team committing a foul should not *benefit* as a result and that the opponents should not be put in *a less favorable* position by play being stopped for a free kick.

Because of these different thoughts about the wording, referees utilized and applied the advantage clause in such a bewildering multitude of ways that players never knew what to expect from one match to the next. That is the way the situation is today, a situation not helped by the way this law is taught.

At many referees' training programs you will hear all kinds of instructions. Prominent among these is: "No advantage in the first 10-15 minutes!" The theory is that this will allow the referee to first gain control of the match, and then to relax and allow the players some leeway later. As a theory, it seems OK. Unfortunately, however, it produces a confusing lack of consistency, not only from one referee to the next—always a major complaint from players and coaches— but also from an individual referee in just one match. The players have a right to know what the referee is going to penalize, but when the official gives a free-kick for a particular foul at one moment, and then allows the same infraction to go unpunished a few minutes later, the players don't know what to expect.

Some instructors believe that you should avoid advantage altogether in a tight or critical match such as a cup semi-final, or in a tough match between fierce rivals. The idea there is that you whistle everything to keep things under control. To the players in such a match, however, the referee is choking the life out of the game. Time and again, the players will appeal: "For God's sake (or worse), referee, *let us play!*"

These theories of advantage (1) are unfair to the players, (2) are not mentioned in the Laws, (3) are wrong, and (4) should not be used. Is that clear enough?

The fundamental problem.

We believe that the first problem is that this clause is over-emphasized in basic referee training. Referees are constantly being told that in assessments, they are judged heavily on their application of advantage. This generally results in referees applying advantage too liberally, because they don't want to be accused of not understanding the clause. The result is predictable: the poor victim in the middle applies advantage (or thinks he applies advantage) all over the place and loses control of the game.

The second problem is that too often, referees confuse advantage with the application of the "trifling and dubious infractions clause" that used to be part of Law 5. We cover this in detail in Chapter 4, but for the moment let us summarize the art of refereeing—the old Law 5, International Board Decision number 8—as being the ability to identify and deal *with only those infractions that affect the game.* If you see a foul and let it go unpunished, you may have decided that the foul was "trifling" or insignificant, and did not affect the players of the play. The recognition of what is significant for the game is one essential skill for all referees to learn. The correct application of advantage is another.

A true advantage situation will occur only a few times in a match, but could occur in the first minute or the last, or any moment in between. Therefore, we must be able to recognize it. It is vital that referees understand that *keeping possession of the ball alone is not advantage.* There must be retention of possession *plus* (1) an enhanced opportunity either to score or (2) a chance to mount an attack that has a good probability of leading to a shot on goal. And (3) it must be clear that if the referee were to stop play and award a free-kick, it would be *less advantageous for the team in possession, and more advantageous for the team that committed the foul.* Obviously, no referee would want to do that. Helping the cheaters is not part of our job-description!

That paragraph immediately above contains a lot of stuff to remember, but there's more. There are other variables to be taken into consideration:

> *the location on the pitch,*
>
> *the skill level of the players* (the particular one with the ball, and the others on both teams),
>
> *the proximity of opponents and teammates,*
>
> *the severity of the foul* committed.

Let's take a closer look at each of these variables.

Location.

Because giving a penalty kick is probably the most disadvantageous position a referee can put any team in, many referee instructors will tell referees never to apply advantage in the penalty area. They believe that the penalty-kick (with a success rate of 94% at all levels of the game) is all the advantage necessary. But it is always possible that the kicker could miss, or the 'keeper make a great save. Nevertheless, we believe that 100% is always better than 94%. If in a match an attacker is fouled in his opponents' penalty-area, but the ball rolls free to a teammate who has the goal open in front of him, or the fouled player recovers to see and shoot at the open goal, or if after the foul, the ball rolls on towards the open net, then let play go on. Playing advantage in the penalty-area is going to be rare, but Oh! Will you look good when it comes off!

In the case of fouls occurring in a team's own half, there is rarely an advantage situation. A player with the ball at his feet after being fouled, but more than 50 yards from the goal and with several opponents in front of him, can hardly be considered to be in an advantageous position. This is especially true in games at a lower skill level, the level at which the vast majority of referees operate. However in games involving players of high skill, there are occasionally conditions for which an advantage ruling would be preferable. Consider the following ones.

THE PERILS OF ADVANTAGE IN THE PENALTY-AREA

The dangers of advantage calls in the penalty area—and the unknown complications that lurk in the background in the professional game—can be illustrated by the following incident that occurred in a match (NASL) refereed by one of us (EB). Midway through the second half, with Golden Bay leading by 6-0, their leading scorer Steve Zungul broke into the Tampa Bay penalty-area. Just as he was getting off his shot, he was challenged by the goalkeeper and also fouled from behind by a defender. The ball rolled free, trickling into the lower left corner of the goal, and so the referee did not whistle for the penalty kick, preferring to allow the goal instead. However, the Tampa Bay defender Glenn Myernick, sprinted in from the right side of the goalmouth, managed to get a foot on the ball on the goal line, and cleared it away!

Play continued and (no surprise here!) Zungul complained about the decision. "You're winning 6-0, and it looked as though it would go in anyway," explained the referee. "Ah yes," replied Zungul, "but I get more bonus money if I score more goals, and I am the one who takes the penalties." Of course, with the recent change in wording of the Law, today's referee could give the penalty kick anyway once Myernick kicked it off the goal-line, but in the good old days, revoking advantage after it had been applied was specifically prohibited at the time. It is so much easier now, for the referee comes out looking good with either decision.

Let's say that many players push into the attack. If one of them commits a foul, this could be exploited by a very quick long ball downfield to fast-breaking forwards who then could get into a one-on-one situation with only the goalkeeper to beat. This is especially true in the case of minor fouls from corner kicks etc., when the goalkeeper gets the ball safely in his hands. A quick throw or a long punt is usually preferable to a free kick. And be aware that expressly in order to allow their defenders to re-organize, many experienced or sophisticated teams will deliberately foul in the attacking area when it is realized that their attacking opportunity is lost. Referees who are unaware of what is going on, blow the whistle to give a free-kick and in so doing blithely fall into the trap set by the players. *When you see a foul by an attacker deep in his opponents' territory, ask yourself: "What was the purpose of this foul?"* And if you believe it was for the purpose of creating time for reorganization, and if the foul was not a severe one, then find a way to keep play going, especially if there is a good, long-ball opportunity for the defenders.

The situation in the case of fouls that occur within 30 yards of the goal is especially difficult (Figure 8-1). The referee must assess the opportunity for a player of tremendous ability, such as Pele and Zico of old, or Roberto Carlos, Stoitchkov, Haji or Beckham of today to take a direct shot on goal and score from these distances, even though the defenders will get everyone back behind the ball and probably form a defensive wall. Clearly the offending team is placed at the proper disadvantage by the decision to give the free-kick, that is, if the attacking team has players with the requisite skill. Here the best decision is the free-kick. In fact, there are so many players who are dangerous at these set-pieces that in top-level professional games, attackers often attempt to draw fouls in this zone specifically to get their free-kick specialist an opportunity (see Chapters 5 and 6).

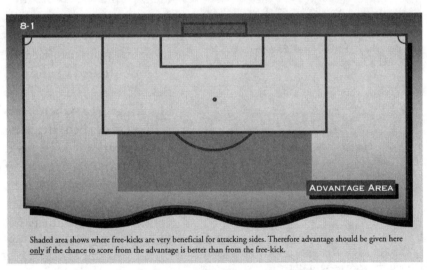

Shaded area shows where free-kicks are very beneficial for attacking sides. Therefore advantage should be given here only if the chance to score from the advantage is better than from the free-kick.

But even if there are no players with the required skill to beat a wall, such as in games of lower skill level, a free kick which could be floated into the goalmouth is likely to be more advantageous than simply allowing play to proceed in a situation where defenders are close enough to continue tackling. Even in low-level amateur and youth soccer, teams do practice free-kicks near goal, and have strategies that increase their chance to score. So give them that chance, unless there is the kind of advantage every referee dreams about.

Level of skill and sophistication of players.

We learned from our playing days that when a player is fouled, he generally expects the referee to punish the offender. A kick on the ankle or shin doesn't suddenly become less painful when the referee shouts "Advantage, play on!" It doesn't take too many of these before the players start to get fed up and take matters into their own hands. This is especially true in games at lower skill levels where—in many cases—they couldn't care less about advantage. The players just don't like getting kicked all the time. It can apply equally well in professional games, since the players rely on their legs and bodies for their livelihood. And as any cynical player knows, in many games there can be volatile players who will react emotionally to being fouled repeatedly, especially if the whistle isn't blown.

But there are rarely more than a handful of occasions in most matches where a true advantage situation occurs. These can occur at any time in the match, which is why the "no advantage in the first 10 minutes" method is flawed. But if a referee realizes what a true advantage is and knows that they do not happen very often, then his decisions will be much appreciated when he applies the clause correctly.

There are times when it is essential to stop play even if a good advantage situation presents itself. One of these is when there is a potentially serious injury to a player. At that point the well-being of the player overrides the expedience of advantage, and treatment of the injury should take place as soon as possible. As with several other examples discussed in this chapter, this is extremely important in amateur matches, where the game is being played for the benefit and enjoyment of the players, but also is important in professional games. Most referees are not medically qualified, but with experience it is possible for a referee to distinguish between a slight injury and one which requires urgent attention, such as a head injury, or obvious possible bone fracture.

Another time to forget about advantage is the case of a really serious foul for which a player should be sent off. This player should not be allowed to remain on the pitch where he could perhaps commit further offenses or could be the target of retribution, which may then produce a flare-up among the players. Note that the laws do allow the referee to postpone the disciplinary action until the ball goes out of play, but it would very rare, and probably unwise in the case of a sending-off.

The delayed caution.

Having expressed our opinion about a sending-off in an advantage situation, it is now appropriate to write about the delayed caution. Imagine a defender trying to stop an attack by unfair means, but not in such a way that he would automatically have to leave the field. The referee knows he must caution the player, but applies advantage. Even if the advantage works beautifully and produces a goal, if the original infraction was deserving of a caution, then it is vital that the referee produce the yellow card as soon as play has stopped.

It can be very useful to indicate to the player and everyone else that you intend do this. As you are running past the incident or alongside the player who committed the foul, shout loudly: "Play on, advantage! Blue number 6, you have a yellow card!" This lets everybody know that you do not intend to permit such infractions to go unpunished. And when the ball goes in the net, calmly walk to the player and show the card.

ADVANTAGE AT A PENALTY-KICK?

Talk to one hundred referees and you may find one who will say that you can apply advantage at a penalty-kick. Be that as it may, but there are rare occasions when by applying advantage, you can beat the percentage of 94% success by the penalty-kick taker. One of those occasions presented itself (to RE) in a play-off match in the NASL.

Fort Lauderdale played Montreal, whose goalkeeper, Bob Rigby, was one of the first really successful American goalkeepers in the league. There was not much dispute about the decision after a defender came in from behind an attacker and tangled him up with both legs, bringing him to the ground. The man taking the kick was Berndt Holzenbein, a member of West Germany's World Cup-winning team of 1974. He shot the ball well to one side of Rigby, but the goalkeeper had moved before the ball was kicked, and dived to save. The kick should have been ordered retaken, but the ball came rebounding back to Holzenbein, who had the goal open in front of him with the goalkeeper on the ground. In an instantaneous decision, the referee—never afraid to order a penalty-kick retaken—allowed play to proceed, even though the ball was a high bouncing rebound. Holzenbein was a world-class player, and there was never a risk that he couldn't control the ball or simply knock it into the goal. Rigby was scrambling to get up as the Fort Lauderdale player calmly played the ball into the net, making the referee look good at a perfect application of advantage.

Note that this was at a time under the old law, when you couldn't revoke the advantage decision. Nowadays you can simply wait a second or two and then order the kick retaken if the kicker doesn't score—that is, if you have the courage

How to make the call.

The referee should indicate that he has applied the advantage by both word and signal. He must loudly call out "Play on!" and use an upward swinging motion with both arms with palms raised upwards. It is also advisable to at least speak to the player who committed the foul. Just a quick word is all that needed, not a lecture.

The recent change in the wording of the Law that allows the referee to award the free-kick if the advantage does not materialize is a gift for referees, from the Great Referee in the Sky or from FIFA, whichever you prefer. Previously, the referees—the all-knowing, wise, psychic prophets that we all are—had to be able to predict what was going to happen. Now the referee can allow an advantage without having to worry about whether it will materialize in the first few seconds. If it does: Great! If it doesn't, blow the whistle for a free-kick, and still look good in the eyes of the player who was fouled! The new wording means that the referee can take more of a chance when there is some doubt as to what may happen, but it does *not* mean that the referee can blow late whistles all over the place, claiming he was looking for advantage.

There is another point to consider, and that is the position of the referee. The old adage "presence lends conviction" has real meaning in this context. The referee must be well positioned and up with play in order to correctly apply or not apply advantage. Players will usually be more accepting of questionable decisions from a well-positioned referee than they will be of one who is not keeping up.

Which laws does it affect?

Although the advantage clause is usually applied in the case of fouls (Law 12), it can be applied to other laws as well. For example, a player may be correctly flagged for an offside violation, but the ball is intercepted by a member of the opposition. If it is clearly better to allow play to proceed—taking into consideration all of the foregoing principles, then that is what the referee must do. In youth games, where the very young players have difficulty making a correct throw-in, you could play advantage if the thrower tosses the ball to an opponent, but more than likely, you would simply allow the infraction to go unpenalized because it is trifling and has no adverse effect upon the game (see Chapter 4).

Note, however, that the advantage clause cannot be applied in the cases of the ball going out of play and coming back in again due to the spin of the ball, or because of the wind. Advantage can be applied only in the case of a breach of the law. In this case of the ball passing out of play, no player has broken the law, and so the appropriate restart (throw-in, corner-kick or goal-kick) must take place.

Clive Thomas, FIFA Referee from Wales, wrote "It takes skill, knowledge of the game, instinct, experience and intelligence to operate the advantage clause to its best effect, and—reluctant as we are to admit it—there also needs to be that little bit of luck." But a good referee can stack the odds for success in his favor if he thinks about and applies the principles that we have discussed in this chapter. Surely nothing can be as enjoyable as a game in which both teams are attempting to play open, flowing football and are accepting skillfully done advantage decisions.

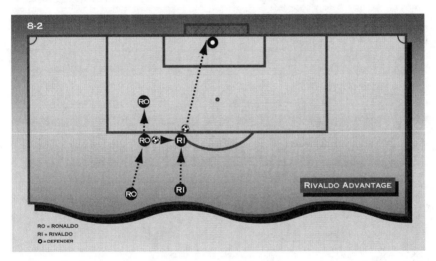

This can be illustrated by a beautiful example from the 1999 Copa America (Figure 8-2). In the semi-final between Brazil and Mexico, Ronaldo of Brazil was brought down by a foul tackle just outside the penalty area and immediately in front of goal: a perfect place for a free kick to be taken by any one of their players with the ability to score directly. However, the ball rolled free to the right and into the path of the oncoming Rivaldo. The referee, Sr. Moreno of Ecuador, saw the opportunity, allowed the advantage and Rivaldo, with a fierce and unstoppable shot, promptly put the ball into the back of the net for a marvelous goal. The TV replay shows Ronaldo on the ground after the foul and turning to appeal to the referee, but the instant he saw the situation, he jumped up to congratulate his teammate. He should have also congratulated the referee for a good decision.

9

THE MYSTERIES OF OFFSIDE REVEALED

Ignorance of the law excuses no man...

John Selden
English historian

A terrible public gaffe.

In a match broadcast to the world, Brazil and Holland played in Dallas during the World Cup finals in the U.S. in 1994. After about an hour of play, with Brazil leading 1-0, there was a wonderful example of how the offside law is supposed to be administered. Unfortunately, although we and others had been teaching offside this way for at least twenty years, not everyone involved in the game knew what should be done.

The ball was headed forward into the Holland half of the field. One Brazilian forward—Romario—was clearly in an offside position as he walked slowly back upfield after participating in the previous attack. The ball was headed high in the air along the path shown in Figure 9-1. Romario knew that he could not legally play the ball, and probably knew that the pass was not intended for him. He made no attempt to play

IN THIS CHAPTER:

- *History of our experience with offside—as players and as referees*
- *How a player breaks the law*
- *When a player does not break the law*
- *When no one can be penalized for offside*
- *When not to penalize even though the player breaks the law*

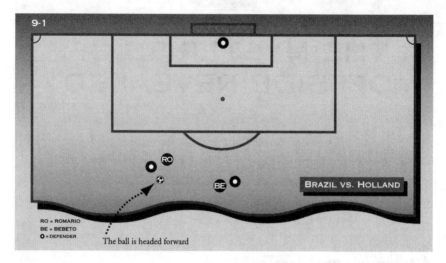

9-1

RO = ROMARIO
BE = BEBETO
O = DEFENDER

BRAZIL VS. HOLLAND

The ball is headed forward

the ball, but casually continued his walk upfield. The ball bounced a few yards from him and the nearest Dutch defender, who by this time had trotted past Romario, but was not looking at the ball. Bebeto, the other Brazilian forward saw the opportunity, ran onto the ball (Figure 9-2), and raced past another defender, who attempted a despairing tackle a yard or two outside the arc at the top of the penalty-area. Bebeto continued on, ran around the goalkeeper and from close in, put the ball in the net.

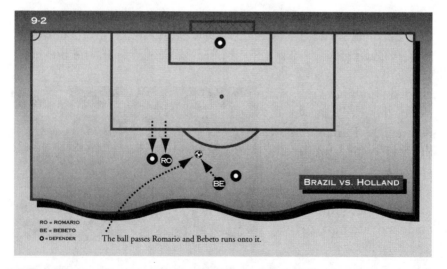

9-2

RO = ROMARIO
BE = BEBETO
O = DEFENDER

BRAZIL VS. HOLLAND

The ball passes Romario and Bebeto runs onto it.

The commentator for the U.S. broadcast—Seamus Malin—was outraged and for the next few moments proceeded to tell the audience that this was a bad decision, even though among his comments he inadvertently explained why the decision was a good one:

"This is going to be very controversial—an offside decision that wasn't given!" [**Because there was no infringement of the law.**]

"Romario was way offside!" [**True.**]

"This is a huge controversy!" [**Only in Malin's mind.**]

"He (Romario) did not attempt to play it. He was in fact, lazily walking back." [**True, and that is the whole point.**]

"The passive offside, I think, was a very dodgy call there. The defenders for the Netherlands surely were entitled to think that it (the ball) was intended to go through (to Romario)." [**Not so. Romario—by walking in the opposite direction from play, and by making no attempt for the ball—made his intention clear. In fact, the closest defender was goalside of him when the ball went through to Bebeto!**]

DOUBLE JEOPARDY FOR A PLAYER...

In the late nineteen eighties, one referee instructor in the northeastern U. S. prepared a set of 35mm slides and went around teaching about offside, including the following case at corner-kicks.

Many times an experienced attacker close to the goal can see as the ball comes over from the corner that he could get caught offside when the ball is next played towards the goal. Under those circumstances, the attacker will step off the field behind the goal-line to indicate he is not going to be involved until the ball is played back upfield. His action is a public statement that he does not wish to be involved in the play; he should *not* be penalized.

This particular instructor, never a player himself and with not much understanding of how the game is played, felt that this was unfair. He taught his recruits to penalize the attacker for offside, *and* recommended issuing him a caution for leaving the field without permission! Both decisions are wrong.

"I would argue that in this situation they (the defenders) have every reason to expect offside." [**Perhaps they feel they do, but not according to the law. They were caught napping and paid the price.**]

You would think that an experienced television commentator, one who had worked US national team matches, many games in the North American Soccer League and Major League Soccer, and who had been the radio voice for the mighty New York Cosmos in the club's heyday, would have a better understanding of one of the fundamental laws of the game. But to understand why he could make such a gaffe, and why there weren't howls of laughter and protest from all the U.S. soccer fans watching the broadcast of the game, you have to appreciate a little bit of history. So bear with us for a few minutes as we review the evolution of the state of knowledge of Law 11—Offside, as we have seen it since the middle sixties, when we first came to the United States.

A little bit of history.

College soccer at that time was a strange game. Platoons of players came on and off the field every fifteen minutes or so, and two men in striped shirts strolled back and forth, too far away from the action to see what was going on. As far as we could tell, the calling of offside was a matter of pure guesswork, but despite that, we have to say that the law was applied uniformly, because when the ball was played forward in an attack, *any* player standing in an offside position was penalized. As the goalkeeper and player-coach of Kansas University Soccer Club, one of us (RE) didn't get too upset by this ignorance of the law, because by calling everybody offside, the referees made goalkeeping a less difficult exercise than normal. And at the other end of the field we had some clever South American graduate students who could take a ball through defenders without passing the ball. By keeping the ball, they avoided the risk of having teammates penalized for offside.

However, EB, playing on a similar team in a mens' league in Minneapolis, was quite often upset by this interpretation, especially when a perfectly good goal was disallowed. In one memorable case the player who had *taken* a corner kick was given offside following a terrific 25-yard shot coming after the original corner kick was weakly headed out. Standing by the corner-flag as the ball screamed into the net, he was judged to be seeking to gain an advantage!

When we talked to college officials and other referees about this law, the general answer was that by penalizing all the players who got into offside positions, the referees were bound to catch the ones who were actually interfering with play! That attitude was widespread, and when we moved to Texas (1969) and started playing senior soccer in the league in Dallas, once again there was no discrimination between players involved or not involved in the play. Since the five or six referees in Dallas at that time didn't have a clue about what Law 11 was supposed to mean, and since they were also the ones teaching new referee candidates, you can imagine what happened on the field! The ignorance was pervasive, but no team suffered more than any other. Only the game, this beautiful game, was deprived when good attacks ended with an unnecessary whistle.

We believed that things had to change, and with the arrival of the NASL, there came an opportunity to start doing things right all over the country. At that time the people in positions of responsibility in the college soccer organizations—coaches and referees both—were for the most part a refractory bunch, unwilling to accept new ideas. So along with other enlightened individuals around the country we made our efforts in the training of new referees for the United States Soccer Federation and in educating officials in the NASL, and gradually began to make a little progress. However unfamiliar with the game they may have been, many new recruits understood that there was something unfair about penalizing a team when a player wasn't cheating or violating the law.

CONVERSATION WITH FIFA

At the National Referee testing session in Colorado Springs in 1989, the National Director of Referee Instruction (RE) made a presentation on offside. In the audience was Tom "Tiny" Wharton, Scottish member of the Referees Committee of FIFA. In the question-and-answer session following the slide show, Wharton asked me if there was anything I would change about Law 11, and if so, what was it? The reply was immediate, because I had been thinking about it for a long time. I would change the wording from "...seeking to gain and advantage..." to "...and gains an advantage from being in an offside position." Wharton smiled and nodded.

I don't suppose for a moment that the conversation influenced the International Board of FIFA, but on March 4th, 1995, the wording of the law was changed so that a player is to be penalized if he is "gaining an advantage..." FIFA produced new offside diagrams showing players interfering and not interfering. I was happy that the principles we had been teaching for years in the U.S. were now being emphasized to the rest of the soccer world.

We have never subscribed to the old dictum that "When ignorance is bliss, 'tis folly to be wise," and so we kept on preaching the message that it is not an infringement of the law to be offside. But even in the professional league it was not until 1979—more than ten years after professionals began playing here—that the NASL media guide had any mention of interfering with play. Of course, we weren't the only ones administering and teaching Law 11 as it is supposed to be administered, for other instructors around the country were also teaching the right way to do things. But well into the eighties there was still a great deal of resistance to changing the interpretation of Law 11. Even today, you can still hear the voices of ignorance state that if the player is simply on the field, he must be interfering, or must be seeking to gain an advantage!

As for the Brazil-Holland game in Dallas and the commentator's error, we have to say that we believe it is rare for television commentators to attend training sessions on the laws of the game. We believe they should. And even though Seamus Malin should have known that FIFA issued a directive to the referees before the 1994 World Cup that only players interfering with play should be penalized, he still came out with the nonsense we have described.

THE INSTRUCTOR IN THE COACHES DEN...

Before the start of the 1978 NASL season, the league held a meeting for all the referees, linesmen, coaches and assistant coaches. The idea was for everyone to get to know each other a little better, to share ideas about how the game should be officiated, and for everyone, coaches and officials alike, to hear how the league wanted the games to be conducted. If everyone heard the same message, then surely there could be no arguments...

One of us (RE) was invited to make a presentation on offside, the same presentation made at various clinics all over the U.S. One of the examples shown by 35mm slides involved a player making a wall pass to one of his teammates who was not in an offside position. The return pass came back to the original player, but a few yards away there was another forward standing in an offside position. The opinion expressed to the audience of more than one hundred was that the intent of Law 11 was to allow play to proceed, that the player in offside position must not be penalized, because although he was close to the play, he was not actually involved in the action.

As soon as the slide was shown and the opinion expressed, uproar took over the room! Some coaches were saying it was wrong, others insisted the instructor was right. Some referees were horrified, while others nodded in agreement with—what was for that time—the controversial interpretation. The place looked and sounded like the floor of the stock exchange at the height of a trading frenzy.

After a few minutes Eddie Pearson, the director of officials for the NASL, took control and established order, but not before we noticed that something revealing had emerged among the coaches. All those who were arguing that the offside should have been called, had been defenders during their playing years, whereas those who insisted that play should go on had been forwards or attacking midfield players! Can there ever be consistency in this game of ours?

But enough history for now. Let's look at the nature of the infringement under Law 11, and then consider *how and when* the referee should call it. We are not going to deal with every detail of offside position and so on, for you can get that from the lawbook. But we *are* going to deal with when a player *is* and is *not* breaking the laws. Finally, be warned—even when the infraction is clear, the referee does *not* have to penalize the offside player! We'll show you that, too.

What is the infringement?

The key words from the law are these: *"A player in an offside position is...penalized if...he is...involved in active play ..."* And then Law 11 defines what "active play" is: interfering with play, interfering with an opponent , or *"gaining an advantage by being in that position"*. That last phrase says everything you need to know, and when we recall the conversations with FIFA VIP's Tom Wharton and Adolfo Reginato (who publicly supported the way we were reading the law) when they came to visit the training sessions in Colorado Springs (see sidebar), those words "gaining an advantage" do our hearts good! We have been preaching this for years, and now the law defines it the way we have been teaching it.

Understanding Law 11 comes down to this single question: *Does the offside player gain an advantage from being offside?* If he does, then he has broken the law; if he doesn't, then he hasn't. It's pretty simple, so let's look at some examples to see how straightforward it really is. In each case we will emphasize what advantage the offside players gains from his or her position, and in the cases where the player is not gaining an advantage, we will explain why.

The easiest case of all is shown in the Figure 9-3. The attacker on the left has only one opponent—the goalkeeper—nearer the goal-line when the ball is played to him by his teammate on the right, and is therefore in an offside position. What advantage does he gain? Because of his position behind the defenders when the ball is played

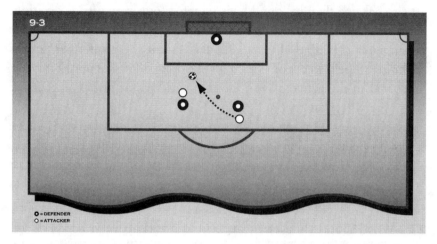

to him, he gets the ball free of any nearby challenge, and will almost certainly win the footrace to the ball. He will then be one-on-one with the goalkeeper, and in a position for an easy scoring opportunity. Had he *not* been behind the defenders, he might have faced a challenge, he might have lost the race to the ball, and he might not have been able to score. *His offside position gave him a great advantage, and so the player must be penalized.*

But now look at the next case (Figure 9-4). The ball has been passed to a player in the right wing. He has three defenders nearer

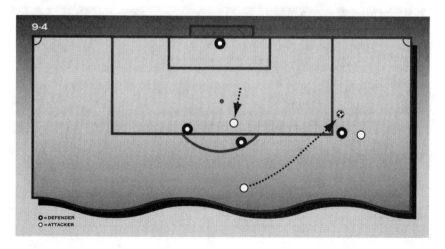

their goal-line than he is and he is therefore not in an offside position. Over to his left however, in the middle of the field, one of his teammates is behind all the defenders except the goalkeeper, and is running upfield to get onside. The player in an offside position is not involved in the active play; quite the contrary, for he is going in the opposite direction to the attack. Even if he were simply standing watching the action, neither he nor his team will gain any advantage from his being in an offside position, and so he must not be penalized. The attack is successful and proceeds because of a well-directed pass to an open player who is onside. The player in an offside position has nothing to do with it.

What about a player in an offside position when a pass is *not* made? Figure 9-5 shows just such an example. The player in the old-fashioned "inside right" position knocks the ball forward past the flanking defender. The assistant referee raises his flag immediately because he assumes that the ball is intended for the right winger, and the referee, neither hesitating nor thinking, stops play, exactly at the moment when the forward who made the pass runs onto his own ball and cuts towards the goal. It is essential that referees keep in mind *that except under rare circumstances, a player in offside position cannot be penalized when his teammate keeps possession.* This applies to a player

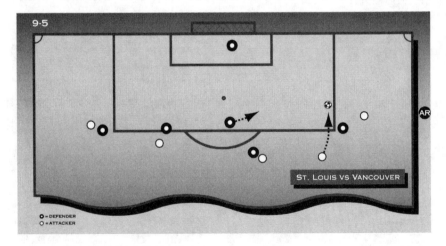

9-5

ST. LOUIS VS VANCOUVER

● = DEFENDER
○ = ATTACKER

who dribbles through the defense by keeping the ball close to his feet, and to a player who knocks the ball forward—even as far as ten or fifteen yards—and then runs onto it. Assistant referees and referees must learn to *hesitate slightly before making an offside decision*, the hesitation being necessary for them to make sure they know where the ball is going and *to whom.*

When not to penalize even though the law has been broken.

Assume for a minute that an attacker is standing offside close to and in front of the goalkeeper as a shot is taken. The ball misses the goal. There is no doubt that the forward was interfering with play, but because the ball missed the goal, the infringement of the laws becomes trifling—it doesn't matter. In such a case, the referee can refrain from penalizing (as you read in Chapter 4) and just give a goal-kick. The ball will be kicked into play from approximately the same spot as from the free-kick for offside, so what purpose is served by blowing the whistle for the free kick?

If any defender spots the offside player and asks (or complains) about it, you can simply say: "Yes, he was offside but the free kick is from the same spot as a goal-kick, so let's just play from there." Or if you want to be smooth, you can give out a compliment: "Hey, good eyes! He *was* offside, wasn't he? Why don't you take up the whistle when you quit playing? Now let's take the goal-kick; it's from the same place as the free kick."

We explained in considerable detail in Chapter 4 that an important task of the referee is to keep the game flowing, without stopping it unnecessarily. In the situation we described immediately above, the referee may choose to ignore the infraction, but the game *will* stop, because the ball crossed the goal-line. Other offside situations give the referee the opportunity to keep the game going.

Think of a long ball through the defence, with a forward in full flight after it. The attacker was in an offside position when the ball was played, and he clearly seems to be gaining an advantage since he

EXAMPLE: DALLAS TORNADO VS. ZENIT LENINGRAD (USSR)

The Dallas flanking defender on the right gave the ball away to an opponent. The attacker cut in towards the penalty-area as shown in the diagram (Figure 9-6a). He looked up and saw the huge gap behind the Dallas defenders, who were in a state of utter disarray after the sudden loss of possession. The forward chipped the ball over the center of the defense into the path of a Leningrad player moving up at high speed from the midfield. The linesman was in perfect position, and saw that in the middle of the field about nine yards from the goal-line, another Leningrad player

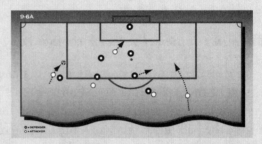

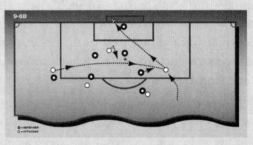

was in an offside position, but starting to turn away from the goal.

Without a moment's hesitation, the linesman raised his flag just as the ball dropped behind the Dallas defenders. The Leningrad midfield player, tearing in like a cheetah after an antelope, hit the ball on the volley with the outside of his right foot. The ball took a curving path and flew into the angle between the far post and the bar as the goalkeeper and the other defenders watched helplessly and in amazement (Figure 9-6b).

But the referee had seen the flag, and so blew his whistle to cancel one of the finest goals ever seen in Ownby stadium in Dallas. The forward in an offside position should not have been penalized, for he contributed nothing to the scoring of the goal. Before he raised his flag, the linesman should have *hesitated* to see where the ball was going.

There is a postscript, for as the referee and linesmen were walking off at halftime, the Russian coach, the very model of discipline and self-control, asked the referee: "Why no goal?" "Offside!" came the reply from the man-in-the-middle. With a scornful toss of his head, the Russian coach said: "Offside, hah!" and strode off the field. *He* knew it was a bad decision and not in the best interest of the game, and so should the referee and linesman. If the referee and linesman needed further convincing, they could have asked the Dallas defenders, obviously embarrassed that this brilliant goal had been disallowed.

has outrun the defenders. But you can see that the ball is going through to the goalkeeper, who is going to get it safely *before* the attacking player can. Let play proceed, even thought the assistant referee's flag is in the air. Just put your arm out to wave the flag down—you might even shout out: "Good flag! Thanks very much!"—and then watch what happens. If the goalkeeper gathers the ball safely, the game will keep going with his throw or kick, and you will look very good indeed. And remember that *if for some reason the goalkeeper misses the ball, or it takes an awkward bounce, or if it looks as though the attacker might win the race for the ball, you can still call the offside.* The breach of the law doesn't go away; you are simply changing your mind quickly, that the infringement was not trifling after all.

You can do the same sort of thing with a defender who intercepts a ball intended for an offside player. If the defender has plenty of space around him and is not under a challenge, then let him play on. He may thump the ball upfield or may pass it to start a counter-attack, in which case the offside infringement has become meaningless, and can be ignored. Again, if something goes wrong, you can still call the original offside, so you come out looking good in both cases!

All it takes to play on in these situations is a cool head and a little patience. A slight hesitation in making decisions about offside is such a positive skill for both referee and assistant referees that we encourage everyone to acquire it. The players appreciate it, the game needs it, and the officials look good doing it. Everybody wins!

HERE'S A TIP: JUDGING OFFSIDE BY "REMOVING" THE OFFSIDE PLAYER

In *almost all* potentially offside situations when a goal has been scored, you can quickly evaluate whether an offside player interfered with play. Mentally "remove" the player from the field, and ask yourself whether the goal would still have been scored with the player absent. If the answer is "yes, the goal would still have been scored", then you can safely conclude that the player did *not* contribute to the 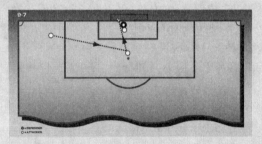 scoring of the goal and should not be penalized. If the answer is "no, the goal would not have been scored without her participation", then the player obviously influenced what went on and *must* be penalized.

For real examples, refer to the Minnesota decision described earlier in this chapter, and the disallowed goal as we described in the opening chapter of this book. In both cases, remove the offside players, and the goals would still be scored. They did not gain any advantage. By way of contrast, look at the goal scored in an MLS match recently (Figure 9-7). A ball crossed into the penalty-area is headed down and toward the goal by an attacker. Another forward is standing right in front of the goalkeeper in an offside position. *The ball goes between the legs of the offside player and into the goal, because the ball is effectively hidden from the goalkeeper until it is too late for him to stop it.* Remove the offside player in this case and the goalkeeper collects the ball easily.

The forward clearly gained an advantage from his position, and he should have been penalized.

The one exception to this way of looking at offside situations is the case where an offside player is directly in the path of a ball on its way into the goal. If the player steps aside or jumps to allow the ball to go into the goal, he clearly has influenced play and must be penalized.

10

CONTROL OF THE GAME-I: FUNDAMENTALS

The depositary of power is always unpopular.

Benjamin Disraeli
Nineteenth-century
British Prime Minister

A referee's success at controlling a soccer match depends upon one thing, and one thing only: *his credibility.* With it, he can do much or he can do little, for the players will not question a single whistle. Without it, he might as well have stayed at home for all the attention any of the participants will pay to him or his decisions, both good and bad. We stated earlier in this book that any referee starts establishing his or her credibility in the first encounter with players and coaches, and we gave you some techniques that you can use before you even start the game. But what else can you do? And how is your credibility affected as play goes on?

> *"Each one of these decisions, ...will destroy the referee's credibility, and ultimately produce nothing but unpleasantness on the field."*

The answers to those questions are the subjects of this first of three chapters on controlling the game. Also in this chapter we will deal with the

IN THIS CHAPTER:

• *The foundation-stones of control: Credibility, Attitude, Accuracy*
• *The five steps in the degeneration of a game.*
• *The "Moment of Truth"—the defining moment in a match*

progression of a game from "in control" to "out of control", what you can do to stop that process, and in the next chapter we will give you some clever and not-so-clever techniques you can use to persuade players to stay more-or-less within the laws of the game.

Credibility—how to get it.

The first thing you have to do is make sure that you know the laws, inside-out and back-to-front, upside-down and right-way-up! If you make a mistake about law, you have no defence, and deservedly so. To the players, such a mistake is inexcusable, and everything you do from that moment on is instantly brought into question. "Excuse me, ref, but you showed us how much you know about the law, giving a drop-ball when you didn't know whose throw-in it was (see example below). Why should we believe you now?"

You can become expert in the language of the laws by studying them, by exchanging questions and answers with your refereeing colleagues, and by attending meetings with more experienced referees. At the beginning of your career, it may seem like hard and sometimes boring work, but believe us, it will pay dividends later on! Here are a few examples of common errors that even experienced referees make, simply because they have not spent enough time with the laws of the game.

1. The ball deflects off two players simultaneously and goes over the touchline or perhaps over the goal-line. What does the referee do? The laws state that if the ball goes over the touchline, play must start with a throw-in, and if the ball goes over the goal-line, play must start with a corner-kick or goal-kick. So we have to start with a throw or a kick. *Whatever* the referee does, he cannot give a drop-ball! A drop-ball is given after a temporary interruption while the ball is in play, it is not the solution for indecision on the part of the officials.

If you are in this situation and neither you nor your assistant knows who played it last, take a second or two to look at the players going for the ball. If only one team (say, red) is going for it and the opponents seem OK with that, then let red take the throw-in. If both teams are claiming it, then signal firmly, giving the ball to the defending side. In the case of a goal-kick/corner-kick, watch the players first, and if they can't decide, then give a goal-kick. The reasoning is that *you have to make a decision, so make the one that is least harmful.*

By giving the ball to the defenders you are making the decision that is least likely to have an immediate effect upon the game. You give a throw-in that is at least half the field away from the goal; you give a goal-kick because there is no threat of an immediate goal being scored, as would be the case for a corner-kick.

2. The referee allows one-too-many substitutes during a match, because he didn't check the rules of the competition, or didn't keep a good record during the game.

3. One team changes its goalkeeper at halftime, but neglects to notify the referee. After a few minutes of the second half, the referee notices the new goalkeeper, and when the player first picks up the ball, the whistle blows for a penalty-kick. The new version of the laws spells out what the referee may do, whereas in older editions it was not written. However, a little understanding would tell the referee that he cannot give a penalty, for if he says that the new goalkeeper is not entitled to handle the ball, then who is? *According to the Laws the team must have a goalkeeper.* The breach in the laws is the illegal substitution, not handball.

4. From an indirect free-kick in their opponents' penalty-area, one team puts the ball directly into the net, and the referee gives a goal.

5. From a direct free-kick outside their own penalty-area, a team attempts to pass the ball directly to their goalkeeper, but the ball goes into the goal. The referee awards a goal.

6. A defender makes contact with the ball with his hand in his own penalty-area. The referee considers the incident to be accidental and so awards an indirect free-kick.

7. A defender slides in for a tackle on a wet field. In his own penalty-area, he misses the ball and brings down the opposing forward. The referee considers that it was accidental and gives an indirect free-kick.

We hope that by now, most of our readers are wincing at the sheer horror of these decisions, all brought about because the referee did not know the laws of the game. We can think of many more, but by now you get the point. *Each one of these decisions, and many others like them, will destroy the referee's credibility, and ultimately produce nothing but unpleasantness on the field. Be warned!*

After credibility—what? It's attitude!

After you have learned all the Laws and their fine points, when you know all about positioning during play and at restarts (because you have read Chapters 13 and 14 in this book), you can recognize fouls (Chapters 5 and 6), know when and when not to give offside (Chapter 9), you are ready to go out and referee a match. Right from the start, the players will recognize that you are a qualified referee, and because of that they will do everything correctly, accepting all of your decisions without complaint. The result will be a good, fair, sporting match with no one intentionally doing anything that violates the Laws of the Game. In your dreams!!

The old stories say that the matches played in the 1860's under the jurisdiction of the newly-formed Football Association in England were played in this manner, but no matches are that way anymore. If one event contributed to the change in attitude, it was undoubtedly the legalization of professionalism in 1885. Shortly afterwards, in 1888, the Football League began play, and the nature of the game changed. It was no longer merely *play*; it was professional sport, with money at stake for players and clubs. The professional approach to the game, coupled with the natural desire to win is now prevalent throughout soccer at all levels, for even in youth and amateur play there is a desire to win, sometimes at all costs. We will confess that as players, we had no qualms about doing whatever was necessary to win—and win we did. We bent the rules, took advantage of our naïve opponents, and accepted—with polite thanks—whatever the referees would give us.

When we were playing we did not have referees similar to the ones we are now trying to encourage: the ones who not only adjudicate the infractions that occur, but who take action to ensure that the players' behavior is within the bounds of acceptability, and, better yet, who attempt *to prevent players from exceeding these limits.* We got away with a lot, simply because we knew more than did the referees we saw each week. (Now that we look back, we can say that we were bending the laws and ignoring the laws for purely altruistic reasons. In playing the way we did, we must have contributed to the referees' education— which is what we were trying to do all the time, of course!)

We have explained how to set the right atmosphere before a game, by being reasonable, friendly and approachable, not overbearing, aloof, fussy and dictatorial. Clearly the former attributes will help controlling the game, but it is amazing how many referees fall into the latter category. But please don't put on merely an *act* of being human, only to drop the pretense once you blow your whistle. Sustain the reasonable approach to the players throughout the entire game, and they will respond to you, even when you make the tough decisions.

We chose the epigraph for this chapter deliberately to remind all referees that in most games, you start off with some of the participants—many of the participants—resenting your very presence. You have power and the players know it. You can screw their game up, or you can make it a pleasant experience. And that is why so often before a game the players ask: Who've we got this week? And back comes the answer: Oh! no, not him again! The first job you have when you arrive at the field is to convert that resentment into at least grudging respect and maybe even a good rapport with the players.

One method we found useful in doing that is to get to know the players' names (see also Chapter 2). If you have seen the team before, try to remember who are their key players. If they are new to you, make a point of listening to the players call to each other in the first few minutes, and put names with the faces and shirt numbers. Then you can talk to them in a more personable manner when you have occasion to. It is much better to say, "C'mon Giorgio, no more tackles like that today please" than to say "Number 9," or "Hey you! I saw that."

Our experience tells us that when you address players by name, they are both pleased and confused. Pleased because you seem to be friendly and want to know them (therefore they must be important), and confused because perhaps they are thinking "Uh-Oh, this referee knows my name. Perhaps he's been watching me. I'd better be careful." It also has a similar effect on the other players who hear what was said. This referee has taken the trouble to learn our names. He must be very keen; perhaps he's not so bad after all. But above all, *it is a personable approach in which the participants become more than mere numbers.* Most players respond to a human approach, and as they do so, the referee's credibility rises.

On some rare occasions, you may meet players who prefer to remain detached from interactions with the referee, and they will ask you not to use their name. When you do, honor their request. Don't talk to them at all, or if you have to, refer to their shirt number. *Do whatever makes the players comfortable, and subordinate your style to their requests.*

Accuracy—the cornerstone of control.

We believe that there is little doubt that correct decisions, made *with* confidence and *without* delay, are the major ingredients in match control. If you doubt that statement, imagine yourself in a tight game as a player, and you see an opponent flick the ball forward with his hand to bring it under control, then pass it to a teammate, who scores. You yell out "Handball, ref!", but all you get in response is: "Good goal. The handball was accidental!" You know absolutely that the referee was wrong, and now your team is one goal down. How would you feel?

You are going to be as mad as a wet rooster, and rightly so. What should be a simple decision for a referee has in this case gone awry, because of his lack of knowledge, or because of his inexperience, poor positioning, or perhaps even because of fear. What is more important is that your feelings are not going to go away immediately. Even the most rational and dispassionate person will retain the feelings of irritation for some time, and during that time in a fast soccer game, he may do something foolish. The first signs of the game getting out of hand will appear, all because of this one inaccurate decision. Players are neither stones nor robots; they are emotional human beings who get upset when they have been cheated.

So you must strive to make accurate decisions that are in accordance with the law, and that convince the players that you have seen one or two soccer matches before. *Especially you need to be correct in dealing with physical contact between players.* You have to be able to determine accurately those players who commit fouls. And how do you achieve this accuracy? Actually, it's quite easy. All you need are two little items: knowledge and experience.

Knowledge comes from study and learning; experience comes from.....well, experience. You took a good first step by training to be a referee, and by reading this book you are taking a second step. Watch as many games as you can, both live and on television. See how players make physical contact with each other and watch the reaction of both players in the challenge. Watch reruns of incidents from professional and international matches. Talk to players, for they are a great source of good information.

As for the experience, there is only one way to get it, and that is to referee matches. Tens and hundreds of them. Youth games, senior games, girls' games, women's games, games with over-the-hill players, any games. Analyze the reaction of players to decisions you make. Watch the faces of players in a tackle. Is there a decision you make time and time again that causes a strong reaction from players? If there is, you might be making the wrong call! Read over the chapters on foul recognition—not once, but twice or more times until you have a grasp of some of the methods we recommend. Keep striving for knowledge and understanding, both of which will bring accuracy to your decisions, and credibility to your refereeing.

Even if a referee never makes a mistake, he would be foolish to expect all of his decisions to be accepted as correct. Most players do not expect perfection, and it has been our experience that players are willing to accept a small number of incorrect decisions, since they equally might get the benefit of similar errors in their favor. They know, as we know, that playing and refereeing soccer are two human activities that produce mistakes here and there. They can live with a few errors, if not too many, and as long as they are not like the ones we have described above.

The five steps in the degeneration of a game.

Eddie Pearson, the former Director of Officials of the North American Soccer League and our first instructor at the professional level, gave us a vivid image about the destruction of a soccer game. In his talks on keeping control of a match, he referred to the referee's role as a five-finger exercise. He would begin by saying that *he knew of very few cases where a player woke up on the morning of a match and said to himself: "I think I will go out today and get myself cautioned or sent off."* In Eddie's view (and in ours, as former players), something had to occur during the game that caused players to do things that get them into trouble with the referee. So what is it?

Holding up his left hand, palm to the audience, with fingers spread, he would grip the thumb with the fingers of his right hand and declare that this position represented the start of the game. Everything is fine, not a foul has been committed and there have been no problems. Then after a dramatic pause, he would say that the referee would never be in this position again at anytime throughout the match. As soon as the first foul is whistled, or any other decision made, the referee and the game go to the next position, depicted by the first finger of Eddie's left hand. This is where the referee should try to stay, in a position where no misconduct has occurred.

The game is still very much under control. There have been no serious incidents, and the most that the referee has had to do is perhaps to speak to a player or two as a warning. If the game stays in this state, the occasion will have been a success for all concerned: the players, spectators and referee. An important point in understanding how a game deteriorates is to realize that you cannot go backwards, and that each step is irreversible. From the ideal game where the referee blows his whistle just four times—to start and end each half of play—every match progresses down the slippery slope of decay. How far it slides can be largely a matter for the referee to determine.

Next, things may get a little heated, a little less under control, and the referee has to resort to the yellow card. Eddie would grasp the middle finger of his left hand and wiggle it to emphasize the point. The referee is still in good control of the game, but he's progressed halfway along the five steps to chaos. The referee might issue some more cautions to keep things under control, but there could come a time when the red card has to be pulled out. Now the game is at stage four, represented by the ring finger.

It is imperative that the referee keep the game at this level, because there is only one finger left, and that one represents ending the match because it is completely out of control. The red card is necessary to prevent any further decay, but if it does not work, if you reach that point where the match is totally out of control, either due to the behavior of the players, or because the spectators are on the pitch, the match has to be abandoned.

We found this "five-finger" exercise a useful concept to keep in our minds when refereeing, because each time we went from one stage to the next, it reminded us of what lay ahead if we didn't keep our minds on what we were doing. It helped us to focus whenever the slightest thing went wrong. And it helped us to evaluate each incident to see if it was the event upon which control of the rest of the game might depend. It made us aware of what is known as the "Moment of Truth", the defining moment in a game.

Where do games go wrong?—"The Moment of Truth."

The phrase is at least several hundred years old, and has come to describe an instant in time when a decision has to be made, a decision that will affect the course of events. It has become popularized by the writings of Ernest Hemingway, who defined a "Moment of Truth" as that moment when the bullfighter decided to kill the bull with a single sword-thrust between two cervical vertebrae of the exhausted beast. If he left it too late, the bull might not have enough energy to stand, and for the matador, a bull on its knees is a disgrace. If he attempted the thrust too soon, the matador would be in danger, for the bull might still be able to toss its head and impale the man close and leaning over the head of the animal. Success or failure for the matador depended upon this one decision.

Although control of a soccer match is not a matter of life and death—as it is for the bull (always) and the matador (rarely)—success or failure for the referee might also depend upon a single decision made at the right time. Once again we owe our former mentor, Eddie

Pearson our gratitude for introducing us to this concept. Experience has shown that in each game there is a particular incident that if handled correctly could determine that the game will proceed to a successful conclusion without much dispute or acrimony. Conversely, if such an incident is mishandled or not appreciated, the game could go all to hell very quickly. It is your ability to recognize these Moments of Truth—and there could be more than one in a particular game—that will determine your success or failure as a referee.

They can take many forms, but usually have one of the following characteristics: injustice meted out; lack of awareness about something that the players react to; or simple error because of ignorance or inexperience. The list of such possible events is long:

1. A goal is awarded when neither the referee nor the assistant is in a position to see that the ball did not cross the goal-line. Players will never accept such a decision, and their subsequent demeanor will show it.

2. A goal is disallowed for a reason that no attacking player saw, nor any defender appealed about. Was it a mysterious foul? An offside player not involved in play?

3. An attacker is brought down in the penalty-area, but the referee does not give a penalty-kick, preferring to find safety in an indirect free kick or by moving the ball outside the area. Players can recognize, and do not forgive, cowardice.

4. A particular foul goes unpunished or is not punished severely enough. Players want justice.

5. The referee seems unaware of the reaction of players to their opponents' fouls. The players give clues that you need to take action. There is a code of conduct among players: "If you won't take care of it, referee, *we will!*"

6. An act of misconduct is not dealt with correctly. The most frequent type is a foul that goes unpunished, especially if the fouled player gets injured and has to go off. His teammates generally know the truth, and usually will begin to seek retribution themselves, for they now realize that the referee is weak and will not protect them.

7. Retaliation is not handled correctly. We discuss this in detail elsewhere (see Chapter 1), but be aware that players seek justice, and when the innocent is punished as the criminal escapes, there is no justice. The players will make their own, as in item 5 and item 6 above.

8. Players attempting to make a fool of the referee, with such acts as holding the ball for him and then dropping it as he reaches for it; tossing it gently so that it bounces off the official; gesticulating to the crowd in derision of the referee. Was it harmless, or was it demeaning?

9. A public display of dissent that the referee seems not to notice. The match then becomes a debating chamber, or deteriorates into the bedlam on the floor of a commodities market. The referee must control the debate.

10. A nose-to-nose confrontation between two players after they have been battling for superiority during play. The referee must take some action in order to be seen to be in control.

We are sure that you can describe other such incidents after training yourself to spot these Moments of Truth in games you referee, and also in games you watch, either live or on television. Sometimes they are difficult to identify, but gradually, with practice, and if you allow yourself to benefit from the advice of an experienced referee (see Chapter 18, where we talk about mentors), it becomes easier to spot them. Eventually they will become very obvious to you, standing out like a beacon in the dark. But however you do it, make certain that you understand and use this most important concept in maintaining control of a match.

11

CONTROL OF THE GAME-II: TECHNIQUES

My object, all sublime, I shall achieve in time
Is to let the punishment fit the crime,
The punishment fit the crime.

W.S. Sullivan

What is game-control all about?

It comes down to this: In order to control a soccer game, the referee has to establish a good *relationship* with the players. It doesn't have to be close, affectionate and intimate, but like all good relationships, it does have to have some fundamental qualities: *credibility; honesty; mutual trust; respect; and a mutual acceptance of our basic human flaws.*

Credibility and how to get it we have talked about in Chapter 10. Honesty should hardly need emphasizing, because no referee can attempt to officiate without it, but be aware that there are players and coaches who believe that some referees are crooked or "bent". Part of establishing credibility is therefore convincing the players that you are honest, favoring neither one side nor the other. The final three qualities of a good relationship—respect, trust and acceptance—need some elaboration.

IN THIS CHAPTER:

• *What is game-control about?*
• *The purpose & use of a yellow card*
• *What to do with a cautioned player*
• *Dealing with dissent*
• *The red card*
• *The much-neglected persistent infringement*
• *The game without a caution*

Put yourself in the position of a player at the start of an important match. It doesn't have to be the World Cup Final; it could be a match in a youth competition, with the two teams contesting the league leadership. As players, we can recall the atmosphere before the second leg of the Texas State Amateur Cup Final in Houston. We had won the match in Dallas the week before, but now we were faced with an unfamiliar field, a hostile crowd, a referee we had never seen, and a player who was mad-as-hell that the previous week, and for the first time that season, he had not scored. We had stifled him completely.

So we walked onto the field and were shocked to see two referees and no linesmen! They were violating the rules of the competition by using a discredited and out-of-date system to work a first-class match that was going to be played at speed. Whatever trust we might have had in these two officials was gone immediately. Matters got worse, for a few moments into the match, one of them gave a free-kick and when asked if it were "direct" or "indirect" responded: "Either, play on!" The man didn't know the laws, and at that moment any acceptance of his human fallibility dissipated as quickly as our trust in him had. Respect was gone. The game was hard, ugly and ended in a confrontation between spectators and various players. The two referees had had little influence on the game, for the players—our disciplined players who refused to be provoked—had controlled the match, which, we are happy to say, we won 4-0.

We hope that when you walk onto any soccer field, you have an aura of trust, respect, credibility and honesty, and that you grant the players those same qualities. What we will do now is show you how to walk *off* the field with the same aura!

Techniques.

The laws give the referee certain powers with which to control the match. But the way these powers are used that determines whether a referee will be successful in any particular match, and in his career in general. These strongest powers provided by the laws are the caution and the dismissal, commonly referred to since 1970, the year of their introduction in the World Cup in Mexico, as the yellow and red cards. But the referee can use other techniques—not mentioned in the laws—to assist him in controlling the match.

The man or woman with the whistle can impose a series of punishments or sanctions on the players, depending upon the severity of their misdeeds, but we will advise you again that *the referee should do the least that is necessary to control the situation.* Just as there is a steady progression from order to chaos in a match that is going badly, so there is in the referee's armament a steady progression of techniques that he can use to maintain control. He must not use the sledgehammer of the red card when all that is necessary is a disapproving look.

Control begins at the very first whistle. Are the players in the correct positions? Does the ball get played forward? Do no players from the opposition run into the center circle before the ball is played? These may seem like trivial offences, but you can be sure that if these simple requirements are not enforced, the players will immediately think that they have a lenient referee and will then begin to try to get away with other infractions. But by correcting these small infractions at the kick-off, the referee sends a different message to the players. Because they are small infractions, he can use humor very effectively, delivering his message in an attractive package. "I know you're eager to get going, John, but stay back until he's kicked it, eh?" or "No, no, fellers! You're going this way, so kick the ball in that direction, OK?"

So now the match is under way, and you can be sure that within a minute or two, there will be some kind of infringement that affects the game, and you will have to stop play. If it is something obvious— a harmless handball in the middle of the field; a player cheekily taking a throw-in that belongs to his opponents; a forward running into the penalty-area too soon at a goal-kick—all you need to do is blow the whistle and point. If you happen to catch the eye of the player who broke the law, you can look at him and give him a slight look of disapproval, shaking your head at him as you do so. If you are close by, you can throw in a word or two, smiling as you speak. "Now, you don't think I'm going to let you get away with that, do you, Freddie?"

You are demonstrating that you are on top of things, that you are relaxed, and that you are not over-officious. Don't be at all hesitant about getting involved with the players by talking, smiling and being in the midst of them. You will be learning names, you will *be showing yourself as a participant not an enemy*, and you will be establishing a relationship that will last ninety minutes.

Next there will come a foul, whose recognition and interpretation we described in earlier chapters. Correctly penalizing such fouls is a major contributor to match control, and in most cases it is simply not enough to whistle and point. In some cases, the guilty player acknowledges his fault right away, and may even go to pick up his opponent. Little needs to be done except for "the look" of disapproval and a nod to recognize the player's act of contrition. But in most cases, you are wise to talk to the player, for several reasons. First, it provides a warning to the player concerned that such fouls will not be allowed, and could possibly lead to a caution if he doesn't change his ways. Second, it sends the same message to all of the other players, and third, it lets the player who was fouled and his teammates know that the referee is attempting to prevent such play.

You don't need to make a speech, or give the player a humiliating public lecture. A short, pithy admonition is all you need. It can be delivered casually as you are standing nearby, or on the run as you get near the miscreant. "I liked that foul....but not very much!" or "OK! He knows you're in the game now, so no more of that!" or "Dave, what are you doing?" Many referees believe that you cannot do anything to prevent fouls from occurring. We firmly disagree with this approach, and believe that referees *can and must* influence the future actions of players. The quick comment with players after fouls is one way to do this.

If the foul or event is more serious, you may have to make a formality out of talking to the player. You stop everything and isolate the player, looking him straight in the eye and telling him what you think. Make it clear that the responsibility for what happens next rests on his shoulders. "If you commit another foul like that, I will have no choice but to caution you. So it's your decision about the yellow card, not mine." At this point we have to emphasize that you do not have to go through all these steps every time. If the very first foul in the match is serious enough, you don't waste time with preliminaries, with nods, smiles, shakes–of-the-head and wagging fingers. You go straight to the card—yellow or red, as appropriate. What we have described are techniques that work in most matches, not all, and with most players, but not all.

The purpose and use of the yellow card.

Despite all of the foregoing, there are some infractions that have to punished by a caution and the showing of the yellow card. But the referee should not take that action without getting something in return. He has two reasons for pulling out the card. The first is as punishment to the individual concerned for the actual infraction, and the second is to establish and maintain control over the match and the other players. The card to the player puts him on notice about the consequences if he doesn't slow down or change his ways, but the public display is for the benefit of all the other participants. Each caution issued should serve both functions.

Infractions that merit cautions fall into three main categories: *fouls, technical offenses and dissent.* Among *fouls* are the well-known offenses such as a late tackle, a deliberate trip, blatant shirt-pulling, a heavy collision, and deliberate handling of the ball. The *technical offenses* described in earlier sections of this book include encroachment at free-kicks, time-wasting, delaying free-kicks by kicking the ball away, etc. *Dissent* is aimed at the referee or his assistants, and may be verbal or by a demonstrative action. Note that some cautions are mandatory, as we described in Chapter 5.

It is essential that referees be prepared to issue cautions for *all* of these offenses, not just certain of them. What do we mean by that? Some referees are known to immediately show the card if any player protests a decision, but seem to allow all kinds of fouls to go unpunished. Others might do the opposite. Still others are keen to show the yellow card for the technical offenses, whereas others never punish such infractions.

If you ask the players—and why not?—they would rather that fouls be punished and prevented, since those can result in injury and pain, whereas the technical offenses and dissent rarely affect them personally. So a game is more likely to stay in control when the referee gives appropriate cautions for fouls rather than for the technical offenses. However, we emphasize that these are not alternatives, for *all* types of infringements should be punished by caution when necessary.

How do you administer the caution? The method is important, for this is your opportunity to get and keep the player's attention for a few moments in which you hope to influence his behavior for the benefit of the game. Don't simply flash the card in his face, as is being done too often in matches at all levels. The card itself merely provides information to everyone involved in the match, *but it is the conversation between player and referee that is most important.* Your words must not be delivered in a manner that is overbearing or humiliating to the player concerned. Approach him calmly without any display of anger (but clear displeasure is allowed!) and tell him he is being cautioned. Ask for his name, and write it down. Speak to the player to tell him why the caution is being issued, be sure he understands, and by putting on his shoulders the responsibility for what happens next, advise him of the possibility that he could be sent off. Then display the card by holding it up above your head, and do not wave it anywhere near the player's face.

It is not sufficient simply to display the card and note down the player's number without saying anything. Even if there is a language barrier, a player will generally get the idea of what you are trying to do. This should not be a prolonged conversation; a few well-chosen words will be sufficient. [Incidentally it is a good idea to memorize and practice many of these little speeches or comments. You will have one or two for a really bad foul, another for encroachment, a third for dissent and so on.]

Be careful where you stand when issuing the caution! Take up a position 1-2 yards from the player; too close is confrontational, and too far away is unconvincing, and could give the impression of timidity. If a player is highly agitated, it is inadvisable to get close enough to where there could be physical contact. There have been several cases of referee assault, ranging from pushes to card-snatching to actual blows under these types of circumstances. Although the referee is not to blame for these incidents, they could have perhaps been prevented by more prudent action. In Latin American countries it is common for players to approach the referee with their hands behind their backs, in order to show that they are not about to molest the official, and also to restrain themselves. In Asia the same gesture signals respect and submission to authority, but since this is not common to other cultures, the referee must be prudent.

Pick a position that gives you the best view of the field of play (see Chapter 15 on vulnerability). As a reminder: If the offense occurred near the touch line, you should face the field during the cautioning procedure, with your back towards the line. In this way you can see most of the other players at the same time as you are talking to the sinner. Similarly, if the offense occurs in the penalty area, be sure to face upfield, or towards the direction where most of the players are. It is also advisable to direct the assistant referees (before the match) to be sure to observe any other areas of the pitch during the cautioning procedure, and *not* to be taking notes at the same time as the referee does.

There are times when a quick display of the yellow card is necessary before you do any talking. Where a player has committed a bad foul, and it looks as though other players are going to react, pull the card out quickly for all to see that you have control of the situation. Then do your talking after you have taken the player aside. We kept such a "fast card" in the side pocket of our shorts, ready for easy retrieval if needed.

The Early Caution.

Many players believe that since referees are reluctant to issue a caution in the first 10-15 minutes of a match, this is the time to get in that hard tackle that could slow down or intimidate an opponent. Whatever those players believe is their business; you be aware that from the point of view of match control, an early caution can be very effective. Don't hesitate if you think the caution is warranted. This action has the effect of letting everyone know that you will not allow any misconduct to go unpunished, and that you do mean business, from first minute to last.

Think for a moment like a player who sees a bad foul early in the game, and sees that the referee is not going to do anything about it except give a free kick. Players use this as a gauge to estimate the referee's level of tolerance and if they see a "softie" or a coward, they know that they too can get away with a higher level of physical play. More such infractions will be the result. Eventually you will have to caution the perpetrator of one of these fouls, so it might as well be the first one. *Note that we are not saying that you should look for an opportunity to issue an early caution, but if one does arise, you should take advantage of it.* A caution in the first half can prevent two in the second half is an old but still appropriate observation. A downside of the early caution is that you have now set the standard, and you will have to be prepared to caution all similar offenses for the rest of the game. If the players are determined not to get the message you are delivering, then you could end up with several more yellow cards. But in our experience, this is seldom the case. The players' normal reactions are to be more careful to avoid the caution.

What to do with the cautioned player: Keep him on the field!

One way of talking about the referee's task is to assert that it is his principal responsibility to walk on the field with twenty-two players who are reasonably sound in mind and body, and approximately two hours later walk off the field with twenty-two players in that same condition. With this in mind, it is fair commentary to say that *most referees do not apply themselves to the task of keeping players on the field after they have been cautioned.* It is easy to send players off; it is a difficult test of your skill to try to keep them under control and playing for the rest of the game.

This is particularly true in the case of the early caution we have just described. You have to "carry" the cautioned player for a very long time, with the risk that he might commit a second cautionable offense. So how are you going to prevent this second caution? It comes down to a statement we made at the beginning of this chapter: the referee has to establish a relationship with the player. Or at least *try* to establish such a relationship, using techniques we can vouch for as being effective. The phrase "man-management" is used frequently to describe these techniques, which can involve devices as positive as praise, persuasion, flattery, manipulation and appeals-to-reason, or as negative as intimidation, ostracism or simply old-fashioned bullying, but all for the purpose of keeping the player on the field for the entire match. Let's look at a few of these efforts.

Say that the cautioned player is still being a bit reckless, and could be getting close to another yellow card. You saunter past him during a break in play and say something like: "Look Derek, I know you were a bit unlucky to pick up that early yellow, so try to take it easy from now on" or similar soothing words. A quick "Oooh, careful, Derek!" might work as he goes into a tackle rather hard, or if he turns angrily towards an opponent who has just fouled him: "Don't do it, Derek, leave him to me!" (And then make sure that you *do* do something.)

Most players who get a card are a bit upset for a few minutes after the event. Perhaps they may feel picked-on, or feel as though you were harsh. Keep your eye on the player after you have cautioned him, and try to gauge how his mood is. When it seems to have quietened down, that may be the time to try a little persuasion and praise. "You alright, Paul?" "Yeh, ref, I'm OK." "Great. When you're on, you are really good to watch." It is a rare player who will not respond to such an exchange, and respond positively.

Opponents of a cautioned player will sometimes try to provoke him into another act of misconduct, so be watchful for such efforts. And when the provocation occurs, you will have a heaven-sent opportunity to help the cautioned player and calm him down at the same time. Make a loud declaration that you know what is going on, and make sure the cautioned player hears that you are on his side. "Chris! I know you're trying to needle him because he's been booked. Now, knock it off, or *you* will be the one in trouble!" And then turn to the cautioned player and praise him for his restraint. "Well done, Paul. Just play your game and leave the bugger to me; I'll sort him out!"

If none of these techniques works, it may be necessary to become hard and ruthless with the player. You can try a really severe public dressing-down, with strong voice, emphatic gestures and not-so-subtle intimidation or bullying. This is especially necessary with very experienced players, the ones who are not averse to trying a little intimidation of their own. More than once we have "invaded" the personal space of tough, old players, getting almost nose-to-nose with them to let them know who's boss and what will happen if they don't straighten up. It is a last resort, and if you have the confidence and the guts to do it, it works. (Of course, we both happen to be six-foot-two, and so when we got that close to most players we met, we were actually leaning over him, which gave us that little extra bit of power for that moment.)

And then a few moments later, when the "hard man" has settled down, you can resume a normal conversation with him, even using some of the manipulative techniques we described above. You will have established your position of authority, and can relax a little when the player has responded. It is as though you are playing "good cop and bad cop" all rolled into one!

The point we wish to emphasize is that you must keep working with the players you have cautioned. It is not sufficient to caution them and then leave them alone to commit another foolish act.

Dissent.

Dissent can be a major problem for referees, for several reasons. First, *because it can have the effect of undermining the authority of the referee*, making him appear weak and indecisive if he doesn't deal with it. Second, hearing a lot of disagreement *can cause the referee to lose confidence in himself* and his decisions, especially when the dissenters are experienced or famous players. Third, *many referees cannot distinguish what is mere banter or conversation from players, and what is real dissent.*

Let's deal with the third one first, the one that frequently gets inexperienced referees into trouble. It is unreasonable to expect that a game—in any sport—be played without some differences of opinion between referee and players. And it is equally unreasonable to expect that a game be played in humorless silence. But it takes experience, confidence and emotional maturity to be able to distinguish between what is serious, destructive dissent, and what is harmless repartee. Keep in mind, at all times, our admonition that *the referee must do the least that's necessary to control the situation.*

You make a call, and a player nearby stares at you in disbelief. "What kind of call was that, ref?" Is this dissent? Most certainly! But does it warrant a yellow card? Probably not, because a confident referee sure of his game would simply look at the player, laugh out loud and say something like: "You didn't like that one? Oh, I've got worse than that up my sleeve!" or: "You didn't see that? Well, don't ever take up refereeing, mate!" One of our favorite responses comes near the touchline at a disputed throw-in. "But I had to give the throw to them; it's right in front of their bench!" All these humorous responses show the players that disagreement will not disturb you. It is almost as if you *expect* them to disagree and you are ready for it. It is harmless banter from players who simply complain or show disappointment in a decision, but who then get on with the game. They are not guilty of dissent.

But it is important to distinguish between the banter that comes from mere grumbling or frustration, and dissent in its real form, which must be dealt with quickly before it spreads. For many players, it is part of their bag of tricks. They complain publicly about every decision, knowing that with most referees, eventually a 50-50 decision will go their way, or they will get away with something that the referee—now intimidated by the constant disagreement—should have called. These players steadily erode the confidence of the referee by constant complaining. Don't put up with it! At some point hold up the game, pull the player aside and let him know what's coming. "I didn't come here to get into a debate with you! If you keep yapping at me, I will have no choice but to give you a caution. So now you decide if your right to free speech is worth a yellow card, OK?"

The same goes for players who shout loudly and directly at the referee, or who run towards the referee yelling and gesticulating. They are guilty of dissent and must be cautioned. If this is done early in a game, the result is usually good, for the rest of the players get the message, and there are no further problems. In a game during which a lot of dissent was allowed to go on unpunished, the administering of a caution for this offence late in the game is not likely to be effective, for it will be seen as "too little too late", and a desperate attempt on the part of the referee to regain control that was rapidly slipping.

The Gang Dissent.

Recently it has become common to see several players rush to surround the referee to protest a critical decision. This action is evidently intended to intimidate the official. In our more cynical moments we believe that this may be a planned, rehearsed or coached event. But what is more likely the cause is that the "wolfpack mentality" takes over some of the players. Initially only one or two protest, but then others join in, shouting and howling when they sense weakness. If this happens to you, be ready to stand firm.

First, do not back away, for as with wolves, this is a sign that you are frightened. (Following a recent well-publicized incident of this type in the Premiership in England, one of the main perpetrators admitted that if the referee had not kept retreating, they probably would not have continued to go after him!)

Second, do not allow yourself to be boxed in either by players behind you, or by the perimeter lines of the pitch. You have to move.

So, third, keep moving in a zig-zag or erratic pattern, and attempt to get the game going again. (see the discussion in Chapter 14 about dealing with protests at penalty kicks.) You are trying to give the players a chance to cool off and drop the protest, but...

Fourth, if the pack still won't leave you alone, pick one of them (but not someone who already has a yellow card) and caution him. This usually will encourage the others to depart the area rather quickly. But if it doesn't, a few well-chosen words such as "If you are still here by the time I finish taking his name, yours will follow his into the book" will get the desired result, especially if you direct the remark to a player who already has a caution. You don't have to be the nice guy in circumstances like this. Be tough, cold-blooded and unyielding. And if he does not get that message, follow through and give him a caution too, and if he has to be sent off, then do it. You gave him the chance to escape by not choosing him to be the first in this pack to get a caution. If he didn't realize how generous you were being, then so be it.

These actions will have the effect of showing that you cannot be intimidated, and that you have sufficient strength of character and confidence in your abilities to deal with attempted intimidation and bullying. That's a reputation to savor!

The Red Card.

The most severe punishment a referee can mete out is to send off a player. Players hate it because it punishes the player *and* the rest of the team, which must play short. As with all such extreme powers, it must be used wisely, and correctly. Correct we can be by following the law; but acting wisely comes only through understanding and experience. Let's start with the laws.

They specify seven offenses for which a player shall be sent off: serious foul play; violent conduct; spitting at an opponent or any other person; denying a goal-scoring opportunity by handling the ball or by fouling; use of offensive, insulting or abusive language; receiving a second caution in a match.

For many years, a sending-off was left to the referee's judgement. But in recent years, certain offenses have been deemed to be "automatic red cards" in order to bring about some degree of uniformity in application. (And—as we have said many times—to write into law what referees *should have been doing anyway!*) The two most prominent are the deliberate prevention of a goal by a defender by handling the ball (or handling by the goalkeeper outside the penalty area), and fouls by defenders on forwards with clear scoring opportunities with no other defender them between them and the goal. Then in 1999, a sending-off was mandated for a foul tackle from behind which endangered an opponent.

Violent conduct includes punching an opponent; treading on opponents; kicking an opponent when the ball is not in play; or other such egregious acts. For these offenses, the players must be immediately sent off, using a simple technique: Blow the whistle forcefully, and immediately display the red card! Your immediate and emphatic stance will have the effect of preventing escalation and retaliation.

Other serious fouls that also merit a red card include the following:

1. A challenge on a fast-moving opponent, with such hard and heavy bodily contact that he is propelled through the air to land very heavily.

2. A hard tackle in which the studs are exposed and make contact with the opponents legs, particularly above the ankle (the so-called over-the-top tackle).

If any players commit any of these fouls, they must be sent off immediately, the referee using the technique described above. Don't hesitate!

A more difficult decision is that of dealing with the second cautionable offense or second yellow card, formerly known as misconduct after a caution. Most of the infractions that can be cautioned are subject to interpretation, and besides which, there can never be consistency, not only between one referee and another, but also with one referee alone. [Now every coach reading this is going to leap out of his chair complaining that two guys who are supposed to know better are saying that we can't have consistency!] Yes, we *are* saying that, and here's why.

If a player is cautioned for a bad foul, and then commits another one, you send him off. When a player gets a card for a technical offence (say, encroachment), and then commits a bad foul, you send him off. Few people would dispute your decision. But let's say you caution a player for a bad foul, and *then he delays a free kick.* Strictly according to the law, you must send him off, but if you do, you will be greeted with a chorus of players and coaches saying: "Surely you're not going to send him off for that, are you?" So, by their reasoning, technical + foul = red card, but foul + technical = ? *There* is the inconsistency, and for a mathematician it is like saying that 2 + 3 = 5 but 3 + 2 = something less!

So what can we do? The referee must not appear to be too quick to dismiss a player, nor must he shirk his duty when it is justified. But our experience tells us that this action is *not always* justified, and because of the incensed reaction of most players when they see it, could produce the opposite effect to what we want. It may result in loss of control, not retention of it, because it is difficult to "sell" the decision to the players. Our recommendation is to deliver a stern, public reprimand with a reminder (in a loud voice) of the prior caution. "Hey, Nobby! You are playing with fire! You've already got a card, and I can send you off for anything like that. Do it again and I'll have no choice. You decide!"

The overlooked infraction – Persistent Infringement.

Among the infractions for which a player may be cautioned is one that the vast majority of referees never enforce. It is the one described by the phrase "..persistently infringes the Laws of the Game." Time and again we have been dismayed that players are rarely cautioned for this, despite our knowledge—as players and as referees—that persistent infringement exerts more of a negative influence on the game than does any one of the isolated incidents for which players are generally cautioned.

We should state at the start that persistent infringement applies primarily to fouls and misconduct and not to offside or foul throw-ins. No player should be cautioned for being caught offside repeatedly, since he is hurting no one but himself and his team. And a foul throw gets a throw-in for the opponents, so it doesn't hurt the game. These are matters best left to the coach or captain to deal with. But fouls can affect the game, and must be the referee's responsibility.

So what exactly is this overlooked infraction? To some, trying to define persistent infringement is like trying to define pornography: "I can't provide a definition, but I know it when I see it" was the remark of a prominent Supreme Court Justice. This may be true for pornography, but clearly it is not true in our game, judging by the number of matches in which the referee doesn't see it, or *doesn't* know it when he *does* see it.

Consider a typical match: statistics show that there are usually about 40 fouls in most matches, fewer in some, more in others. Now let us assume that these fouls are evenly distributed around the 20 outfield players (knowing as we do that goalkeepers seldom commit fouls). This means that each player committed two fouls. We know that after a foul, the ball is usually dead for about 15-30 seconds, the time taken for it to be brought back to the correct place, players to take up their positions, referee to be satisfied, and so on. So for 40 fouls, we lose about 10-20 minutes of actual play. Because of all the other stoppages in a match, the ball is probably in play for no more than 60-65 minutes in a 90-minute match.

This simple calculation shows that fully half the active playing time lost in most matches is lost because of fouls. This is generally accepted as reasonable, a normal part of the game. Now let us see what happens if we were to have 60 or even 80 fouls in match. Then there would be 15-30 or even 20-40 minutes lost due to fouls. Clearly the upper values of these estimates would be unacceptable, since almost half of a match would be spent on free-kicks. This would spoil matches for both players and spectators.

Let's take the average of two fouls per player as acceptable, three fouls marginal, and four fouls unacceptable. We know that in any match there will be a few players who commit only one or no fouls, then some others must be committing three or four. But this kind of reasoning we would have to say that any player who commits more than four fouls has had more than his "fair allocation." But so far, all we have considered is the effect of persistent infringement on lost playing time. We must also consider the pernicious effect it can have on the referee's control of the game.

In many matches the type of player we are talking about does not commit a flagrant foul for which he would be cautioned. He commits the less-noticeable ones, usually minor fouls: a trip here, a push there, an occasional obstruction. However, these can have the effect of gradually chipping away at the referee's control of the game, but chipping away so imperceptibly that it is not noticed. Not noticed, that is, until it may be too late.

For be assured that the opponents *will have* noticed, and may respond by adopting similar tactics of their own, reasoning that the referee will not do anything about it. Or worse, opponents may become exasperated and react directly by clobbering the player, or may aim an outburst of dissent to the referee. And who gets the yellow card? The persistent infringer? No, it always seems to be the retaliator or the speechmaker! Their crimes may deserve punishment, but who was the real culprit? If you don't recognize the source of the problem, another crime against the spirit of the game will go unpunished.

Now let's deal with this overlooked infraction. Our rule of thumb was that *a player who commits four fouls—any fouls—in a half, or six fouls—any fouls—in a game should be cautioned,* if he hasn't already been. If this seems harsh, consider that four fouls in a half, would be a rate of eight fouls for a match, clearly way too many. If only half of the outfield players committed that many, you would have 80 fouls! And for a whole game, if four is an unacceptable number, six is also excessive, and should be where the line must be drawn at an absolute maximum. *No player should be allowed to commit six fouls in a match, and remain unpunished.*

"But I am not a human computer, I can't keep track of every foul committed by every player throughout a match." This was the response of some referees when we introduced this concept at clinics. To those faint-hearted skeptics we replied that it was not as difficult as it seemed. After all, we are not talking about twelve persistent infringers! Generally it is only two or three players who are doing the repeated fouling, four or five at the most. What we did was to mentally tell ourselves the identity of the player committing a foul: "Red number four", "Blue number six" and so on. Without our being aware of it, the brain noticed repetitions of numbers and colors, and we *knew* when to speak to an offender about repeat offenders. Sometimes the players will tell you about one of their opponents. "C'mon, ref! That's four times he's kicked us!" Use that information. All it takes is practice, concentration and commitment, all the attributes of refereeing in general, right?

THE CAT HAD NINE LIVES!

In a professional match in the NASL, one of the midfield players was a former international and player on championship club teams in his previous country. He was nearing the end of his career, and like many of that ilk, had decided to play in the US to earn a fistful of dollars, and enjoy the climate without exerting himself very much. However, he often found himself up against younger, faster, keener players and found it difficult to keep up, especially in the heat and humidity of southern US summers, which were a marked contrast to the colder climate—even in summer—of his familiar northern Europe.

There was no doubt that in his prime he had been a much better player than those he opposed in the NASL, but time had taken its inevitable toll on him, as it does on us all. He made up for his physical deficiencies by substituting guile and cunning, including a series of little fouls like those described above. Also he kept up a running dialog with the referee (EB). Although sympathetic with his plight, the referee nevertheless warned him regarding persistent infringement, and eventually cautioned him.

Unfortunately, he chose to ignore the friendly advice and the caution. With about ten minutes left in the match, when he realized he was too exhausted to get the ball legally, he reached up over his head to pull a ball down to prevent it going through to an opponent in a dangerous position. Out came the red card, and although he left without comment, his team-mates protested on his behalf. "That didn't deserve a red card! He didn't kick or injure or punch anyone" went the cries.

As was the custom in the NASL, the club protested the red card, and even the Director of Officials felt the punishment may have been too severe. When all the details were explained, the red card was upheld, the Director grudgingly admitting the referee was right. Nevertheless he still expressed sentiments about how difficult it is too "sell" such a decision. The estimate of the referee was that this was his eighth foul, well above the reasonable allocation we have advocated, and even above what would probably be allowed by referees who were not routinely aware of persistent infringement. Close scrutiny of the TV video tape revealed that it was actually his tenth infraction!

A good idea is to have a quiet word with the player who has committed three fouls. "That is your third foul and we have only been playing X minutes. If you commit another before the half is over, you'll be cautioned." The player has been warned, and if he does not heed the warning, issue the caution! This will be noted by other players and will serve as a deterrent. If he heeds that warning, but commits two further fouls in the second half, the warning should be repeated. "That's your fifth foul; one more and you are in the book!" Again, follow-through is vital, and it is important to tell the player he is being cautioned for persistent infringement. If our assessment of games is correct, it may never have happened to him before.

We must stress that the referee must not flinch here, even though the particular foul after which the caution was issued may seem to be minor and not normally be worthy of a caution. If anyone questions you, let him—and everyone else—know that persistent infringement is the call, and if you know the number of fouls, tell the players. This can prevent you from being the target of unfair criticism from persons—club owners, spectators—ignorant of the Law (see sidebar for an example).

A cautionless game—the ultimate satisfaction.

What every referee should aspire to but what seldom occurs, is the game in which everything goes so well, that he has to issue no cautions. We do not mean a game where cautions should have been issued but were not! We refer to a game in which there was no need for disciplinary action because the players all played well, and were respectful of the referee's decisions.

This is a good sign that as a referee you have done a good job, not only in the game in question, but also in your previous games. For as the old saying goes "A referee makes his own reputation." In our experience this only comes after several seasons of refereeing in a particular league, and will seldom come in a tournament game, where you are unknown to one or both teams, and they will therefore "try you out." In a regular league program, the players and coaches get to know you and your reputation. The players avoid doing those things that they know will get them cautioned, and as a result, they play in accordance with the Laws and in full awareness of your standards.

NOTES

12

CONTROL OF
THE GAME-III:
BENEFICIAL HERESIES

*It is the customary fate of
new truths to begin as heresies.....*
T. H. Huxley

Comments by way of introduction.

We have hinted here and stated there, that we believe many things are wrong with the way that referees are prepared and trained. Or rather, that changes should be made to bring refereeing up-to-date and capable of dealing with players in the modern game. What is being taught at the moment is fine as far as it goes: referees *do* need to be taught the Laws of the Game and some of the history behind them. They *do* need to be shown certain basic techniques about positioning and movement, and they *do* need to be made aware of the powers they have—and the responsibility—for dealing with misconduct. But we believe that they should be taught much more.

Their role in the game is the first thing: that they are subordinate to the players, that they are not put on the field as dictators, that power is not their most valuable asset. We have dealt with this at some length in Chapters 2 and 3.

IN THIS CHAPTER:

- *Flash-points and flare-ups*
- *Two player flare-up and retaliation*
- *"Round up the usual suspects!"*
- *The problem of the star player*
- *Use of humor*
- *When all else fails*
- *The "needle match"*

A more compassionate and thoughtful approach in their dealings with players—especially in the amateur and youth game—is second. That players and coaches are not the enemy of referees, that we are all *participants* in the same sport. Referees should attempt to put themselves into the minds of players in order to understand why things happen, why players react the way that they do. We have written about this, too, notably in the previous chapter where we introduced the reader to the idea of working to keep a cautioned player on the field. Some referees have been *accused* of "thinking like a player"; we believe that that is not an accusation, but a compliment!

And third is the idea that our profession—and refereeing is a profession—must innovate or else it will stagnate, damaging the very thing it is supposed to take care of—the sport of Association Football. New ideas about conducting a match must be experimented with, tested, then used and taught. We know the value of this, for we have both been fortunate in our other work to see profound changes in the way that our respective professions conduct their business. Since we started our research careers we have witnessed the discovery that the DNA molecule, the single genetic code connecting all living things, could be manipulated to move genes between species, thereby giving rise to the exciting new field of biotechnology (EB). And we have learned that the crust of what we thought was the solid planet earth is a moving, dynamic thing in a constant state of creation, rearrangement and change (RE). What would biochemistry and geology be if those ideas and many others had never come to light?

So it is, we believe, with refereeing. It may never have the importance of fundamental biochemistry and geology, but it does directly affect the pleasure of millions upon millions of players, and perhaps billions of spectators on the planet. *The game of football is changing and we the referees must change with it.*

In this chapter we are going to introduce you to some new ideas about handling difficult situations in the field. Some we learned from other referees and instructors, but some we devised ourselves. They involve anticipation, understanding, manipulation, preparation and finally, a determination to keep a strong grip on a game without damaging either players or teams. At the moment you will find few of these techniques taught in referee training courses, but one day you will, of that we are sure. Several of them are regarded as heresies, and this explains why we chose Huxley's comment as the epigraph for this chapter. But these ideas and techniques worked for us, and we are pleased to pass them on!

But several words of warning are needed here. We must emphasize that these techniques are not to be used without due consideration of the circumstances, and of your own personality. They can backfire if used at the wrong time, or with the wrong people. We suggest that if you decide you can use them, you should introduce them into your game gradually, being careful at first, and then later allowing yourself more freedom. A true story will illustrate these points. Gordon Hill was an excellent referee who enjoyed a great reputation with players in the Football League because of his easy-going banter with them. He kept firm control by developing and maintaining a good relationship with the players.

After he left the Football League, he immigrated into the USA, refereed in the NASL, and also went around giving talks to referee groups across the country. Unfortunately more than one referee became a cropper when they tried in their own leagues to imitate Gordon and his easy-going methods. The players and coaches, accustomed to one style of refereeing from these officials, suddenly found themselves dealing with something completely different, a new person almost. Players did not respond as they had responded to Gordon himself; some games went to pieces as a result. So be warned.

Flash-points: Be ready for them!

We have described (Chapter 10) several situations or incidents that we called "Moments of Truth". Handle them correctly and you keep control of the game; mess them up, and all hell breaks loose. But we talked about those incidents as events that had already occurred. Now we are going to suggest ways to prevent some of them from even happening. Our entire Chapter 15 describes situations where the *referee* is vulnerable and has to be careful. Now let's consider what we call "potential flash-points", where the *game itself* is vulnerable and in danger.

Whenever a large number of opposing players gather in a very small area, there is the potential for problems. This happens in the goalmouth at corner kicks. Also near the wall at free kicks near goal, and in the area to where the ball may be directed after the kick. Think also of the gathering around a player who is down after a hard foul, with the victim's teammates wishing to have a word with the player who committed the infraction, and his teammates coming to his aid.

In all these situations, *you do not wait for bad things to happen. You try to make sure that they don't happen!*

Try and get as close to the group of players as you can. At corner-kicks this is easily done, because for many of them, you will be seeking a position on the goal-line close to the goal (see Chapter 14). If you anticipate an inswinging corner from the left wing to the near post, you can walk right through the crowd at the front post. Talking as you go, you let the players know that you are close by, and let them know what's on your mind. "Well, there's quite crowd down here, isn't there? I'd better stay close to the action!" "Hey, John! You've got your hands all over him! Does he like that kind of caressing?" "Jackie, get that pushing over with in the next few seconds, because once he kicks the ball, you'll be giving away a penalty!"

In similar fashion, an inswinging corner taken from the right wing should get you close to the goal-line and to the players. Don't miss the chance to talk to them and let them know you are watching. The same applies from a close free-kick out on the right, with a group of players on the far post side of the goal waiting for the cross. You should make those players on the left aware of your position, and if some contact between them is taking place before the ball is kicked, tell them the consequences if they don't stop pushing and shoving and manhandling each other.

At most walls erected at free-kicks close to the goal, you are necessarily going to be close at hand to take care of the encroachment. While you are there, you can comment on other things: a forward jostling for a place in the wall, or a defender holding the shorts of an opponent. Do it with humor, but make your presence known. "Hey, number five! If you had hold of my shorts for that long, I'd think you were hoping for a date!" And if the situation warrants your going downfield of the wall (see Chapter 14), you can talk and be a mysterious voice coming from behind the players to convince them that illegal activity would be very unwise!

Some referees (and instructors) disagree with techniques such as this, because they say that the referee is convicting the player before the crime. Or in other words, the referee is guilty of pre-judging the innocent. We have only one response to criticisms like that: it is naïve and old-fashioned. We will refer you to the complete statement of the brief but wise words at the head of Chapter 15, the words of Emile Chartier (Alain), the French philosopher:

> And that is the way we live; we dodge a misfortune at every moment because we anticipate it; thus what we anticipate—and this certainly makes sense—does not happen.

By anticipating problems at these crowded situations, you prevent them from happening. No matter what anyone says, *the prevention of problems is good refereeing.*

In those hot moments after a bad foul, when players from both teams begin to mill about, shouting and gesticulating, we advocate getting in the middle of them, talking all the time and blowing your whistle in someone's ear if he doesn't seem to be paying attention. Don't just stand there and take names, because all that does is let things go on! You want to stop anything serious happening, and you won't do *that* by merely *watching.* Make your presence felt, spin around frequently to make sure you see all the activity, and yell at anyone who seems to be close to doing something silly. As people back off from the confrontation, compliment them for their restraint. With you in the middle of things taking charge, the ugliness will not escalate to violence.

Two-player flare-up and retaliation.

Frequently, after one player has been fouled, perhaps once too often in his opinion, he will react in some way towards the opponent. He makes a comment, or gets nose-to-nose, staring at the other player, or perhaps pushes him away. Most referees have experience of such incidents, and—sad to say—most of them make the wrong decision. All too often the second player is the one that ends up with the caution—or worse—while the instigator of the mess gets off scot-free, and with a smirk on his face.

Even if the player who retaliates is deserving of punishment, a referee should always consider *why he reacted.* The fictional television detective Theo Kojak once stated "If there is no justice, there will be violence." He was referring to crime on the streets, but it can equally well apply to soccer matches, and the person who is there to deliver the justice is the referee. Games will go wrong when there is the perception among the players that there has been a miscarriage of justice. *Most situations involving retaliation end up with the players feeling that there has been no justice.*

Make sure in these incidents you punish the instigator, the real culprit. The other players know all too well what has been going on, and so should the referee. In fact, this could all have been a deliberate attempt to provoke a particular player in order to get him booked or sent off. You should know that such a plan will never succeed without the complicity of the referee. If you decide to caution or send off both players at such an incident, *it is important that the instigator be dealt with first, and spoken to more severely than the retaliator.* Then the retaliator should be dealt with, and spoken to with a little more empathy, but still emphasizing that the discipline should be left to the referee. In many cases, where the response of the fouled player is merely anger, words, or a slight push, you may not have to caution him. Book the original criminal, and sympathetically lecture the retaliator. The players will know that you have administered justice!

If both players are actually fighting and some other players are attempting to intervene, you need to act quickly to restore order and maintain control. Blowing the whistle hard, fast and furiously, while running toward the site, usually has a calming effect. If you can get to the two players involved before any other players get there, inform everyone quite loudly to leave them both to you, that they are going off. Use every attempt—including getting between the pugilists—to stop the altercation. Continually blowing the whistle right in their ears (!) usually does the trick. Then simply display the red card and order both players off.

This action generally has a beneficial effect in several ways. First, no team has a numerical advantage, so nobody feels that the referee has favored the other team. Second, the remaining players are aware that the referee is not afraid to send someone off to restore order. Third, no one can doubt your sense of justice. And fourth, 10 vs. 10 often makes for a more open and attractive game than does 11 vs. 11!

"Round-up the usual suspects."

As anyone who is an admirer of classic movies will know, this command was issued on more than one occasion by the wily police captain Louis Renault (played by Claude Rains) in "Casablanca." Why? He knew that some individuals commit a disproportionate number of the crimes, and he knew that you can save much time and aggravation by investigating those persons first. And what is true in police work can equally well be true in soccer, as we will show here. (Incidentally, Captain Renault also uttered another famous line which most certainly should NOT be used as a guide by referees. He said "the winning side would have paid you much better" although some factions of the game still accuse us of it!)

In any league or competition, there are certain players who commit more fouls than anyone else, who receive more yellow cards and red cards than the rest of their team combined. These players are now currently known by the politically correct term *"serial transgressors!"* Probably all of you reading this book could immediately name two or three such players in each of the leagues or competitions in which you regularly officiate or watch. Also, in the professional competitions, even the spectators know who the so-called troublesome players are. One of these players in England made a commercial video showing all his "talents" for everyone to see. Not long after that, he appeared—a masterpiece of casting, this!—as a thug in a black comedy about crime in London. Time and time again such players create problems in games. What are referees supposed to do about it?

Traditional referee training tells referees that every player starts each game with a clean sheet, and all of them—the good, the bad and the ugly—are to be treated the same. We believe that this is naïve and a recipe for disaster. We realize that what we about to say is considered heresy, but referees are there to control the game, and they should use all the information available to them, including information about a player's track record. But before you accuse us of being prejudiced officials out to "get" some bad boys, read on and see what we were about.

First you have get to know who the problem players are in the competitions you regularly work, and keep an eagle-eye out for these guys. When you go to unfamiliar leagues or cup tournaments, you will have to determine the identities of such players by talking to other referees and by watching other games. After you have found out who these players are, then when you referee them, the moment they show signs of stepping out of line you must deal with them, *but without mentioning that you know anything about their reputation.* The best time to stop a runaway train in when it starts moving, and before it has built up a head of steam.

If you can bring the player under control with a comment, so much the better, but if he doesn't respond, don't hesitate to give him a caution. We are sure that you will hear all the usual complaints from the players and the managers that like all the other referees, you are picking on the player unfairly. But your answer to this criticism is that *you took action only after the player stepped out of line.* You did not prejudge him or talk to him about his past. You did not convict him before the crime. "I'm not having that kind of play in this game! You know what happens next…" is all you need to say. Get on with your job and ignore the criticism.

Just as a referee does, a player makes his own reputation, and it is nobody's fault but his own if he continually gets into trouble. Leopards in soccer uniforms rarely change their spots, and referees should know who the leopards are. Just one or two hard-men who play ruthlessly all the time can ruin a game for the other players, *if the referee does not restrain the thugs early.* If more referees did what they are supposed to do, and did not listen to the naïve comments of disinterested observers, perhaps some of these players would begin to change their ways, or better yet, perhaps coaches would not be as keen to put them on their teams.

This may be heresy at the moment, but eventually—as the great scientist Thomas Huxley said—it will be the truth. Of that we are sure.

The star player problem.

In every competition there are certain star players, the ones of exceptional ability. In professional and international soccer we have been fortunate to encounter some of these greats: Pele, Cruyff, Maradona, Moore, Beckenbauer, Best, Eusebio, Cubillas and others. How should the referee treat such players, who simply by name alone bring in thousands of spectators to any game? Should they get special treatment from referees? This is a question that has been debated for years, and according to some referees in the professional league here, is still the subject of argument. Our answer is an unequivocal "Yes!" But hold on now! We may not be saying quite what you think...

We are not saying that if they are guilty of misconduct, we should ignore it. Nor are we saying that they have the right to make comments to the referee that no other player would be allowed to make. We do not advocate the idea that since they are stars, and lots of people pay money to see them play, we should not take action that may get them suspended. Quite the contrary, for the rules of misconduct are the same for them as for any journeyman player.

What we do say is that because of their great skills, they are frequently the victims of harsh treatment by their opponents, simply because it is almost impossible to stop them by fair means. The special treatment they *should* get from the referee is careful and thorough protection. It is a foolish referee who makes statements such as: "Ronaldo is just another player as far as I am concerned", because that is just not true!

No, star players should not be allowed to hand out their own justice, or be allowed to commit serious offenses without receiving the same punishment as other players. We are aware that they may get away with things in certain other sports. Did Michael Jordan or Kareem Abdul-Jabbar ever "foul out" of a basketball game? Not often! However, in a soccer game this kind of "special treatment" should never be allowed. There cannot be one set of rules for some players, and another set for different players. This was well illustrated in recent World Cup games where Zidane of France, Kluivert of Holland and Etcheverry of Bolivia, each a star player of his team, were dismissed for unprovoked serious foul play.

But the sending off of Beckham of England in the 1998 World Cup was not for an *unprovoked* action, and the Argentinian player who committed the original foul on Beckham was guilty of a terrific acting job after being feebly kicked by Beckham, who was laying face down on the ground at the time. A superficial analysis of this incident, and in accordance with the strict interpretation of the Laws, might lead to the conclusion that Beckham should have been sent off. However, a deeper insight into this incident leads to a different conclusion.

Look at the factors: 1. a star player; 2. provocation; 3. tournament play at the single elimination stage. At such tournaments, and this applies equally well to youth matches, when the teams are down to the single elimination stage, competition is tough. One way to gain an advantage is to attempt to get an opponent sent off, and if it happens to be their star player, so much the better. Thus we see an unusual amount of over-acting after minor fouls in these tournaments in order to induce the referee to pull the red card. This is not seen so much in regular league play, since the result of one isolated match is less significant, and there seems to be a sort of gentleman's agreement in domestic pro leagues, that you do not attempt to get a fellow professional sent off. But all such agreements are off in major tournaments. So in the Beckham incident, had the referee been aware of all these factors, and had he recognized, as we are recommending to you, that a star player did need some form of special treatment, he would have recognized the cynical acting by the Argentinian and not been fooled. As it was, however, he became—unwittingly perhaps—an accomplice to the crime.

Use of humor.

If you have any sense of humor at all, try using it. It has been our experience, and the experience of others, that a humorous remark can obviate the need for a caution to a player, or can defuse a tense situation. It is especially effective when players are complaining to you, or getting close to what other referees might call dissent. If you can respond with a smile and a quick joke, many players will simply shrug and get on with the game. You will have demonstrated that you are not perturbed by their comments, and that you can live with a certain amount of back-and-forth banter. You will have demonstrated that you are a human being enjoying himself.

To give you the idea of what we are talking about, here are some examples, most of them true stories. The one in the sidebar is a classic!

At a free kick and caution:

It is sometimes worthwhile to deliberately take your time while pretending to write in your little book, in order to allow time for tempers to cool before the ball goes back into play. During one such delaying action by a referee, the player waiting to take the kick became impatient and said: "C'mon Ref, what's the problem? There are only five letters in his name!" Came the reply: "Yes I know, but I have to write slowly 'cos the bloke who gets the reports can't read very fast!"

At what a player thinks is an obviously unfair caution:

"Aw, c'mon ref, you're not going to book me for that! What did I do?"

"I'm sorry, George, I shouldn't book you just for kicking him up the air like that, but if I don't send in two cautions every game, I don't get paid!"

Criticism from a player:

A player started to tell the referee that he was having a nightmare of a game. The comments might have been worthy of a caution, but instead, the referee looked the player straight in the eye and said: "Now let me see...you are two goals down, you are the central defender, both goals have come down the middle, and *I'm* the one having the nightmare?" In other cases you might point out goal chances he has missed, or bad passes, or missed tackles, or giving away the ball—whatever is appropriate to the player concerned. In many cases when we did this, the same player asked about our observations later on in the match. Apparently he believed that if the referee has noticed his mistakes, the coach will have also! His insecurity then gave us a perfect chance to reassure him that we were only kidding, and to establish a friendlier relationship with him.

[Few players enjoy anyone pointing out their shortcomings, and rather than risk another retort like the one above, most will make no further comments.]

But one must be careful with smart remarks, because some players are totally humorless, and such comments can backfire. So try to get a feel for a player's personality before trying this approach. If one of the humorless ones complains that you can't talk to him like that, simply give him an artificial apology: "You're quite right, number 7, I do apologize. I forgot that the laws allow only players to make sarcastic remarks!"

More criticism from a player:

Many inexperienced referees have difficulty in dealing with comments from players because they can't distinguish what is destructive and what it merely a player's way of letting off steam to ease his own frustration. Unless the criticism is so loud and public that you have to caution the dissenter, we recommend trying to handle the problem with repartee.

"Referee, you really are pathetic!"

"Yes, I know. That's why they won't let me referee *real* players...." or: "Yes, that is why I only referee in the 2nd division", or whatever lower league it is you are in. Of course, this won't work if you operate in the top division of your local competition, so you will have to use your imagination to find something along these lines to say. But you get the idea: *humor may save you the use of a card.*

Idiotic explanations:

We described in Chapter 11 a disputed throw-in where the referee explained his decision as being necessary because the throw was right in front of a team bench. Another silly explanation you can use to disperse dissent is to claim that you are alternating your decisions just to be fair: "No, no, Alex, you got the last one!" Try this one: "Yeah, I know it should have been a corner, but they are at home!" If this is said with a wry smile just before you quickly run away, the players usually understand what you are doing. In some cases, a player may seem to believe what you are saying, assumes therefore that you are totally useless and decides that further discussion is pointless!

HOW A STRIKER GETS PREGNANT...

Peter T. Johnson, FIFA Referee for Canada in the days of the NASL, was a marvellous humorist. At more than one pre-season clinic, when things got tense or dull, he would take the stage to regale the audience of serious referees and even-more-serious coaches with patter, jokes and impressions. He frequently used his humor in games, and in one match in Dallas, was able to control a player's fouling by a wisecrack at the right moment.

Dallas used Kyle Rote, a fast and athletic young American player, as one of two target men in the attack. A great jumper and skillful in the air, he would use his head to knock balls off to one side or the other to his partner, an old pro named Richie Reynolds. Reynolds was not nearly so agile as Rote, but was experienced and wily. When the ball came to him, he had to compete for it with taller defenders who could always out-jump him....unless, of course he did something about it (see Chapter 6 for a discussion of this kind of conflict).

What Reynolds would do was to lean backwards into the central defender, keeping him away from the best position to take the header. This is known as "backing in" to a taller opponent, and when it is followed by bending forward it makes it look as though the defender is leaning all over the striker unfairly. Peter Johnson, however, an experienced old pro himself, was wise to what was going on and penalized Reynolds several times. But the fouls continued. Tired of blowing his whistle for the same infraction time after time, Johnson eventually cried out in his London accent: "Look 'ere, Reynolds, if you don't stop backing into him like that, you're goin' to end up pregnant!"

All the players nearby erupted, and even Reynolds had to smile. But the "persistent infringement"—for such it was—stopped, and Reynolds and his teammates left the high balls for Rote. Johnson's humor saved the use of a card.

On more than one occasion, we have chattered our way out of a disagreement by overloading a player with information he can't possibly comprehend. If you were a player, imagine how you would respond to something like this from a referee who is trotting upfield after the defenders had made a loud appeal for offside: "Well, you might think he was interfering with play, but if you had looked at the eyes of the feller with the ball you would have seen that he glanced over to the right, then cleverly shifted his eyes to make me *believe* he was going to pass the ball to the left to the winger who was offside. As the light caught his eyes, I saw that he winked at the winger, shook his head slightly and played the ball the other way. I mean, there's no way I could give the winger offside for that....." On and on you go with utter nonsense until the player gives up in disgust. *Humor may save you the use of a card.*

Killing the Game.

Occasionally, you will be involved in a game which has been very heatedly contested, with several yellow cards, and perhaps a red card or two. The players are very frustrated, and several may be about to lose their composure. Tell-tale signs are when they appear to be more interested in kicking each other than playing the ball. When these games are in tournaments, or play-offs or end-of-season matches, things can go totally awry near the end of the game. The usual sanctions of cautions or red cards do no good, because there may be no tomorrows, so to speak, for the players who are losing. In high school or college games, the players may be graduating; in youth games, they may be moving up to a different level, and even in adult contests, discipline such as suspensions may not be carried forward to the following season. If the result is essentially beyond doubt, it is sometimes wise to "kill" the game in the last 10-15 minutes.

You can do this by calling a free kick for every minor infraction. At several of those kicks you pick up the ball and hold it, taking ten or fifteen seconds longer than usual to get the game going. There's not much that can go on when you have the ball in your hands. At another stoppage, you can ask to see a player's footwear, because you thought you saw a dangerous cleat. Hold up a throw-in until you have consulted with an assistant referee, making a show of consulting watches. Insist on the correct placement of the ball at corners, even though you will allow it eventually to be taken from the same place it was put originally.

In these tense few minutes, make sure also that you run to every foul and free-kick to prevent any hint of a confrontation. Slow things down by any means you can think of. If you feel uncomfortable as you read this advice, *remember that one of your principal roles is to keep order. When the result of a game is beyond doubt, yet things are still in danger of getting out of hand, no one suffers if you choke the life out of the contest as it draws to a close. Better that than to have to abandon the game due to a major fight, with players or others injured on the field because the benches unloaded or spectators came on.*

The "needle match."

This can be an ugly affair, with a lot at stake, and often full of left-over feelings from a previous encounter. There is no love lost between the teams or among the players, and it shows even before the game: no friendly greetings between opponents, just sullen glaring back and forth, a few provocative comments tossed here and there. If you have done your homework (see Chapters 3 and 18), you should know what's coming and be ready for it. But being ready doesn't necessarily means that you will have control.

You can start by whistling everything to show you mean business, talking to the players committing fouls, loudly proclaiming your intent to keep the game within bounds. If that doesn't work, then go to your cards, three or four in quick succession for heavy fouls, dissent, late tackles and so on. Let everyone know in no uncertain terms that you will book every last man of them if they decide they don't want to play. And most important: *Be prepared to do it!* In most cases, things will settle down, and the players will begrudgingly accept what you are doing.

But if things don't quieten down to a dull roar, you have one more weapon at your disposal—the captains. Call them together and tell them that they had better help in getting control of their players, or else the match may not last the ninety minutes. Be aware that many referees (and referee instructors) feel that this is a sign of weakness on the part of the referee, because he appears to be admitting publicly that he cannot control things. However, we ask you to remember that the game is played for the players' benefit, and that on their behalf, the referee must make one last attempt to prevent the game deteriorating into an ill-disciplined debacle that will have to be abandoned. But as with some of the other heretical advice we have given in these pages, we advise you to use it rarely, not as a general practice.

NOTES

13

MOVEMENT, PLAYING-TACTICS AND THE REFEREE

Isn't it bliss? Don't you approve?
One who keeps tearing around, one who can't move...

Stephen Sondheim

Ask a group of referees or referee instructors and assessors about the *Diagonal System of Control*, and you will hear familiar words, like the refrain from a well-known song. "The *Diagonal System of Control*," they will say, "keeps the referee close to the action, and it allows him to see the play and one assistant referee at the same time. The referee runs from the top corner of one penalty-area to the same top corner of the other penalty-area. In order to talk to players, he may deviate from the diagonal when necessary, but in general, his path of movement will take him through the center-circle. He should be fit enough to stay within twenty-five yards of the action at all times. Two pairs of eyes looking at the action are better than one. There will

IN THIS CHAPTER:

- *Advice about the Diagonal System of Control is generally not enough for the modern referee to know how to move on the field.*
- *Movement of the referee should be planned to enable him to see as much as is possible, near the ball <u>and</u> away from it.*
- *The referee must understand enough about tactics to learn to stay out of the way of players and the ball.*
- *Techniques for spotting off-the-ball fouls, and techniques for staying out of the way of the play.*
- *Advice on anticipating where play is going next.*

be no duplication of effort or responsibility by the referee and linesman." Ah, yes! These are familiar words, and they've been around for decades.

No matter how true those statements may be, they miss the point. Like all clichés they do contain elements of truth and good advice, but coming as they do from a time when soccer was a different game from what we see nowadays, they are woefully inadequate for the task at hand: the task of the modern referee. They are deficient because they are not backed up by any analysis of *why or how* the referee moves about the field in the first place, except for the vague assertion that he should be "close to the play" at all times.

They are also deficient because they do not consider how the movement and position of the referee affect the play of the players, and the tactics of the teams. Nor do they consider how the referee can use his knowledge of the game and the teams to be in a position to make better decisions.

But stay with us, and we'll show you both *why* and *how*. If you want to avoid getting in the way of the players, and if you want to be in a position to make better decisions, then read on for an introduction— and it is only an *introduction*—to the art of moving around the field in a more effective way than you've been doing. We can summarize the purpose and method of movement of a referee by the following:

The referee must move around the field to see as much as possible as clearly as possible, and must do so without getting in the way of the players or the action.

Now we are going to take many pages to explain that single sentence, because its truth and beauty are not obvious at first reading.

Take a look at the illustration (Figure 13-1), a drawing of a moment during a match between Manchester United and Manchester City in the Football League in England. The midfield player has the ball at his feet and has to make a decision about where to pass the ball

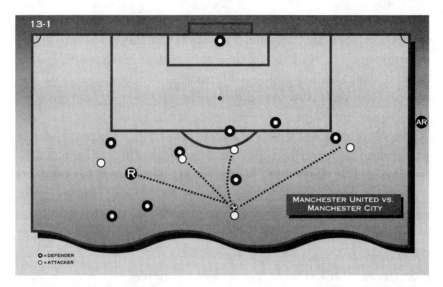

next. If he played the ball to the right, to his team-mate on the wing, he runs the risk of having the ball intercepted by the defender who is only three yards or so off the path of the ball. If the midfield player attempted to pass the ball immediately forward to his team-mate on the penalty-arc, he would have to make a lofted pass or a chip to get the ball over the defender between the passer and the intended target. Such a pass would place the recipient under pressure to bring the bouncing ball under control before the defender lurking a few yards behind him came in for a challenge.

The choice of a pass to the forward closest to the midfield player is not a good one either, because that man is tightly marked. The best choice would seem to be to the forward on the extreme left. He has stepped away from his marking defender, he is only twenty-five yards away from the passer, and is in a good position to turn and pursue the attack. Unfortunately, the referee is directly in the path of the intended pass, and in all probability, his position would inhibit the passer from delivering the ball in that direction. *The referee has had a negative influence on the play. Stated less politely, he has disrupted the attack by being in the wrong place.*

Yet if we describe the position of the referee by referring to the basic principles of the *Diagonal System of Control,* there would seem to be little wrong with it. He is close to the play, a mere twenty yards from the ball. He has positioned himself so that he can see both the play and the assistant referee on the right. He is in a good situation to see many of the players involved or about to be involved in the action. According to the best of the old clichés, therefore, his position would seem to be perfect. But nevertheless he disrupted the attack. So what did he do wrong? *Quite simply, he did not see what the players saw, especially the player with the ball. And because of that, he ended up in a space that the players would like to use.*

Be patient, and we'll show you how to avoid doing this yourself. We'll show you how you can stay out of the way of the players *and* their passes. But let's look at some other examples.

This one comes from the North American Soccer League, a game between Hartford and Chicago (Figure 13-2). The left wing of Chicago ran at a bouncing ball going towards the right flanking defender. The referee was in an excellent position a few yards behind the play. As the defender came in for the challenge he lifted his foot head-high to touch the ball away from the forward, who saw the boot coming and pulled back to protect his nose. The action by the

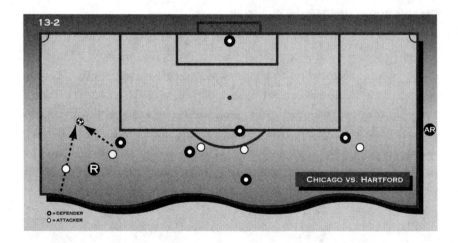

defender had all the necessary elements for "dangerous play" (see Chapter 5) and the referee blew his whistle. As the shrill blast echoed around the empty stadium (it was Hartford, remember?), the ball rolled away towards the touchline, where a Chicago defender, streaking down the wing, was ready to latch onto the ball and enter the penalty-area. He heard the whistle as he reached the ball, and when he knew that his moment of glory was taken away from him, his comments to the referee were short, choice and not-very-sweet. The referee had missed a perfect opportunity to apply "advantage", and had screwed up a great scoring opportunity for Chicago. But more than "advantage", what did he do wrong?

He had failed to notice and understand the tactics of one of the teams playing, regularly employing defenders to overlap their attacking forwards.

Thirty thousand fans were in the Kingdome in Seattle when this next disaster occurred (Figure 13-3). A Seattle forward attacked on the right and laid the ball off to his teammate, who was tightly marked by the flanking left defender. The player who made the original pass ran into the penalty-area, expecting a return pass ("wall pass") from the winger. As the forward penetrated the area, the defender realized that the attacker was going to get past him and would probably receive

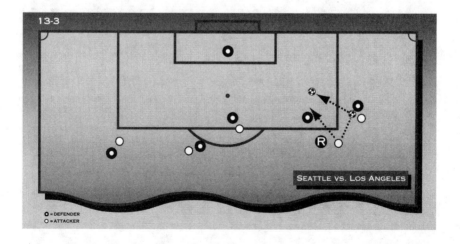

13-3

SEATTLE VS. LOS ANGELES

○ = DEFENDER
○ = ATTACKER

a pass that would create danger for the Los Angeles defence. He did what all perceptive defenders do when faced with a danger they can't control: he grabbed the forward, first slowing him down, and then hauling him down. The referee, however, was intent on watching the action between the flanking defender and the flanking forward, and alone among all the people in the stadium, he missed the penalty-kick infraction. It was a critical decision for this particular game, which never recovered, spiralling downwards from that moment into violence, dissent, sendings-off, abuse and turmoil. What went wrong?

The referee had failed to act on a basic tenet that defenders understand: that the most dangerous attacking player is often one who is not in possession of the ball.

Consider one last example of this disease of refereeing before we go into describing its cure. Imagine an attack down the wing (Figure 13-4). The principal danger to the defenders is that the ball will be swung behind them across the goal, for other forwards to reach. In this theoretical example, we show an attacker on the left, running past the flanking right defender. If the forward has the beating of him with speed, the only recourse for the defender is to impede the progress of the attacker by holding him, by getting in his way or by using some other unfair means. The referee in this example is a fairly

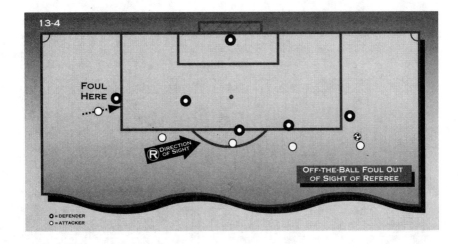

13-4

FOUL
HERE

DIRECTION
OF SIGHT

OFF-THE-BALL FOUL OUT
OF SIGHT OF REFEREE

O = DEFENDER
O = ATTACKER

normal position, dutifully watching the action over on the right wing, keeping the play between him and his assistant referee and so on. But he will miss the most important action, the off-the-ball foul by the defender on the forward penetrating the defence.

The referee is looking in the wrong place because he does not understand how attacks are made, how forwards defeat defenses, how defenders commit fouls away from the ball in order to break up dangerous attacks. As we said in the paragraph above, the most dangerous attacking player is often one who is not in possession of the ball.

But enough of this disease; let's go to the cure, which will not be found in the simple statements about the *Diagonal System of Control.* And we must point out that this disease and its cure are the same at all levels of the game, because the principles of attack and defence are similar throughout the sport, and what the referee needs to see is the same. The real problem is that too many referees don't understand how this game is played, and too many referee instructors don't teach anything except the laws and some basic techniques. And as for the many assessors who haven't played or understood the game, well, that's another book...

We believe that in order to referee effectively, it is essential to know something about what the players are trying to do, what the tactics are, and so on. Referees must see what is important and should become aware of how their position may affect tactical decisions made by the players. So where are referees supposed to learn these things, learn about *the game and how it is played?* The best sources of good information are experienced coaches who were themselves players. Like Ron Newman, player and coach of professional teams in this country continuously from the late sixties, and a man who is known deservedly as the "Dean of Coaches."

Ron came over from England in the early days of the North American Soccer League. He had been a player in the First Division in the Football League in England, and subsequently coached NASL teams in Dallas, Fort Lauderdale, and San Diego. He also coached the

Kansas City Wizards of Major League Soccer. We knew him during his tenure in Dallas, when we played against him and his team, when we refereed matches involving his teams in the NASL, and occasionally when we would meet him at soccer events. Always eager to talk about soccer, he has a wonderfully simple view of the game, a view that is useful for referees.

"It's a race for space and time," Ron says. "The more space you have, the more time you have to do things. And the quicker you do things, the more time you have and the more space you can create. If your opponent shuts down the space you have, then that cuts down the time you have to move the ball." One of the things that this means is that we must recognize how players can play very effectively even when they don't have the ball. Some studies have shown that an individual player may be in possession of the ball for less than thirty seconds *in a whole game.* When players are not in possession of the ball, they may be spending their time running into space, they may be drawing the attention of defenders, thereby creating space for others, or they may be using small areas of space by being in one-touch contact with the ball.

Referees, too, can think about time and space to be more effective in our movement about the field? Think of these two questions or problems:

(1) How can we make sure that we do not occupy *space* that the players may want to use? (And particularly: Can we learn to see the space that the players see, to see the action, the movement of opponents, and so on?)

(2) How can referees watch and protect the players during their *time* away from the ball? (Especially since most officials concentrate on watching the ball and the action immediately around it.)

THE PENALTIES
HARDLY ANYBODY SAW—OFF-THE-BALL

Several years after the Seattle incident described above, we were both now on the International list, and more experienced at dealing with skilled and experienced players and their tactics. In an NASL game refereed by one of us (EB) there was a similar incident. This time after about five minutes of play, the ball was played out to the right, and as another forward was sprinting into the penalty area, away from the ball, he was brought down from behind. With the ball still out on the right wing, the whistle blew and a penalty kick was awarded. Again many of the players including the captain had not seen the incident and he asked what the penalty was for. But the referee simply pointed out the forward still on the ground, gestured toward the guilty defender and said "Ask him, not me." The guilty player simply lowered his head as his captain looked at him, knowing that his rash action was about to put his team a goal down so early in the game; nothing was said, nothing needed to be said. They all now knew and they knew the referee knew, and they knew the referee knew that they knew. The penalty was converted and there was not one further dissenting comment for the rest of the game from either team.

Something similar happened in the match between Brazil and Norway in the 1998 World Cup in France. The referee, Esse Baharmast, from the USA, awarded a penalty kick to Norway that initially was questioned by almost everyone at the stadium, including the press and TV announcers, because they had all been watching the ball. These doubts were soon erased when a photograph was published, taken from directly behind the goal, that showed clearly what the referee had seen: a Brazilian defender, Baiano, pulling the jersey of the Norwegian forward, Flo, in order to prevent his run into a dangerous position. Interestingly, Baiano himself did not protest the decision!

The space problem.

Any time the referee is in front of the ball, he may be using space that the players could use. Notice the phrase "*any time* the referee..." There is not a referee in the world at any level of the game who has not seen a player first coming towards him with the ball, but then suddenly veering off in a different direction. The player changed direction because the referee was in space that the player wanted to use. *The position of the referee forced the player to alter his plan.*

How can we solve this problem?

One solution is to *remain behind the ball.* Let's say the defenders collect a stray pass from their opponents and start to move forward. The referee should *wait for the player in possession to move ahead* past him, and then follow the player downfield. Or, alternatively, the referee can actively *seek a position behind the player in possession of the ball.* In other words, run in the opposite direction to the player with the ball, until you are behind him and can then turn and follow him downfield. It may seem strange for us to advocate moving in the opposite direction to the way that play is going, but it is often the right thing to do, and is a very effective way of not disturbing what the players are attempting. And better yet, it works in youth soccer, senior soccer, professional games and international matches! Figure 13-5 shows an example.

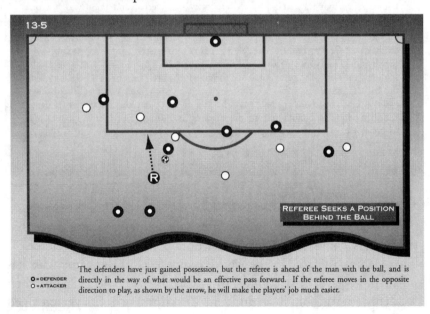

O = DEFENDER
O = ATTACKER

The defenders have just gained possession, but the referee is ahead of the man with the ball, and is directly in the way of what would be an effective pass forward. If the referee moves in the opposite direction to play, as shown by the arrow, he will make the players' job much easier.

It is always a source of surprise to us that more referees—at all levels—don't use this simple technique, and we can only assume that it is not being taught. We are aware that some instructors and assessors are concerned that a referee who waits for play to pass him may get caught out of position by a long pass downfield. Our response to that is to emphasize physical fitness (see Chapter 16) and to say that the advantages outweigh the disadvantages: the referee slightly behind the play won't get in the way, and will be able to see more players, more off-the-ball action than will the referee caught in the middle of traffic and close to it.

A second solution is particularly useful when the referee does not have time to allow play to go past him. Quite simply, he can "hide" from the player with the ball, by moving behind an opponent. He may have to move only a few yards to take himself out of the potential path of the ball, but in doing so he opens up space for the player and the ball. Figure 13-6 shows how this can be done.

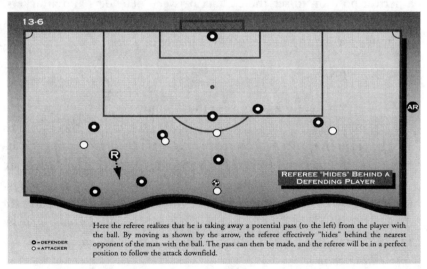

Here the referee realizes that he is taking away a potential pass (to the left) from the player with the ball. By moving as shown by the arrow, the referee effectively "hides" behind the nearest opponent of the man with the ball. The pass can then be made, and the referee will be in a perfect position to follow the attack downfield.

O = DEFENDER
O = ATTACKER

A third solution is for the referee to make sure that he uses space that the players cannot use, or are not likely to use. Consider the situation in the next Figure (13-7). The attack is down the left wing, with the winger being chased by a defender. All the other forwards are

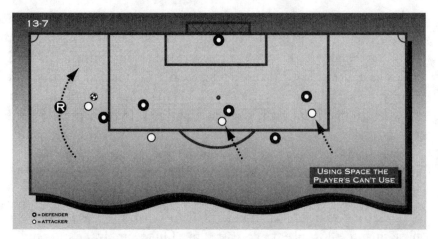

to the right of the man with the ball, and the referee can see that all the space to the left of the man in possession is not likely to be used in the attack. It is a perfect place for the official to go. He can outflank the attack and the defenders, and he can penetrate to the goal-line to be in a perfect position to see the contact between defenders and attackers, or to make a judgement about any shot on goal. He can do all this without once getting in the way of a player or a pass.

The time problem.

In basic referee training there is so much emphasis on staying close to the action around the ball that you wonder how any off-the-ball fouls ever get seen in games where the players are a little more sophisticated and skillful than the average ten-year-old. Players are held, they are impeded, occasionally completely blocked, but always in places where, for the most part, the referee is not looking. Soccer is a game of movement by players who are not close to the ball, *so how can we watch them and protect them during that time away from the immediate action?*

The first solution is one that we have already described, *for whenever he stays behind the player with the ball,* the referee can see downfield without difficulty. Not only will he be out of the way of the players and their passes, but he will also be able to *see what the players see*, including the movement of players up ahead, the actions of defenders near them. The referee can watch players who are not near the ball, and can also anticipate where the play is going to go next. Behind the player with the ball, the referee can see most of what is going on off-the-ball. From that position he can *read the game and where it is going.*

The second solution is especially useful when the referee is on the opposite side of the field from the play. He may be on the left wing as play is on the right. From this position the referee will not be able to position himself behind the player with the ball. So what else can he do? He can take advantage of situations *where the player in possession is not under pressure* from opponents, or has no one near enough to make a challenge. Under these circumstances, the referee can safely look downfield away from the ball, and see what is going on elsewhere. In the one or two seconds it may take the official to do this, he can get a picture of where the attack is going, where the players are moving, what the defenders are doing, and other useful pieces of information. Most important, he will be able to see any off-the-ball fouls occurring downfield from where the ball is. This is a technique that should become part of every referee's bag of tricks, no matter what kind of game he or she is refereeing.

Where is play going next?

General patrol pattern.

It should be clear from the foregoing discussion that a major goal for the referee is to avoid getting in the way of the play. Most referees are instructed to adapt a diagonal path across the field, and most referees do exactly that. However, this path takes the referee through the areas of greatest congestion, specifically in and around the center circle. A far better patrol path is a more Z shaped pattern, as shown in Figure

13-8. By generally following this pattern, the referee can still observe the play, but not be in such a position that he will interfere with the players movements as much. It is important to emphasize that the referee should get across the center circle as quickly as possible, to reach the other side of the pitch. Referees should treat the center circle as though it were filled with hot coals, spend as little time in there as possible. If during a match you find yourself in the center circle a lot, your overall mobility and positioning is probably at fault. In this case you should request a more experienced referee or assessor to work with you on this point (see Chapter 18, section on mentoring). As with many other of the suggestions we make in this book, this requires the referee to be very fit, and to be able to change his running speed rapidly. But, we can hear the protests now, what if the ball goes down the right wing? Won't you be too far away? Well, then the referee simply goes over towards the play to get a closer look. But what if the ball is suddenly crossed over to the center or to the left? Then go over there after it. Again fitness is paramount in this level of refereeing.

Penetration to goal lines.

Furthermore, this patrol pattern allows the referee to penetrate down to the goal lines near the corner flags in those cases where there are challenges for the ball down in the corners. Far too often referees can be seen watching the action in the corners from somewhere near the edge of the penalty area, and this can result in dissent when the ball goes out of play and both teams claim it. However if the referee is right down there with them, but off the field, there will seldom be an argument, because most players will accept a decision with which they may not agree, from a referee nearby, rather than from one making decisions from a distance. Also there will be the added deterrent of proximity which might inhibit a player from delivering a gratuitous kick or elbow in the ribs of an opponent.

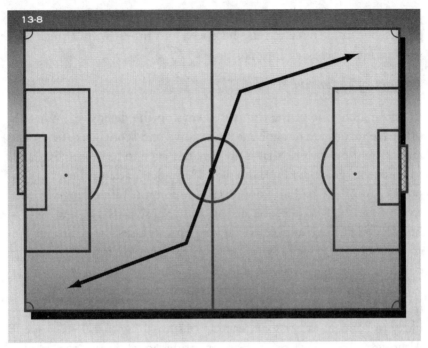

13-8

Observation of the attacking tactics is very helpful to the referee in deciding where to position himself. If the team has one or two forwards who are good in the air, it is quite likely that there will be plenty of crosses delivered into the penalty area from the right side, to be met by oncoming forwards. (There will obviously be some crosses from the left also but this discussion concerns the referees position during crosses from the far side of his patrol pattern.) This move provides a very good opportunity for the referee to get into a good position without getting in the way. He simply reads the play, watches the actions of the central attackers. If they are calling for a center into the penalty area, the referee can sprint past and wide of the forwards to the goal line. From there he can see the ball coming over, and *at the same time* observe the actions of defenders, goalkeeper and forwards. He is in general perfectly positioned to make judgements of all kinds because the play is now coming towards him rather than going away. If the ball is quickly cleared by a defender or the goalkeeper, the referee can use his speed and fitness with a quick 30-yard sprint to get back into position.

Impact of defensive tactics.

In any match, one of the teams is always on the defensive. Whereas offensive tactics are designed to be creative and score goals, defensive tactics are the opposite; that is they are designed to be destructive, and to prevent goals being scored. Defenders attempting to win possession of the ball are more likely to commit infractions. In this section we shall take a look at various defensive tactics, and how a knowledge of these and what can happen can assist the referee in the control of the game. Nowadays, these types of tactics are being coached at all age levels, so referees are likely to encounter them at most levels of competition, not just in professional matches. We refer to this as pro-active refereeing, that is knowing in advance what is likely to happen, rather than reacting to something that does happen. Although derived from our other professional areas, the phrase "chance favors the prepared mind" applies equally well to refereeing.

From this section you will learn what you need:

- to control games more efficiently by acquiring a better knowledge of team tactics
- to become familiar with and understand the consequences of different types of defensive tactics
- to appreciate what steps referees must take to recognize and accommodate these tactics

Five general types of defensive tactics are in common use:

1. Immediate Chase

2. Fall-Back and Delay

3. Man-to-Man Marking

4. Zone

5. Attack Man and Ball

A well-known principle goes "defense begins the moment the team loses possession of the ball." So let us consider what is likely to happen next. When a player loses the ball by interception or tackle, that player or a nearby colleague will usually attempt to get it back immediately. This is what is meant by *immediate chase* and it happens at or near to the place where the ball was lost. There is the immediate possibility of a foul occurring here, either out of annoyance, lack of tackling technique (especially if a forward is involved), or due to tactical reasons. The latter is designed to deliberately concede a free-kick in order to allow the rest of the team time to organize their defense. Quite often, this is a 'mild' foul, a gentle jersey tug, or simple obstruction, not intended to hurt the opponent. This can be a perfect opportunity to apply an advantage (see Chapter 18), but if this is not the case, then the referee has to award a free-kick. But a caution should also be given to the offending player. While this may seem harsh in comparison to the nature of the foul on the opponent, the deliberate intent aspect must be considered.

Now a team may employ *fall back and delay* defensive tactics. This is essentially territorial, with the objective being to cut out space and opportunity for the attackers. The principle in use here is get as many defenders behind the ball as quickly as possible, allowing the opponents to bring the ball forward essentially unchallenged, and to force them into tight situations where mistakes can be made and the ball won back. Meanwhile the attackers are attempting to counteract this by movement into space to draw defenders away. In these situations there is the possibility of so-called "off-the-ball fouls." (See above for examples). At this moment, when the player with the ball is not being actively challenged, the referee must scan the entire field and observe the movements of the players. There is likely to be holding, bodily obstruction and in some instances, deliberate tripping of the attackers by the defenders.

Overlaid on top of the foregoing are the concepts of man-to-man marking, and zone defenses. Both of these provide potential problem areas for referees. Let us look at each of them in turn. In permanent man-to-man marking, one player is assigned to a particular opponent. Usually, only one or two players have such assignments, and the idea is to neutralize the opponents' star player, usually a mid-field general or prolific striker. The marker follows his prey all over the field. Quite often, the marker is a recognized tough player, or enforcer. With this method in use, there is severe potential for problems.

The most common of these is persistent infringement, too many fouls by the marker. (We discuss the principles of identifying persistent infringement in Chapter 11). Also there is the distinct possibility of retaliation from the marked player, not to mention complaints and dissent by that player. How often have we seen a marked player cautioned or even sent off after enduring 60 or more minutes of sometimes brutal treatment when the real guilty player, the one who has been kicking him, escapes scot-free, his job now successfully completed for him by the referee? In cases like this, the referee has failed to realize or to deal with what is going on. In this context it is worth remembering the words of a former member of the FIFA Referees' Committee: "a star player can be stopped only with the complicity of the referee."

We have found it very useful in cases like this to actually let the players concerned know, usually after a foul has occurred, that we are fully aware of what is going on and the consequences. This technique has the effect of both issuing a warning to the marker and providing reassurance to the marked player that he will be protected. Sometimes the marker ignored the referee's friendly advice, preferring to follow his coach's instructions. After the caution had been duly issued, the coach substituted the player, not prepared to risk subsequently having the player sent off. When this happened we felt a sense of pride in knowing that we had made a positive contribution for the good of the game.

In other cases there is what we refer to as *transient man-to-man marking.* Here, different players mark opponents each time – tight marking of the nearest player especially when close to goal. This can cause problems on set plays such as corners, throw ins and deep free kicks. Fouls are highly likely by both attackers and defenders, on and off the ball.

Zone defenses are organized differently. Players stay in assigned zones or areas and deal with the ball and whichever opponents when they enter that zone. This technique provides cover for the close markers and tacklers, and generally the player involved attempts to intercept rather than directly dispossess. So this seems to be less of a problem for the referee at first glance. But we must consider the mind of the defender, and take note of the instructions and threats given by the coach. "Do not leave your zone, and let no-one pass through it. If you don't do it, I'll find someone who will! I will hold you responsible for any goal conceded that comes through your zone." So the defender will adopt a "stop them at all costs" attitude, and will resort to fouls if beaten or seems to be beaten by an opponent.

Finally, when all else has failed, defenders have to resort to a last desperate attempt to win the ball or *stop the opponent by a tackle.* Players in this situation can be careless, ruthless and incompetent. Hence fouls are highly likely particularly on opponents of high skill and those in shooting position.

How does the referee apply all of this knowledge? First, he must be aware of it. Make note of it in games that you watch. Be prepared for it. Study the team rosters and see if you can anticipate the tactics. When are the danger times? After a goal has been scored, both defenses get tighter for a while. Near the end of a close game, when players are tired.

Take into account the relative abilities of the players. For instance, are there older, slow but experienced defenders, trying to deal with young fast forwards? One example of this we saw in the 1994 World Cup quarterfinal match between Brazil and Holland played in Dallas.

Holland had two old warriors in defense, Wouters and Koeman, both veterans of previous campaigns. Brazil had Bebeto and Romario, both young and fast. Before the match we predicted what might happen, and sure enough early on Bebeto was heavily brought down with a bad foul and was off the pitch for several minutes receiving treatment. The intent was clear, to slow him down. Unfortunately the referee appeared unaware and simply gave a free-kick.

In summary, a knowledge of tactics employed by teams can enable a referee to control a game much better, by knowing what is likely to happen, the reasons for it, and taking the appropriate steps to deal with it and more importantly, prevent it. Then when you encounter the same teams again, they will realize that you are wise to their tactics, and it is no use to continue to use them. Again, the old adage applies "A referee makes his own reputation." Make sure you make the right kind.

14

POSITIONING AT
SET-PIECES

A poor life this, if full of care,
We have no time to stand and stare.

William H. Davies

Old Ideas.

As recently as 1993, the official instructions on the *Diagonal System of Control*—published by the F.I.F.A. and distributed to all its members—included the following directive to referees at corner-kicks: "Position of officials the same no matter at which corner-area the kick is taken. Referee (R) along line shown." The accompanying Figure 14-1 shows the diagram illustrating this instruction, which had not changed for at least as long as we had ever owned what was called the "Referees' Chart and Players' Guide to the Laws of the Game", thirty years or more. Imagine that: no changes in positioning at a corner-kick for the referee of a game that has undergone profound tactical changes since the early sixties!

> "Before any game, gather all the information about the teams that you can, and then use it!"

IN THIS CHAPTER:

- *Where to "stand and stare" at corner-kicks, and at free-kicks near goal.*
- *Where to be in order to see almost everything and everybody at certain throw-ins.*
- *How to prepare yourself for special tactics that teams employ at set-pieces.*

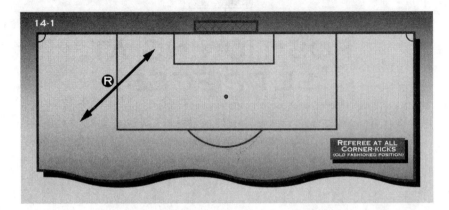

14-1

REFEREE AT ALL
CORNER-KICKS
(OLD FASHIONED POSITION)

The instructions for a free-kick near goal were just as creative. The referee "takes up his position just off his diagonal so that he is placed accurately to judge off-side. Linesman…is more advanced but can watch for off-side and fouls and also is in a good position to act as goal judge in the event of a direct shot being taken." Those sentences are almost a perfect prescription for failure in trying to sort out what happens at these set-pieces in the modern game. So, let's apply a little creative thinking to these situations.

The corner-kick in its multitude of forms

The accompanying figures show six versions of a corner-kick from the referee's side of the diagonal. No doubt many readers can add some other variations on this set-piece, but for now, the six versions shown are sufficient for our purpose. Remember, however, that six similar corner-kicks could be taken from the other side of the field also, making for a total of *at least* twelve different strategies that the defenders *and the referee* have to deal with. And the first step in dealing with these corners is to decide where to stand (and stare, as Davies the poet said).

Number 1 (14-2):

A short corner, involving a quick pass to a teammate a few yards away. The effect of this is to draw the defenders away from the goal as they

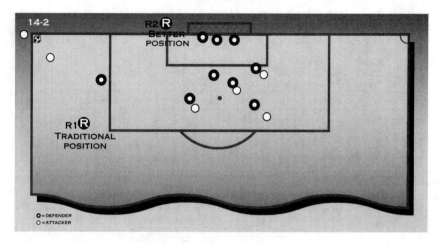

seek to challenge the player receiving the pass, and as they try create an offside trap for any forwards near the goal. If the referee were in the old-fashioned position, he would be close to the action involving the two players taking the corner. And if the ball were then crossed deep into the goal-area, he would be badly positioned to see what was going on between defenders and attackers. *A much better position is on or near the goal-line somewhere close to the six-yard box.* He would be out of the way of the players, he would be behind most of the defenders (and therefore they couldn't see him!) and since most of the action would then be coming towards the goal, the referee would be able to see things clearly, *and* be able to act as goal judge should a shot be taken.

Number 2 (14-3):

The corner is struck hard and fast towards the near post, where another forward back-heads the ball (or flicks it) across the face of the goal. This was known as the "Tottenham Corner" after the team that perfected it: a dangerous ball for the defenders, and a ball that creates chaos in the goalmouth as forwards and defenders battle for a ball in the air in the goal-area. Get as close as possible, preferably *right next to the post and on the goal-line or just over the line and off the field!* There you will see everything, and your presence near the middle of the action will give great credibility to any decision you have to make.

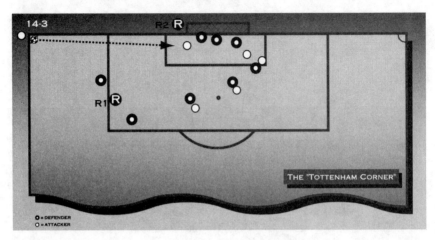

Number 3 (14-4):

An inswinging corner aimed at the front post. The same position as for number 2: off the field, but close in to the action.

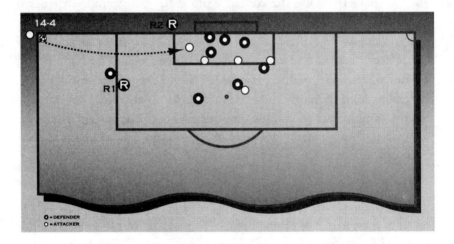

Number 4 (14-5):

Here is a case where *the referee may have to move during the corner-kick.* Starting from a wide position near the edge of the penalty-area about 6-8 yards off the goal-line, he can move in towards the goal-area as the ball comes across. Then if need be, he can quickly sprint the few yards to the line as the action gets close to the goal. He can see the activity and can get down to the line to act as goal judge.

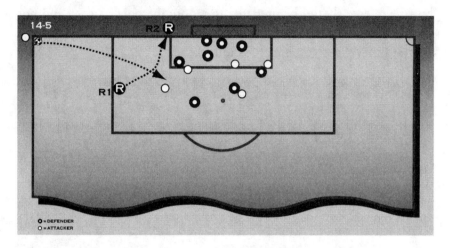

Number 5 (14-6):

A wide view of an inswinger to the area of the far post may be useful, so a *position in the top corner of the penalty-area on the referee's diagonal* may give the official a fine view of the action. He *can encroach forward once the ball has crossed the face of the goal,* or even sprint to the goal-line if need be.

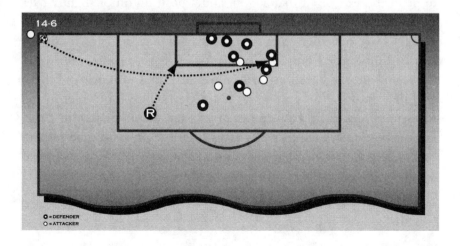

Number 6 (14-7):

Again, a *wide view is best for the ball struck to the far side of the area,*
but the referee should be prepared to ignore the poet's advice and not
stand still. Be ready for the quick sprint to the goal-line to the
position that gives you great credibility.

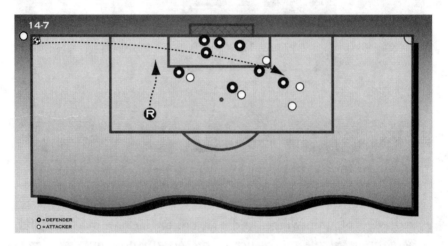

Taken from the other side of the field, corner-kicks number 1, 2,
3 and 5 are all going to end up close to the goal, inviting lots of
activity between attackers and defenders. The referee does not need
to be in the way of all that action, and a position on or slightly over
the goal-line, close to the goal will enable him or her to see what is
going on without interfering with the play or players. For the corners
that end up at the front post for the kick taken from the right wing,
the referee (at the back post) can move forward a yard or two off the
goal-line onto the field to get a better view, always, however, being
ready to nip back off the field out of the way should play come close.
For the two outswinging corner-kicks from the right (numbers 4 and
6) a wide position at the left-hand side of the penalty-area is a good
one, provided that the referee is ready to move to get closer or to get
our of the way.

The important principles here are:

(1) adopt a position that suits the particular corner-kick being taken, and then

(2) be ready to <u>move</u> to improve your view or get out of the way.

In simpler terms: Be alert, and don't be lazy!

Thousands of readers (we hope!) are now muttering to themselves, saying something like this: "That's all well and good in theory, but how am I supposed to know what corner-kick is coming up next? How can I predict where the ball is going, and know the best place for me to be?" That task may seem daunting, but it can be done. Read on!

In the ideal case, you will be refereeing teams in your local league, or the league you are most familiar with—amateur, youth or professional. You should have a lot of knowledge of the teams and players because you may be seeing them week after week. That being so, you should notice the style of the teams at corner-kicks. Do they have a regular pattern of playing inswingers to a particular striker? Do they frequently play short corners? Is it always the same player taking the corners on the right, and a different one on the left? Study them and you will know what to expect, so that you can decide where to go. This should be part of *your preparation for the game.* Hundreds of years ago a philosopher said: "Knowledge itself is power". He wasn't kidding, and we are foolish referees if we go into games without some knowledge of the teams we are about to officiate. *Before any game, gather all the information about the teams that you can, and then use it!*

When you are refereeing teams you have never seen before, you have to pay particular attention early in the game to see what the players are going to do at corner-kicks. First, watch where in the corner arc the player places the ball before the kick. If it goes on the goal line—on the left side of the field or the right—you can be sure that the kick is going to be an inswinger. Because of the proximity of the flag, it is difficult for a player to take an outswinger from the goal line without running the risk of putting the ball out for a goal kick.

Similarly, the flag pole prevents a player from putting the ball in the arc but away from the goal line, and then taking an inswinger. So take a look at the ball placement and then position yourself accordingly.

Second, start watching the tactics at corners. Ask yourself the same questions as in the paragraphs above, to identify the patterns of play that the teams have. Then use that information to make decisions about your position at every corner-kick for the rest of the match.

Third, some teams use signals to tell their players what is coming next. If they use an upraised arm or shout out a number, or use some other obvious signal, then take a note of what happens next. Quickly learn their pattern and use it to make decisions about your positioning.

If none of these techniques works, and you end up in a position that you know is wrong immediately the ball is kicked, *then move to another!* Don't stand in one position like a third goalpost.

The free kick near goal

Free kicks near the goal but wide out on the wings can be treated much like corner kicks, except that the defenders dictate where the last line of defence will be. With Law 11 (Offside) in operation at these close but wide free kicks, the attackers cannot simply crowd the goalmouth as they do at corners. But free kicks around the top of the penalty area—within shooting distance and at shooting angles—create a particular collection of problems for defenders and referees alike:

1. A shot on goal: Did it cross the line?

2. The wall of defenders: Is it back ten yards, and will anyone run to the ball?

3. Attackers in the wall: Are they messing with the defenders, and vice versa?

4. The chip over the wall: Are any attackers offside?

5. Location of the ball: Will the attackers move it?

6. The ball is cleared away: Who is covering offside?

7. Attackers running in after a chipped ball: Are any defenders obstructing them?

8. Attackers at the end of the wall: Are they physically holding defenders in place?

That's a lot of stuff for two officials to watch for! What's the best way to do it? The most obvious things that *have* to be covered are the offside line and the goal line, because to make an accurate judgement of whether the ball has crossed the goal line, or whether a player is in an offside position, somebody has to be *exactly* in the right position. But of those two, the offside line is the most important, because a potential offside situation occurs more frequently than does a shot on goal that may or may not have crossed the line. Shots on goal are frequent, but of all the ones that are taken, how many produce a disputed situation? The main problem is: Who is to take the offside?

The traditional arrangement for referee and assistant referee is for the referee to take the offside line, generally off to one side of the defenders' wall, and for him to send the assistant referee down to the goal line. In fact, one senior member of the FIFA Referees' Committee, the man who used to be responsible for assignments all over Central America, North America and the Caribbean, would advocate that the linesman (as he was then called) should move to the line *automatically* when the referee was in line with the defenders. We believe that this is wrong, for reasons that will become apparent, but also we should state that the curious instruction he gave out was perhaps more related to the fact that he had never refereed a single game in his life, than to any years of experience in top-level matches. (Beware the instruction and assessment of those who have never been out on the field that you are walking....!)

The assistant referee who goes to the goal line—and who may have nothing to do there—must resume his offside position as soon as it becomes clear that there is not going to be an immediate shot on goal. *But*, until the assistant gets back into position, the referee is effectively stuck in line with the offside line. He has to stay there, because at any moment there could be a ball popped forward, creating an offside situation. And if the referee is to do the "offside" job properly, he has to be looking across the field, concentrating on the last-but-one defender. While he is doing that, he cannot be doing his other tasks—watching for fouls, surveying where the ball might be going next and so on. It is a bad arrangement; it should rarely be done, if ever, especially since there is a better way—a proven better way.

Quite simply, it is this: Leave the assistant referee in his normal position of watching offside. Then you assume a position, or move to various positions, to take care of the other tasks. Vary your position depending upon what is needed, or what is most likely to happen:

1. If the kick is going to involve a static wall of defenders, and the attackers don't seem to want to play a quick free kick, then hold up the kick until everything is set.

2. Keeping your eye on the ball to make sure that the attackers don't move it once it has been placed, go to a distance of ten yards from the ball and bring the defenders back (verbally, not physically!)

3. Keeping your eye on the ball and the wall, back into a position deeper down the field than the wall, but not all the way down to the goal line.

4. Signal for the kick to be taken, and based upon how the players are shaping to take the kick, be prepared to move quickly—towards the goal line, if you anticipate a shot coming; closer into the goalmouth if you think the ball is going to be chipped behind the defenders.

With this arrangement, everything is taken care of smoothly and efficiently: offside; the wall; the potential shot on goal (but not if you're too lazy to move!); and activity in the wall. And if that is not enough, the referee in this position deeper downfield than the wall, has a wonderful psychological advantage over the defenders: He can see them, but without turning around (which they won't do in this situation), they can't see him. His position is a deterrent to fouls and other messing about in and around the wall.

Take a look at Figure 14-8. It is an analysis by a professional-level player and coach, and it shows the danger area for defenders at free kicks near goal. The wall is intended to take care of the shot on goal, and in most cases it does. It takes an exceptional player to curve the ball over or around a well-placed wall, and so most teams try to defeat the wall in other ways, especially by playing the ball into the "danger area" immediately behind the defenders. That area spells trouble for defenders because they will have to turn around and play the ball while moving towards their own goal, because the ball will be too far out for the goalkeeper to venture to it safely, and because in the act of turning they will have to try and read what the attackers are planning, just as the forwards are in full flight towards the ball and the goal.

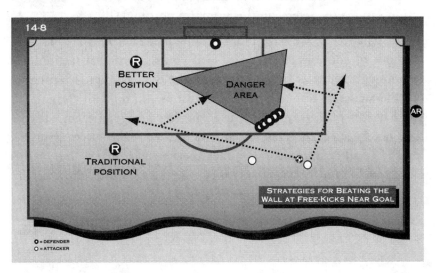

With four or five men momentarily stuck in the wall, the defenders are also outnumbered by midfield opponents who have come forward.

In these cases of the ball being played away from, and then behind the wall, most of the activity is going to take place in the shaded area shown on the diagram. If the referee adopts the traditional position off to the left, on his diagonal, he will have a good view if the ball is played in his direction, but a poor view if the ball is played to the right. The assistant can cover offside well, but if the ball eventually reaches the goal area or the goal, the referee will not be able to get there in order to make a critical judgement.

In the position recommended, deep behind the defenders, he can see everything that the man in the traditional position can see, and then more. In accordance with one of our principal themes about referees' mobility and positioning, he can see every player on the field except the defending goalkeeper. He is close enough to the goal line to reach it if necessary. When the ball is played behind the defenders, the referee will have all the action and all the players coming towards him. And he is close enough to the goal line that if necessary, a few paces of backward movement will take him out of the way of any of the players. What a deterrent to unfair play when all the players in the action can see the referee in this watchful position!

In Chapter 7, we gave more details of the referee's actions and methods of control at free kicks, so if you skipped that section, we recommend you refer back to it. Also, use the technique of scouting out the tactics of teams at free kicks, just as you do with corners. If you have refereed them before, use your knowledge of them. If you have never seen them, then pay attention to what they do early in the match. Gather information, gather their signals, make note of the players taking the kicks and how they take them. Use all those details to guide you to the best position and action at these free kicks near goal.

Throw-ins within twenty-five yards of the goal.

The tale in the sidebar recounts an incident that on the face of it, is hilarious, but in reality, exhibits a very serious deficiency in the way we prepare referees, for tradition is a powerful influence on officials around the world. You should derive no comfort from this incident having happened in faraway Nigeria, because we are certain that something similar could happen and has happened in our own backyard. So take heed!

The traditional position (R1), as shown in the diagram (Figure 14-9), is fine as long as nothing happens. But referees should be prepared for the unexpected, and since the unexpected happens because of *players*, we should keep as many of the players in view as we can *at all times*. Therefore, at *every throw-in within twenty-five yards or so of the goal line on the referee's side of the diagonal*, the official should go ahead of the throw and stand out of the way on the touchline (R2). From there he can see almost every player on the field, can advance quickly to the goal line as necessary (R3), and if the attack breaks down, he will be able to follow the counter-attack downfield without having to worry about being in the way of the players or the play.

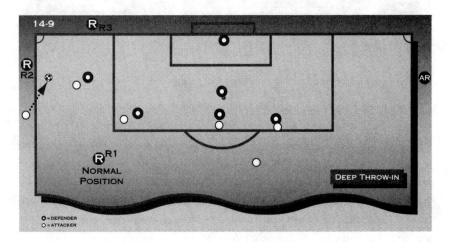

Throw-ins – a special case.

Getting ahead of the throw-in when it is to be taken on the opposite touchline is virtually impossible, but nevertheless, when it is necessary, the referee should be prepared to assume a position that is not the usual one. Here's a case in point.

Swindon is a southern English town famous for its railway yards and not much else. But it does have a team in the Football League, and a few years ago, the team came up with a special throw-in tactic that produced 12 of the 60 goals the team scored on one season. The diagram shows the scheme (Figure 14-10).

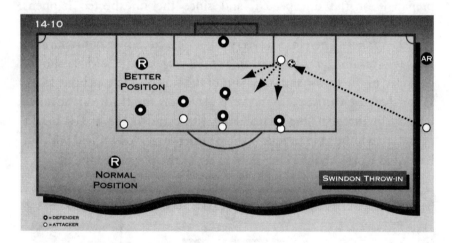

At a throw-in deep in their opponents' half, Swindon used a specialist to make a long throw to a forward who had drifted behind the defenders. From that position, the attacker would lay the ball back away from the goal and towards his onrushing teammates. The defenders had to turn towards the goal to deal with the threat, and the attackers had a momentary advantage, because they knew what was coming, and they were moving towards the ball coming at them. In the few seconds of confusion in match after match from these throws, and similar ones from the other touchline, Swindon scored goals.

SEE NO EVIL...

At a match in the highest division in Nigeria, one of the teams prepared to take a throw-in on the left wing deep in their opponents' half. The referee assumed a position as shown, slightly off his traditional diagonal, and watching the thrower and the few players nearby. Suddenly, just before the throw, there was a great shout in the stadium, from the spectators and from some of the players. The referee held up the throw-in and turned to look behind him to see what had happened.

In the penalty area lay the prostrate form of a defender rubbing his head. Standing over him, with an expression of beatific innocence on his face, was a forward, his arms out and palms turned upwards in that universal gesture of all criminals wrongfully accused. The referee strode over to him, by which time the defender was on his feet, loudly pointing to the forward. The linesman stood impassive, and when the referee raised his head at him, asking, in effect, what had happened, the linesman simply shrugged. No assistant, he! So the man-in-black did the best he could, wagged his finger ferociously under the noses of both players, returned to his position, and signalled for the throw-in. Suddenly, there was another great shout from the crowd.

The referee turned again to see what had happened. There on the ground in the same spot as the first mugging, was the forward, holding his head and pointing at the nearby defender, the same one who so recently had been mugged himself. The linesman looked at the sky, no doubt seeking divine guidance. The defender gave the customary gesture of innocence. All that the referee felt he could do in the absence of any useful information, was to wag his finger ferociously again at the two players and resume his position for the throw-in, which proceeded without further incident.

This is a perfect example of an incident occurring because the referee was not in a position to see as much as possible, or as many players as possible. Had he been nearer the goal line than was the thrower, he would have been looking upfield and would have had twenty players in his sight. As the ball went out of play, all he had to do was trot a few yards past the position of the throw-in, go to the touchline and turn to look upfield. He would have had the two criminals in view, but because he could see them, and because they could see that he could see them, the attacker and the defender would both have been deterred from mugging each other.

The normal position for the referee at such throw would be as shown. But is it the best one to witness what is going on? He would be screened by the defenders and attackers, and could easily miss something important. But if he assumes the position shown, closer to the goal line, he has a much better view. All the players are in front of him, with action coming his way. He can see everything, just as a referee positioned on the goal line at inswinging corners can see almost everything. And if the ball is played close to the goal, what a perfect position he will be in to make a critical decision!

"Yes," say the skeptics, "but how the hell am I supposed to know that there is a long throw coming to a space behind the defenders?" You know because you have studied the teams you are refereeing. You know because you are *prepared*. You know because you have talked to referees who have seen this team before, and you know who takes the throw. When you see him approach the ball, you can expect that this tactic will be used, and so you change your position to take care of it. And even if the long throw does not come about at every deep throw-in, you don't lose anything by going behind the defenders (except that you will have to run a little bit further when the attack breaks down. But then, with the fitness training you do (Chapter 16), you will be prepared for that too...).

Penalty kicks.

Because the awarding of a penalty kick is usually one of the most disputed decisions a referee can make, many referees shy away from awarding penalties, even when they are justified. We see a free kick eighteen yards out, with the ball placed just outside the box, or we witness an indirect free kick, and sometimes nothing at all, as though the grass or the painted line committed the foul.

But if you are confident, and know how to deal with the protests without having to use cautions or red cards, there is nothing to fear in awarding the penalty kick. Not only will you be able to do a better job of refereeing, but you will soon develop a reputation among players and coaches for being both courageous and imperturbable. And when you get such a reputation, strangely enough, the players avoid committing fouls that would result in penalty kicks!

Among several things that you should do when you award a penalty, deciding where to stand is perhaps the least of your concerns. And in truth, there is *no one best place* from which to watch the action and do your duty. But, let's deal with first things first...

Once you are satisfied that the defender committed one of the ten offences for which a penalty kick shall be awarded, and that he committed the infraction within his own penalty-area, and that advantage does not apply[1], *blow long, hard and without hesitation, pointing to the spot as you do so. Then separate yourself from most of the players by running towards the edge of the box. Do NOT run to the spot!*

The penalty-spot seems to be a favorite gathering-place for criminals and protesters, as though they expect the officer of the law (you) to show up there. If you made the mistake of going to the spot, you would find several players including the goalkeeper and perhaps the player who committed the foul, all anxious to engage you in conversation. Avoid them by moving quickly off to one side. If you are lucky, no one will come over to confront you. (In our research for this book, we did find one referee—from Ouagadougou, Burkina— who awarded a penalty-kick without protest.) But despite this, we think it is wise to be prepared!

If players do come over to where you are off to one side of the area, *do not stand still, attempting to wave them away.* We guarantee that they will not obey your waving arms, and if they persist—which is most likely—the next step for you is going to be a caution. Remember that biology teaches us that everyone makes a meal out of a tree or a shrub, because they can't move. So don't imitate one!

---

[1] Statistical analysis of penalty kicks shows that the success rate is about 94 percent at most levels of the sport. Even at the very lowest levels of youth play the success rate is still very high. So in deciding advantage, you have to be able to say that by allowing play to go on, you are better than 94 percent sure that the attackers will score. That's a tall order, which is why you rarely—but not never—see advantage applied at a potential penalty-kick. However, with the new method of analyzing advantage, the courageous referee can afford to hesitate a little, and if no advantage materializes, then award a penalty-kick.

As you see them coming, *do not retreat,* but start to move purposefully back towards the goal. Ignoring the protesters as if they were not there, make yourself very busy organizing the procedures. Keep moving and start talking. "Where is the ball? Who's taking the kick? Number eight? OK, now make sure you wait for my signal, OK?" Get all the players out of the penalty area, and behind the arc. Identify the kicker again, position the ball if necessary, ask the goalkeeper if he is ready. Act as though you are too busy to listen to protests. If they have been trying to follow you about as you walk, talk and give instructions, after a few moments they will usually give up, or—and this is better—some teammates will pull them away.

At this point you will hear comments such as: "It's no use, he won't change his mind. You're wasting your time, you don't want to get carded." This is good, for it means that you are winning the dispute. However, the protesters may choose to make a few sarcastic parting-shots, which—if you are wise—you will ignore. Let the player have the last word, even if it is something you don't like. "That dumb bastard wouldn't know a penalty if he were doing it!" or "He's got his money, and now he's giving them the game!" Comments like that are worth laughing at because they are so childishly asinine. Show that you are not the slightest bit perturbed by them, then take up your position to supervise the kick, and signal for the kick to be taken.

If you have a situation in which the player who committed the foul must be cautioned or sent off, you have to deal with it before the kick is taken. In this case, you should first go directly to the player concerned—again ignoring all the protests—and after you have shown the yellow or red card, go about the remaining business of organizing the penalty-kick.

And as for that least important of all questions: What is the best position for a referee to take for a penalty kick? No one knows. As is the case for a free kick near goal, there are more things to watch for than can be done by two officials. The assistant referee usually stands on the goal line about 18 yards out and acts as goal judge. The referee is left to watch for illegal movement by the goalkeeper (rarely penalized), illegal actions by the kicker (rare), and encroachment by the remaining players (always happens but seldom enforced).

A position near the edge of the penalty-area, about 9 yards from the goalline allows the referee to see both the goalkeeper and the penalty arc. But some referees feel that this position is too far away from the action to act as a deterrent. (As far as we know, no one has ever systematically tested the notion that a player won't encroach if the referee is close by, but nevertheless the idea survives. We've always wanted to ask someone who believes in this deterrent if he *would penalize* encroachment at a penalty-kick!) Assuming the notion is correct, then a position nearer to the intersection of the penalty arc with the 18 yard line would allow the referee to see all the action, *and* be close enough to act as a deterrent to encroachment. We recommend giving a verbal reminder prior to blowing the whistle, but if you are not going to penalize the infraction, the prior warning is a waste of breath.

In a high proportion of cases, the player taking the kick scores. The referee should then run quickly—running backwards if possible—towards to center of the pitch, to avoid listening to complaints (see Chapter 15 on vulnerability) and to be sure to observe everyone in case of a flare-up. If a goal is not scored and the ball comes back into play off post or goalkeeper, you must be very alert to get out of the way while still keeping all the players under observation. If the ball misses the goal altogether, give a signal for the goal-kick, and once again move rapidly upfield. You do not want to be close to hear the comments of the defenders, usually referring to "true justice" or "God corrected your cheating" or some other such similar sentiment.

Goal kicks.

Since the recent changes in the laws about the goal-kick, and about passing the ball back to the goalkeeper, positioning for the referee usually does not present much of a problem. He no longer has to supervise the placement of the ball on the correct side of the goal-area, since the kick can be taken from anywhere within the six-yard box. And because a goalkeeper cannot pick up a ball played to him by a teammate, we rarely see a short goal-kick kicked towards the side or top of the penalty-area for a defender to give it to the 'keeper. Nowadays the referee rarely has to hang around deep in that half of the field.

Most of the time the kick is taken and the ball goes high and towards mid-field. For these the best position for the referee is to be near mid-field, with a sideways view to closely observe where the ball will land to produce the inevitable contest (and contact) between the defenders and forwards.

But one or two situations do demand extra observation. If you do see a team preparing to take short kick, either towards the top or the edge of the penalty area, you must be sure that the ball has left the penalty area before it is played by anyone else. This job can usually be left to the assistant, but you must be on the lookout for fouls if there are opponents in the vicinity. It is a good idea to try to read to intentions of the defending team during a goalkick, so that you are not already at mid-field when the action is occurring near the penalty-area.

The other situation is the case where the goalkeeper or another one of the defenders is capable of kicking the ball deep into their opponents' half. (You know this from your preparation, or from watching the first few goal-kicks they take.) Since there is no offside from a goal kick *(many referees and assistants forget this!)*, a forward can position himself behind the defense and get a good chance for a run at goal after a long goal-kick. The defenders will appeal for offside, because they forget where the ball came from, or are not aware of the exception to the offside law, or will just appeal out of habit. You and your assistant must make sure that the flag does not come up to create much embarrassment for all.

SUMMARY POINTS:

- *Vary your position at set-pieces to suit what is going on*
- *After taking a position, be ready to change it quickly as the need arises*
- *Position yourself so that you can see as many players as possible*
- *Prepare yourself by studying teams before and during the match you are refereeing*

NOTES

PREVENTIVE REFEREEING: KNOWING WHEN YOU ARE VULNERABLE

*...we dodge a misfortune at every
moment because we anticipate it...*

Alain
French philosopher

What would life be like during a match for a referee who could see into the future? Let's say he could see that ten minutes hence, player number five was going to lose his cool and punch an opponent. With that knowledge, any sensible referee would decide to stay very close to the player, talking to him all the time to make sure that when the incident arose, he would not punch his opponent. Ah! you say; what a wonderful attribute that would be for every referee! (Of course, any philosopher reading this would say that if the referee *changed* the future, then in fact he had not actually previously seen the future, because the one he created was not the one he thought he had seen....)

We are not qualified to start a discussion about clairvoyance and epistemology (the theory of knowledge); but we *are* going to show you how you can *change* your future several times during a game, and change it for the better. We are going to

IN THIS CHAPTER:

How to prevent a problem when:
- *An injured player is treated or removed*
- *Leaving the field at the end of play*
- *Cautioning a player*
- *A disputed goal is scored*
- *Sending two players off the field*
- *Deciding a disputed re-start*
- *You can see fewer than five players*
- *Two players are "getting into it"*
- *You get a flag you don't want*

describe things you can do at certain situations when you or the game are vulnerable to conflict, techniques to make sure that unpleasantness does not happen, nor misconduct, nor argument. If those statements intrigue you, pay attention....!

The injured player.

Especially in youth games, the referee has to be careful about a potentially serious injury. The culture of the U.S. is a litigious one, with matters that would be mere disagreements in other countries being settled only by legal action here. No referee can ignore that possibility when faced with a young player prostrate on the grass, or crumpled up holding her ankle. He *has* to stop the game to have the player attended to. In adult competitions, where the players are more aware of the seriousness or triviality of injuries, the referee can afford to wait for a moment or two to see first how the player is dealing with the injury. Only when it is clear that the player cannot continue without treatment or attention, does the referee need to stop the game. Not so with the youth!

So the referee goes to the injured young player, verifies that he or she cannot continue, and calls to the sideline for the coach or parent or trainer to come on with the magic spray or bucket-and-sponge. So why should this be a potential problem for the referee, doing his duty by taking care of the player? It could be a problem because the coach—accompanied in most cases by a parent of the injured player— might believe that the referee was responsible for the incident that led to the injury, especially if the game has been a bit rough. And the parent, understandably concerned and upset about the fate of her little one, might choose the moment to let loose with an emotional outburst about the official's neglect of her precious offspring. Within seconds, the referee could be in a position where he might have to take disciplinary action against the coach, or might have to try to remove an irate parent from the field.

So what? Some will say. I'll deal with it *if* I have to, and *when* it happens. And well he might, but why wait for trouble when you can easily avoid even the *possibility* of it, by taking a simple precaution? Having determined that the player needs attention, call the coach onto the field, and then *move away from the injured player a distance of at least twenty-five yards.* From there you can observe the coach or trainer working on the player but you are not so close that you invite comments or dissent. After a decent time, you can slowly approach the coach to "encourage" him to move things along, but in most cases, the incident will take care of itself, the player will be on his feet, and you will be able to get the game going again, all without any unpleasantness.

Leaving the field.

Either at half-time or full-time, the unaware referee can walk into trouble by doing no more than leaving the field. Many players and coaches believe (erroneously) that since the action has stopped, they can now talk to a referee in a way they couldn't when play was going on. And others, who may *know* that the referee at the half and at the end of the game still has authority over the players, simply cannot resist the temptation to express their opinion about some controversial decision or event. Make it your habit to try to prevent such confrontations.

You start by making sure that your equipment—your bag, sweatsuit and other stuff—is placed far away from either team bench or area. On local parks, you may have to choose a parking spot that is inconvenient, or put your bag behind the goal on an adjacent pitch, and not the one you are working on. The purpose is to prevent easy access to you by the players or coaches, and to make sure that when you are walking off, you are moving in a direction opposite to that of most of the players. It then becomes an inconvenience for anyone to confront you.

Then before the game you instruct your assistants that *at the sound of the whistle they must run to your side in the middle of the field in order to accompany* you off the pitch. Three people together may deter disagreement in a way that a single individual may not. And, if there should be a discussion, three pairs of eyes and ears are more effective than one!

Finally, when you are all together, look for a way to leave the field without encountering any players or coaches. If necessary, walk to a corner of the pitch and wait until everyone disperses. Than walk to your equipment or car as a group. Many, many referees hang around on the field hoping that someone will come up to them to tell them what a fine job they did. Too many times the only plaudits they receive are the ones congratulating them upon their guaranteed acceptance through the gates of hell. Don't martyr yourself by wanting praise from those who may not wish to give it. When your duty is done, leave the field in the company of your colleagues, and do it with dispatch.

For ninety-nine out of a hundred games, this ritualized exit at halftime and at fulltime may seem like an unnecessary precaution. But in the one-hundredth match, the one where angry players curse at you, or irate coaches confront you to tear a strip off your hide, where you are forced to take disciplinary action, to try to get names from people who refuse to give them, write long reports and then attend the subsequent hearings, if you use this procedure, you will not have those problems.

The caution.

In several places in this book we advocate a pattern of movement that will enable you to see as many players as possible. This is good advice for when you are moving around, and is excellent advice for when you are standing still. As, for example, you will be when warning a player, when issuing a caution, and when sending someone off the field.

Those moments may be instants of tension between players, when opponents can jaw at each other or gather round someone they believe is a criminal and causing problems. If you are talking to a player or taking disciplinary action, *make sure that you position yourself properly to see most of the players.* Near the touchline, move outside the player so that you can see into the field. Over the player's shoulder you will be able to see others talking and moving, and at the slightest hint of confrontation, step forward a pace or two and blow your whistle loudly, or shout out that you can see what is going on. (We favored the whistle, because stepping forward a pace or two meant that we would be blowing the whistle right next to the ear of the player we wanted to talk to or caution. The blast from close by then served as additional punishment!)

If the incident is near the end of the field and you are behind play, go past the player and turn so that you are looking upfield past him. From such a position you may be able to see all the players except one goalkeeper. Perfect!

In midfield, you will have to assess which way to turn based upon the distribution of the players at that moment. Whichever way you turn at midfield, don't stand stock-still. As you are talking, turn your head or look over your shoulder to make sure that you don't miss anything developing, and to make it clear to the players that you are "all eyes".

The disputed goal.

It may be after a scramble in the goalmouth, or after a contentious penalty-kick, or after a loud appeal by the defenders for a foul or for offside. Whatever the circumstances, it is clear to you that the goal is going to be disputed. You look across to your assistant and see that he is giving you a definite confirmation that the goal is good. You have seen nothing to justify cancelling the goal.

Once you are satisfied that the goal is legitimate, *run away from the defenders and any other player who may want to question the decision.* Move upfield towards the halfway line as quickly as possible. If you can run backwards easily, then do so. If you have difficulty doing this, then run normally, but keeping your head turned so that you can keep the players under observation. If a player runs after you seeking a confrontation, don't stop at the halfway line, but continue ten yards or more into the other half. It has been our experience that the halfway line seems to act as an invisible barrier to players, for they stop there as the ball comes out for the kick-off. They may stand and stare, glowering at you in anger, but for some strange reason, they rarely come across to confront you and express their opinion.

By running away from the potential dispute, you will have avoided an ugly incident and will have saved yourself some paperwork. And the players will have had a few moments to rid their systems of momentary anger. They know you are not going to change your mind, and they give up in disgust or resignation. In Chapter 14, we describe this technique for a goal scored after a penalty-kick.

Sending two players off.

One day, despite your best efforts in a match, and even after you have read everything in this book and taken it to heart, you may witness an unpleasant scuffle between two players. You feel you have no choice but to send them both off. Do not think for a moment that because you have taken action, the players have ended their dispute! Even as they are going off, there is potential for another flare-up.

If the team benches are on opposite sides of the field, the players leave in different directions and all is probably well. But with benches on the same side, you should walk some distance with the two players, keeping between them, or closely alongside one of them, until you are certain that they can no longer reach each other. Talk to them if there is any hint of another confrontation, but do not leave them until all is safe and orderly. As you walk with them, turn occasionally to view the other players. An ounce of prevention.....

The disputed restart.

You have made your decision, and awarded a goal-kick. The game is close; a corner-kick might have given the attackers a chance to even the score or break the game open with a late goal. But you did not hesitate in making up your mind: goal-kick. However, as you point to the goal-area, you notice that one or two attackers turn in protest, looking at you in anger.

We guarantee that if you stay where you are, you will have a dispute on your hands, a dispute that may lead to a yellow card or two, or if you have previously issued cautions, perhaps even a red card. Is this what you want? Is it necessary? Better yet: Is it necessary when so easily avoided?

The answer to all three questions should be a resounding "No!" When you notice the demeanor of the attackers who are disputing your call, *turn your back on them and run upfield to a position anticipating the goal-kick. Get away from them as quickly as you can.* The attacking players have things to do at a goal-kick—marking defenders, covering various areas and so on—and they will not chase you over a decision they know you will not change. Your action will end the dispute before it begins.

But suppose you are not quite sure what the correct decision is. You have to make some decision, but you don't have to rush into it, making the wrong one and provoking a dispute such as the one we have described. Take a short moment and watch the demeanor of the players.

If the forwards move away from the goal after the ball has crossed the goal-line, this is a sure indication that they believe the correct decision is a goal kick, not a corner. If they are happy, the referee should be happy, so give the goal kick! Similarly, if the defenders are taking up positions to defend a corner-kick, then a corner-kick it should be.

Sometimes the goalkeeper gives the decision away. Did his hand touch it as the ball whizzed over the bar? Quite often (surprisingly!) the goalkeeper who knows he touched it will not go after the ball, but will leave it for the attackers to collect for their corner. If one task of the referee is to decide disputed points, then where there is no dispute, he has nothing to decide.

Note, however, that you must gather this kind of information as quickly as possible, so as not to appear hesitant and uncertain. Take a look, read the players' actions, make your decision, and act as though that was the only decision on your mind.

How many players can you see?

In our long discussion of tactical thinking and movement in Chapter 13, we emphasize the importance of seeing as many players as possible at any one time. After all, *the more players you can see, the fewer there are who can do something out of your sight or behind your back.* This is something to bear in mind at every moment you are on the field. Ask yourself the question while running, and certainly at every stoppage in play: "How many can I see?" If the answer is "fewer than eleven", then there may be a better position for you to assume, one from which you can see *more* than half of the players. The smaller the answer you get when you ask the question, the greater is the certainty that there is a better position for you to be in, one that will give you more visual control over more players. The more visual control you have, the lower the likelihood of an ugly incident.

One specific case is where you have awarded to the attacking team a free kick closer than eighteen yards from the goal line, but outside the penalty area (Figure 15-1). Most referees would go to the wall and try to get the players back ten yards, but if the official adopts the

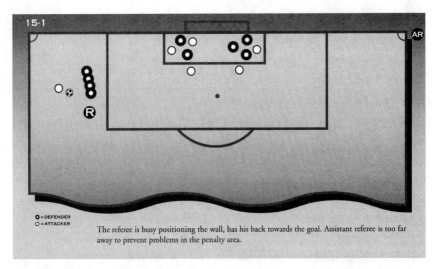

O = DEFENDER
O = ATTACKER

The referee is busy positioning the wall, has his back towards the goal. Assistant referee is too far away to prevent problems in the penalty area.

position shown, he will have many players out of his sight, milling about in the goalmouth. This is a potentially dangerous situation, with the likelihood of dead-ball fouls, elbows, retaliation for the original foul that produced the free kick, and so on. In order to oversee everything, the referee would have to be looking behind him, over his shoulder, and try not to get distracted by supervising the free kick. A better position might be at the *other end of the wall*, facing away from the ball and looking into the field and the goalmouth. There he can take care of the wall and see any potential problems in the goalmouth, An occasional glance over his shoulder will ensure that the kicker does not try and cheat by moving the ball from its original position.

Two players "getting into it."

You probably know the signs: they start talking to each other after their first challenge or tackle at each other. After that, and frequently at stoppages, they have conversations colored with aggressive comments: "Don't try that again!" or "You couldn't beat a bunch of girls..." or "Come down the middle again, and we'll see how tough you are." Perhaps one may "shoulder" his way past the other, getting a slight push from his opponent for his trouble. You get the feeling that tension between the two players is increasing, and that it is only going to get worse. What can you do to stop the rot? What can you do to avoid having to settle this dispute with yellow and red cards?

Our recommendation is to hound the two players into peaceful docility. Get close to them on the field and run around with them for a few minutes, talking to them all the time. "Now what are you two arguing about?" "No, he's not going to touch you with me standing right here!" "Don't even think about doing that! Even a blind referee could see what you're doing from here." And if one of them gets irritated by the constant attention, and asks what you are doing, tell him! "I'll leave you two along when you decide to stop jawing at each other and get down to the business of playing soccer. Deal?"

You will have to do this for no more than a few minutes, because the players quickly get sick of seeing and hearing the referee so close by. Then you resume your normal pattern of movement, but keeping an eye on the two bad boys just in case they start again. It has been our experience, however, that they won't. All that attention from the referee is bad for their reputation! We have used this technique in youth games, in amateur games and in professional matches. Believe us! It works as a great deterrent to escalation of hostilities. *By recognizing the potential for trouble, you take action and prevent the trouble from happening.* You predict a future that will not now happen....

The flag you did not want.

Whenever you work with assistant referees with less experience than you have, there is the possibility that they will raise a flag when they shouldn't. One of them may call a foul incorrectly, or at a time when you are close and can see the incident clearly yourself. You may get a signal the wrong way for a throw-in that is right in front of you. Perhaps worst of all, as the ball flies into the net from a wonderful shot from twenty yards out, the assistant raises a flag because someone is standing offside ten yards out from the goal.

Inevitably in all these examples, some players will see the flag and raise a fuss. And why shouldn't they? It appears to them that the officials disagree; one of them might change his mind in their favor. And no matter how quickly you extend your arm out, telling the assistant to lower his flag, you will have to deal with the players. This case is slightly different from the ones we have described above, because in those, you see the potential for a problem and head it off. Here the dispute has started, and all you can do is to prevent it from escalating into a major incident between you and the players.

First, *there is one thing you must not do. You must not bring discredit to your assistant by publicly declaring that he made a mistake.* All that will accomplish is to increase the players' skepticism about you and your assistants, and to alienate you from one of the people you depend on. Never say anything like: "No, no fellers, he's got it wrong! It's this way."

Second, *do not try to defend yourself or your assistant by insisting that the players leave the decision-making to you, or by telling them to "get on with the game".* All that does is to provoke the players into further discussion or argument with you: "Don't tell me to get on with the game. I'm the captain, and I want to know how you two can screw up like that!" When you hear that, you might get irritated, say something back, and the next thing you know, you are pulling out a card.

Our third point is to suggest that humor is the best escape from these kinds of disagreement. Here's what we mean....

So with a player standing offside ten yards from goal, the ball goes flying into the net, and out on the touchline is the upraised flag waving for all the defenders to see. The players begin shouting at you and pointing at the assistant. "OK, lads," you say, "I'll go and find out what's up." Then you walk over to the assistant, making sure that the players stay away or at least out of earshot, and tell him: "Just shake your head, and point into the field." When he does that, you run back to the players, who will immediately ask what the assistant said. You reply, as you turn to run upfield: "It's OK fellers, there was no offside. He was calling for a foul by one of the defenders!" If anybody asks "Which one?" you shout out "Number five!" and keep going.... By the time the defenders realize they may have been tricked, you are in the middle of the field signalling for the kick-off.

The ball crosses the touchline, you point one way, and the flag points the other. "Hey, ref! Look at your bloody linesman!" Without hesitating, you shout back: "No, no, we're on the same wavelength. He was pointing to the team that's going to *take* the throw." And as for a flag that signals a foul when you are in a better position than your assistant, simply take a quick look at your watch and say something like: "That's a signal for me that twenty minutes have gone." Then follow-up that nonsensical statement with a shout to your assistant: "Thanks for the information, Freddie." With a little bit of humor, you accomplish a lot: the players have nothing to argue about, your linesman feels good at hearing your compliment, and you defuse a dispute.

Important points:

- *The referee should not simply wait for things to happen. He must anticipate potential problems in order to prevent them.*

- *Always maintain a position on the field to allow yourself maximum visibility of the players.*

- *From your own experience, draw up a list of situations where disputes frequently arise, and try to imagine what you might do to prevent them from happening. Be your own prophet!*

- *Humor can often extinguish the flames of disagreement.*

16

FITNESS: CAN YOU KEEP UP WITH THE PLAYERS?

Many shall run to and fro, and
knowledge shall be increased.

Daniel, 12:4

The need.

There's no getting away from it: if you want to referee effectively, you have to be physically fit. This is obvious for top-level matches involving professional or international teams, but is also true for youth games and adult amateur competition. Professional games are played at a very high speed, the ball in constant motion, with rapid changes from end to end. Likewise, the players nowadays exhibit tremendous physical capacity, both in endurance and speed. And whereas youth players may lack some of these qualities, they make up for it with limitless energy and enthusiasm. Likewise in the Sunday afternoon adult games in the park, although the players may not be as fit as youngsters or capable of emulating the pros, the games can still be

> *"A referee's objective should be to organize training to ensure he or she has the fitness, not merely to pass tests, but to referee soccer matches."*

IN THIS CHAPTER:

- *The physical demands upon a referee*
- *How your body works during exercise*
- *What your body needs for energy*
- *An infallible training and nutrition program to give you superior fitness and improve your performance as a referee*

physically demanding for the referee since they quite often involve long balls played from one end of the pitch to the other, and then back again, without much mid-field play.

The sad thing is that many referees choose to deal with these tactics by simply staying near the middle of the field, but as anyone who has ever observed such a game can attest, these referees seldom have the respect of the players nor do they have full control of the game. Furthermore, as the unfit players in these games become tired, they can be replaced by substitutes with fresh legs, which can put additional demands on the referee, particularly near the end of the game. And finally, in some local associations, referees are often called upon to officiate in two or more games back-to-back. Yet despite the physical demands that the game places upon referees, the average standard of physical fitness is not high, even at the national level. Let's examine why.

The test.

In the United States and many other countries, referees are required to pass certain physical fitness tests every year. FIFA initially introduced fitness testing for international referees in the 1970s following concern at the fitness levels of referees participating in the World Cup. FIFA chose to adopt the fitness criteria set out by Dr. Kenneth Cooper, a sports medicine specialist, and author of several books on health and fitness.

Dr. Cooper developed a method of testing and a set of standards based upon the concept that the distance run in 12 minutes is a good overall indicator of general aerobic fitness. So a 12-minute run to demonstrate aerobic capability, together with a 400-meter run (subsequently replaced by two separate 200-meter runs) to simulate long speedy runs that referees are occasionally required to do in a match, a 50-meter sprint (to demonstrate raw speed), and a simple agility test were combined to become what was known in refereeing circles as the "Cooper Test." (We found it quite amusing when participating in various international tournaments where the test was given, to hear referees from other countries discuss, usually with some degree of trepidation, the "Cooper Test", always using the English wording, and usually without realizing that Cooper was actually a person's name.)

The standards based on those set by Dr. Cooper (published in his book "The Aerobics Way") were age-dependent. The older a referee was, the shorter the distance that was required in the 12-minute run. But for the USSF, the standards became progressively more stringent the higher up the promotional ladder you went, the idea being that a referee needed to be fitter to officiate at a higher level. In some respects, this made sense, but in other respects it did not. (Nowadays, at the National and International level, referees have to achieve the same standard regardless of age.) But it didn't please the referees; they complained at the mere fact of *having to take a fitness test.*

But if you wanted to remain registered as a referee, you were compelled to get to a track and be evaluated. Compulsion is a great convincer, and so they reluctantly went along. We never understood what the fuss was about, because it was clear that anyone who was reasonably fit could pass these tests. You didn't have to be a five-minute miler! But there was an inadvertent consequence of using the Cooper standards as a measure of fitness: Some referees trained simply to pass the test, and nothing more. The original measure of fitness became the qualification you needed to referee. To put it another way, *referees trained with the goal of passing the Cooper test, rather than with the goal of being able to referee a match.* Nowhere in the training of referees was the message passed that if you train to be fit to perform the job on the pitch, passing the fitness test is not a problem. *A referee's objective should be to organize training to ensure he or she has the fitness, not merely to pass tests, but to referee soccer matches.* If you keep reading, you will see the methods of training that we *guarantee* will give you match fitness for any level of competition.

AHEAD OF OUR TIME:
A research study by RE

In our real lives, Ed and I are both research scientists, and as is the case with most people in the scientific world, our way of looking at *any* problem is to examine it as though it were a matter of science. After watching the referees in the early years of the NASL, it occurred to me that there was a tremendous variation in mobility from one referee to the next. The fittest was undoubtedly John Davies, who had emigrated to the U.S. from Canada, after serving there as a FIFA Referee. Even though he was then well into his forties, John was incredible, covering the field from goal line to goal line, always on top of things from the first minute to the last. But some of the others....well, let's be polite and make them anonymous, and use an Australian term to describe their mobility: *walkabout*. So I decided to see if I could measure the fit and the unfit, and then use the information to teach other referees.

It wasn't a difficult exercise. I devised a way to make a grid over the field, make a map of the path that the referee took during the game, and then to mark his track with symbols for the kind of movement: walk, jog, stride and sprint. I simply measured the track, calculated the total distance in each of the four categories of motion. Then I did something that no one has done to this day. I shaded the map of the field to show the areas where the referee was positioned most frequently. These shaded maps provided a convenient visual aid to show to referees and to emphasize the need for physical preparation for a match. As you might guess, the contrast between the map of NASL games for John Davies and the one for the "Walkabout Wonders" was dramatic. Simple research it was, but I thought I was on to something useful, so I decided to share it with the soccer world.

What better way than through "FIFA News", the official monthly publication of the International Federation? As a research scientist whose work had been published in many technical journals, I knew what to do. So I prepared a short paper in non-technical language describing everything, I included small professionally-drawn illustrations of the mobility maps, and sent it off to FIFA headquarters in Switzerland. A few weeks later, back came the reply, and I quote:

> The member of the FIFA Referees' Committee I consulted finds that the procedure described in your article is rather too technical and covers only the physical aspect of the referee's supervision of the game — and even that seems too scientific. It is therefore impracticable and the member did not recommend publication of your article in FIFA News.
>
> (signed) R. Courte, P.R. & Press Officer, FIFA

It was my first encounter with the backward thinking ("...scientific...and therefore impracticable...!) that I encountered too often in soccer— locally, nationally and internationally. New ideas and the concept of change are frightening to many people, especially in tradition-bound things like sports. Shaking my head in wonder, I had a good laugh about it, put this important historical document away in a drawer somewhere and forgot about it. Ed and I did, however, use my slides when teaching referees in the U.S. And then more than *twenty years* later, some genius thought that FIFA ought to start measuring the mobility of referees—imagine that!

What the referee does.

In a normal soccer game of two equal halves with a 10-minute interval, the referee does not have to run continuously. Any referee with a bit of experience will describe the game as a series of stop-and-go sequences, in which the official may run hard and then get a slight breather. But beyond that crude description, what do we really know about how the referee moves? Well, precious little! No matter that the world has had professional soccer for more than one hundred years, it was only in the seventies that anyone applied scientific research to the movement of referees in soccer. And, we are happy to say, the first such study was done right here in the U. S. of A., in Dallas, Texas (see sidebar).

In the years since that first study, other sociologists and scientists have analyzed in detail the movements of referees in matches in professional leagues and in the lower echelons. In England, Tom Reilly and three of his colleagues at Liverpool John Moores University studied matches in the four professional divisions, and two semi-professional leagues (1). In Japan, T. Asami and his colleagues at the University of Tokyo tracked referees in The J-league and in some international matches (2). Then in Australia, no doubt trying to quantify the tendency for "walkabout" in the country where it originated, Liz Johnston and Lars McNaughton looked at referees in the Tasmanian State Soccer Association (3). In all three studies, the average for the referees studied was a total distance of approximately. 10 kilometers (about 6 miles) per match. John Davies covered eight miles, our walkabout friends four-and-a-half.

The researchers also analyzed the type of movement that the referees utilized during the games: walking, jogging, sprinting/striding and moving backwards (the administrators' specialty!). Although there were some variations in the numbers, by and large they paint a common picture of motion for referees. Jogging accounts for about 48% of the referees activity, walking 20-30%, sprinting/striding 18% and backwards movement about 18%. The overall conclusions were that refereeing a soccer game is an aerobic activity (jogging) intermingled with several periods of anaerobic-type high intensity effort (sprinting/striding).

Two of the studies included measurements of heart-rate, and these showed that the average heartbeat of the referee was in the region of 160-165 beats/minutes throughout each half of the match with occasional values over 180 being reached, similar to what was found for players. When you consider that in most games, the referee is usually 10 or more years older than the players, the need for fitness is more apparent. It is widely held that the maximum heartbeat for any person is the number obtained by subtracting the age of the person from 220. Thus a person aged 40 should have a maximum heartbeat (HB_{max}) of 180, whereas one aged 20 would have HB_{max} of 200. This means that referees are operating at values close to their HB_{max} on several occasions, again emphasizing the need for excellent fitness ratings for referees.

What does all of this mean for referee training? Clearly, from the scientific studies and common knowledge, refereeing *should* demand a high level of physical fitness. But it must also be a wide range of fitness types or categories. A long distance runner does not sprint too much, except at the end of the race, and a sprinter does not run for very long periods of time. But a referee must cover the 10 kM *and* include several sprints or speedy runs during that time period. Whereas the distance runner knows that the race ends at the end of his sprint, and that he can run himself to exhaustion at that time, the referee and the players know that there will still be more to come after a fast run. How do they prepare for that? To answer that question, let's take a quick look at how the body works.

How the body uses energy.

The essential source of energy for biological processes is the sun. Plants capture light and use it to convert carbon dioxide from the air into sugar, which is the fuel for living things, including referees. When we eat plants, or eat animals that eat plants, our digestive system breaks the food up into the bits and pieces we need to build cells, and the bits and pieces we use for energy. Inside our cells, food molecules are broken down into smaller components and energy is obtained from them during this process. The end products are carbon dioxide and water, because—and this is important for athletes (and referees)—oxygen from the air is involved in the energy-extracting process. We "burn" our food with oxygen, just as we burn the fuel in our automobiles with oxygen. Here's a key: *The body prefers carbohydrates as the fuel for exercising our bodies.*

And when we need a lot of energy for running and any other exercise, we have to keep a ready supply of oxygen flowing in our bloodstream to the places where we need to burn our sources of energy. Sometimes, however, we use oxygen faster than the blood can supply it. So here's another key: *We can increase our supply of oxygen by the simple act of regular physical training.*

Our day-to-day requirement for energy is met by stores of a substance called glycogen, a large molecule made up of branching chains of sugar, which consists of carbon, hydrogen and oxygen. Normally we have enough glycogen stockpiled in our system for about half a day's worth of energy, but after that the body starts breaking down fat to use as fuel. So let's set a referee in motion and consider what happens to the fuel and the oxygen in his body.

At the start of a run, the carbohydrate fuel is "burned" with oxygen and converted completely into energy and carbon dioxide, a gas that is transported in the blood to the lungs, where it passes out into the atmosphere. This kind of activity is called "aerobic", meaning "with oxygen". After a few minutes, our referee decides to pick up the pace a bit (he's been reading the training schedule at the end of this chapter), but unfortunately, he begins to ask his body to do more than it is capable of. He does not have enough oxygen in his blood to completely burn the fuel he needs for energy. He begins to incur "oxygen debt", and he begins to run "anaerobically", meaning "without oxygen". Now you would think that fuel is useless without oxygen to burn it, for we know that in a car or an airplane, when the fuel and air mixture gets fully rich (all gasoline, no air), the engine stops. But not so in the referee's body.

The body can still derive energy from the *partial* oxidation of carbohydrate, but that still leaves some unburned fuel: hydrogen and a substance called pyruvate. Even though they are short of oxygen, the referee's muscles combine those two into a substance that has stopped more referees training than all the excuses we can come up with. The muscles make *lactic acid.* But the build-up of lactic acid in the muscle impairs performance, for the tissue can now obtain only 7% of the energy obtained from carbohydrate during aerobic activity. Our referee keeps running, but slower and slower, with more and more pain in his legs from exhaustion. Eventually, he has to stop, panting and panting as his body tries to get more oxygen. And when he can't go on, there is nothing left to do but quit and become an assessor—as we have done!!

Is systematic training really necessary?

Time and again, when we brought up the business of physical fitness and the need to change the way we think about training, we heard the usual complaints. "All you'll end up with is a bunch of rabbits who can run but can't referee" and other similar words. Those comments were usually from people who thought they were good referees, but wouldn't care to admit they were not in good physical condition, and certainly wouldn't admit that they weren't inclined to do what is needed to get into good shape. Y'all know someone like this.

We have to say that although *we do know some <u>very fit people</u> who are not good referees, we do not know many <u>good</u> referees who are <u>unfit</u>.* You need refereeing ability *and* fitness. One or the other alone is not good enough. This book is intended to show you *everything* that you need to become a good referee. Most chapters deal with refereeing technique, but this one deals exclusively with the other essential element—fitness and how to get it.

The training program.

Right at the start let us emphasize that *it is not enough for referees to train simply by going for a gentle jog in the park or around the streets for a few miles.* That will give you an aerobic base upon which to build *real* fitness; by itself it is not sufficient. Your training should include substantial anaerobic training also, in order to overcome and tolerate the periods of anaerobic running described earlier. Fortunately, a sophisticated and effective method of training has been developed that is ideally suited to soccer referees. It is known generally as *interval training*, and involves a repetitive series of short runs at sub-maximal pace, with various periods of recovery between each repetition. This method of training was used with wonderful effect by Olympic-class athletes for many years. The great distance runner, Emil Zatopek, who won the 5,000M, 10,000M and marathon at the 1952 Olympics, would train by running 40-50 repetitive 400M runs, each separated by a 1-2 minute interval of slow jogging. This method of training builds both aerobic capacity and anaerobic performance, building the body's tolerance to accumulation of lactic acid.

Computerized training programs based on the interval training concept were published several years ago by James B. Gardner and J. Gerry Purdy (Computerized Running Training Programs, TAFNEWS Press, 1970: ISBN 0-911520-00-7). Gardner and Purdy devised systems of training that allowed for an athlete—sprinter or distance runner—to tailor the training program to his specific needs They showed that a certain number of 400M runs at 85% pace with a 2-minute interval was equivalent to a longer sequence of runs at a 70% pace with a 3 minute interval. Furthermore, one can substitute 800M, 200M, or 1000M runs with different numbers of repetitions and different intervals at different pace levels for equivalent workouts. This is shown in the sample page depicted in Figure 16-1 below (reproduced by permission of the publishers).

FIGURE 16-1

340 POINT LEVEL PACING TABLE

SPEED	REPS	REST	110 YD	150 YD	165 YD	220 YD	275 YD	330 YD	352 YD	385 YD	440 YD	495 YD
95.0%	0- 1	----	13.9	19.3	21.3	29.2	38.1	48.1	52.3	58.8	1:10.1	1:21.8
92.5%	1- 2	4- 5 M	14.3	19.8	21.9	30.0	39.2	49.4	53.7	1:00.4	1:11.9	1:24.0
90.0%	2- 3	4- 5 M	14.7	20.3	22.5	30.8	40.2	50.8	55.2	1:02.1	1:13.9	1:26.3
87.5%	3- 4	3- 4 M	15.1	20.9	23.2	31.7	41.4	52.2	56.8	1:03.9	1:16.1	1:28.8
85.0%	4- 5	3- 4 M	15.5	21.5	23.9	32.6	42.6	53.8	58.5	1:05.8	1:18.3	1:31.4
82.5%	6- 7	2- 3 M	16.0	22.2	24.6	33.6	43.9	55.4	1:00.3	1:07.8	1:20.7	1:34.2
80.0%	8- 9	2- 3 M	16.5	22.9	25.3	34.7	45.3	57.1	1:02.1	1:09.9	1:23.2	1:37.1
77.5%	10-12	1- 2 M	17.0	23.6	26.2	35.8	46.7	59.0	1:04.1	1:12.1	1:25.9	1:40.3
75.0%	13-15	1- 2 M	17.6	24.4	27.0	37.0	48.3	1:01.0	1:06.3	1:14.5	1:28.7	1:43.6
72.5%	16-18	60-90 S	18.2	25.2	28.0	38.3	50.0	1:03.1	1:08.6	1:17.1	1:31.8	1:47.2
70.0%	19-21	60-90 S	18.8	26.1	29.0	39.6	51.7	1:05.3	1:11.0	1:19.9	1:35.1	1:51.0
67.5%	22-24	45-75 S	19.5	27.1	30.0	41.1	53.7	1:07.7	1:13.7	1:22.8	1:38.6	1:55.1
65.0%	25-29	45-75 S	20.3	28.2	31.2	42.7	55.7	1:10.3	1:16.5	1:26.0	1:42.4	1:59.5
62.5%	30-35	30-60 S	21.1	29.3	32.4	44.4	57.9	1:13.1	1:19.5	1:29.4	1:46.5	2:04.3
60.0%	36-40	30-60 S	22.0	30.5	33.8	46.2	1:00.4	1:16.2	1:22.9	1:33.2	1:50.9	2:09.5

SPEED	REPS	REST	550 YD	660 YD	880 YD	1100 YD	1320 YD	1.00 MI	1.25 MI	1.50 MI	1.75 MI	2.00 MI
95.0%	0- 1	----	1:34.0	1:58.9	2:49.3	3:42.4	4:36.4	6:27.5	8:21.1	10:16.6	12:13.1	14:10.2
92.5%	1- 2	4- 5 M	1:36.6	2:02.1	2:53.9	3:48.4	4:45.8	6:37.9	8:34.6	10:33.3	12:32.9	14:33.1
90.0%	2- 3	4- 5 M	1:39.2	2:05.5	2:58.7	3:54.8	4:51.7	6:49.0	8:48.9	10:50.8	12:53.8	14:57.4
87.5%	3- 4	3- 4 M	1:42.1	2:09.1	3:03.8	4:01.5	5:00.1	7:00.7	9:04.0	11:09.4	13:15.9	15:23.0
85.0%	4- 5	3- 4 M	1:45.1	2:12.9	3:09.2	4:08.6	5:08.9	7:13.0	9:20.0	11:29.1	13:39.3	15:50.2
82.5%	6- 7	2- 3 M	1:48.3	2:16.9	3:15.0	4:16.1	5:18.2	7:26.2	9:37.0	11:50.0	-----	-----
80.0%	8- 9	2- 3 M	1:51.6	2:21.2	3:21.1	4:24.1	5:28.2	7:40.1	-----	-----	-----	-----
77.5%	10-12	1- 2 M	1:55.2	2:25.8	3:27.6	4:32.6	5:38.8	7:54.9	-----	-----	-----	-----
75.0%	13-15	1- 2 M	1:59.1	2:30.6	3:34.5	4:41.7	5:50.1	-----	-----	-----	-----	-----
72.5%	16-18	60-90 M	2:03.2	2:35.8	3:41.9	4:51.4	-----	-----	-----	-----	-----	-----
70.0%	19-21	60-90 S	2:07.6	2:41.4	3:49.8	-----	-----	-----	-----	-----	-----	-----
67.5%	22-24	45-75 S	2:12.3	2:47.4	-----	-----	-----	-----	-----	-----	-----	-----
65.0%	25-29	45-75 S	2:17.4	2:53.8	-----	-----	-----	-----	-----	-----	-----	-----
62.5%	30-35	30-60 S	2:22.9	-----	-----	-----	-----	-----	-----	-----	-----	-----
60.0%	36-40	30-60 S	-----	-----	-----	-----	-----	-----	-----	-----	-----	-----

Thus it is possible to develop a workout schedule that matches the individual's needs, and provides for a way to gradually and measurably increase performance. We were fortunate enough to be made aware of this valuable workbook by Professor Peter Raven, a sports physiologist at the University of North Texas Health Sciences Center, and himself a top Rugby referee. Once we heard about it and saw its benefits, we devised for ourselves training regimens that were extremely productive.

Well into our forties we both scored in the top 5% of results in referee fitness testing at the NASL and USSF sessions every year in both the 12-minute run and the long and short sprints. But, more importantly, we found that the ease with which we completed top-level high-pressure games also increased. We were better able to keep up with play, reach deeper into the corners of the pitch, follow fast breaks and recover from them, and still be running well at the end of the game. Players often commented on our fitness, and in some cases worried that they were too tired themselves to keep up, and we would make them look bad in the eyes of their coach! This was especially true near the end of a game, when we would run past midfielders attempting to recover their positions after an attack had broken down. (Of course, we will never admit that we sometimes accelerated deliberately just to rub it in!) Our fitness was also noticed by assessors who would remark that we appeared to be running as well in the last 15 minutes of the match as we had in the first 15. (See Chapter 18 for more on this!) And furthermore, we are convinced that our levels of fitness were a major factor in our appointments to the FIFA list.

Even if you do not have to have aspirations to be a professional or international referee, you can and should take advantage of this knowledge to improve your fitness for refereeing. It will also improve your general health and enjoyment of life.

The training schedule we devised for National referees in the US is shown in Table 16-1. It is a progressively increasing schedule to be used pre-season, or to get into shape initially, and then a weekly schedule to maintain your level. It includes both interval training and some continuous running training. It should also be combined with some agility training, running backwards (for when you retire and become an administrator...) and sideways (in case you go into the political side of the game...), and if possible, some light weight-training to maintain overall muscle tone. As with all activities, these sessions should be preceded by warm-up exercises and stretching to avoid injury.

TABLE 16-1

TRAINING SCHEDULE

Week	Day 1	Day 3	Day 5	Day 7
1	1.5 miles 10-12 min	2 miles 15-16 min	2 miles 14-15 min	2.5 miles 20 min
2	3x 800M 4 m I=3m	4x 800M 4 m I=3m	4x 800M 3.5 m I=3m	3 miles 24-26m
3	4x 800M 3.5 min I=3m	1 mile 7-8 m 2x 800M 3.5 m, I=3-4m	Same as 3-3	3 miles 24-26m
4	3x 800M 3.5 min I=3m 2x 400M 90s I=3-4 m	Same as 4-1	2x 800M 3.5 min I=3m 3x 400M 90s I=3-4m	3 miles <24m
5	1 mile 7.5 m I=4 2x 400M 85s I=3-4 m	Same as 5-1	1 mile 7.5 m I=4 3x 400M 85s I=3-4 m	3 miles <24m
6	0.5 mile 7.5 m I=4 4x 400M 85s I=3-4 m	Same as 6-1	5x 400M 85s I=3 m	3.5 miles 28m
7	5x 400M <85s I=3 m	Same as 7-1	6x 400M 85s I=3 m	3.5 miles 28m
8	4x 400M <85s 2x 200M<40s I=3 m	Same as 8-1	4x 400M <85s 4x 200M<40s I=3 m	3.5 miles <28m
9	4x 400M <85s 2x 200M<40s 2x 100M<18 I=3 m	Same as 9-1	4x 400M <85s 3x 200M<40s 3x 100M<18 I=3 m	3.0 miles 24m
10	4x 400M 80s 2x 200M35s I=3 m jog 0.5 mile	Same as 10-1	4x 400M 80s 2x 200M35s 2x100M 18s I=3 m jog 0.5 mile	3.0 miles 24m
11	1x 400M 80s 2x 200M35s I=3 m Rest 5-7m 1 mile ,8m	Same as 11-1	2x 400M 80s 2x 200M35s I=3 m Rest 5-7m 1 mile ,8m	3.0 miles 24m
12	2x 400M 80s 2x 200M35s I=3 m Rest 5-7m 1 mile ,8m	Same as 12-1	2x 400M 80s 2x 200M35s I=3 m Rest 5-7m 1.5 mile ,12m	3.0 miles <24m
13	2x 400M 80s 2x 200M35s I=3 m Rest 5m 2 miles ,16m	Same as 13-1	2x 400M 80s 2x 200M35s 2x50M I=3 m Rest 5m 1 mile ,8m	3.0 miles <24m 8x10 shuttle <28s
14	2x 400M 80s 2x 200M35s 2x50M I=3 m Rest 5m 1.5 mile <12m	Same as 14-1	2x 400M 80s 2x 200M35s 2x50M I=3 m Rest 5m 2 miles<16m	3.0 miles <24m 8x10 shuttle <28s

TABLE 16-1 (Continued)

TRAINING SCHEDULE (Continued)

15	2x 400M 80s 2x 200M35s 2x50M I=3 m Rest 5m 1 mile 7m	Same as 15-1	2x 400M 80s 2x 200M35s 2x50M I=3 m Rest 5m 1.5 miles 11m	3.0 miles <24m 8x10 shuttle <28s
16	2x 400M 80s 2x 200M35s 2x50M I=3 m Rest 5m 2 miles 14m	Same as 16-1	2x 400M 80s 2x 200M35s 2x50M I=3 m Rest 5m 2.5miles <20m	3.0 miles <24m 8x10 shuttle <28s
17	2x 400M 80s 2x 200M35s 2x50M I=3 m Rest 5m 2.5miles 18m	Same as 17-1	2x 400M 80s 2x 200M35s 2x50M I=3 m Rest 5m 3miles 24m	3.0 miles <24m 8x10 shuttle <26s
18	Repeat 17-1	or 17-3 all	week	
19	2 miles 14 m Rest 5-7m 4x 400M 80s 2x 200M35s I=3 m	Same as 19-1	2 miles 14 m Rest 5-7m 4x 400M 80s 2x 200M35s 2x100 18s I=3 m	3.0 miles <24m 8x10 shuttle <26s
20	Repeat 19-3	all week		
21	3 miles 22 m Rest 5-7m 2x 200M35s 2x100M 18s 2x 50M 9s I=3 m	Same as 21-1	3 miles 22 m Rest 5-7m 2x 200M35s 4x100M 18s 2x 50M 9s I=3 m	3.0 miles <24m 8x10 shuttle 24s
22	3 miles 22 m Rest 5m 6x100M 18s 2x 50M 9s I=3 m	Same as 22-1	Same as 22-1	3.0 miles <24m 8x10 shuttle 24s
23	Alternate 21-3	and 17-3		

INSTRUCTIONS: TRAINING SCHEDULE

1. Always warm-up and stretch out properly before beginning these exercises

2. Be sure you have access to liquids before, during and after the exercises.

Continued on next page

TABLE 16-1 (Instructions Continued)

INSTRUCTIONS: TRAINING SCHEDULE (Continued)

3. If you are unable to complete the schedule on any day, slow down or take longer intervals between events.

4. On the days not listed either rest, have a very light workout, or do weight work. Day 6 should be a rest day.

5. Some of you will find this program to be easy and will progress more quickly or you may wish to start somewhere down the list if you feel capable. That is okay. If you get to the performance level given for weeks 17 and 22 earlier than that, just stay at that level or try to improve on it by adding more intervals or by increasing the running speeds or both.

6. Abbreviations are as follows: M = meters; m =minutes; s = seconds; I = interval between runs; 4-1 means "week 4, day 1 " etc.; < means "less than".

7. The various runs MUST be done in the order listed, otherwise they will not be of use.

The nutrition program.

Good nutrition is an essential part of the make-up of any athlete, and that includes soccer referees. But there have been studies done on what nutritional factors are important. During a soccer match, most of the energy is obtained from carbohydrate, with smaller amounts from other nutrients. As we described above, fatigue is associated with depletion of our principal fuel, glycogen. Recent research (4) into the fatigue experienced by soccer players tells us a lot about fatigue in referees, for the distances covered by referees during a match are close to the distances covered by many players.

Amounts of glycogen in the thigh muscle after a match were depleted to as little as 10% of pre-game levels, with an average occurring at about 30% of pre-game value. This is a primary cause of fatigue, since muscle cannot operate for more than several seconds without a good supply of glycogen. In other words when your glycogen level is low, you are unable to move about as well. Also, as would be expected, the depletion was most apparent in the second half of the match. Furthermore, it was determined that glycogen levels do not return to their original values even after 24 hours. It takes 36-48 hours together with an adequate intake of carbohydrates to restore glycogen levels.

This is significant for referees who officiate one high-level match a week, but it is also important for those who do several games in one day in their local associations. Studies of this type now indicate that no referee can perform at his best for the long periods of time over two or even three matches, a point we argued for many years locally—to no avail. Indeed this practice was severely criticized by coaches of competitive-level youth soccer teams in the North Texas area. They pointed out that their players and coaches had spent the week training hard and preparing for the one weekend match, only for it to be refereed by an individual who had just worked the previous match on the same pitch and who was clearly not as his best. Assignors may have difficulty covering all the matches, but *it is not fair to the players when a referee operates in less-than-optimum physical condition, either because of lack of training or because of the inevitable effects of fatigue.*

For several years, while travelling around the country doing professional matches, and travelling out of the country for international matches in Central America, the Caribbean, Europe and Asia, we were rarely assigned to matches in our local North Texas senior league. The reason? We requested that we be assigned only one match on any one day, and the assignor, an individual who had neither refereed nor played, refused to do it because it was too much trouble to get officials. So the players were denied the opportunity of having two very experienced referees. *We'll ask again: Who is this game for?* Certainly not for the convenience of assignors.

However let us jump off our soapbox and move on. So how can we combat the glycogen depletion effect? Probably the best known method is "carbohydrate loading". The principle is simple. If you exercise hard, and severely deplete your glycogen level, the body responds by going into overdrive to replace it. So if you ingest a large amount of carbohydrate during the 24-48 hour period after heavy exercise, not only do you replenish the lost glycogen, but you actually produce and store a higher level than you had originally. During this time of loading, carbohydrates—in the form of pasta, potatoes, rice etc.—should comprise about 70% of the calories eaten. This is around 700 grams per day. If you normally referee on Saturday, you should train hard on Wednesday and Thursday. Carbohydrate loading should begin after training on Thursday, to be followed by light exercise on Friday. Eat a light meal consisting mainly of carbohydrate 3-4 hours before the game.

If you were to start a match with a higher-than-normal glycogen level, then you would also have a higher level at the end of the match, and would therefore not be as tired, or could work harder and run more during the match. It's just like gas in a car. The more that's in the tank, the further the car will go. In games that have the possibility of extra time a referee must be careful to be sure he has enough in reserve; run conservatively in the final 10-15 minutes of regular time in such games if the score is close.

Another way to combat glycogen depletion is to provide a supplementary source of energy. Experiments with players, who were given a drink containing a 7 percent solution of a complex carbohydrate 30 minutes before the match, and again at half-time, showed that they suffered less glycogen depletion (5) and were observed to cover 25% more distance overall than players who drank only water (6). Even more significant was that distances covered at higher intensity—cruise/sprint—in the second half were 40 percent higher for the players who received the carbohydrate drink. Since we know that referees cover similar distances to the players, what is true for the players should also be true for the referees.

Note that full replenishment of glycogen takes 36-48 hours, although there is partial replacement after 24 hours. This is important for referees who officiate on Saturdays and Sundays, and for those who participate in tournaments where you may be called upon to referee more frequently. In general, it is not advisable to referee more than one game in a 24 hour period, and a minimum 48 hour period of rest is preferred.

Fluid intake before and during a game is also vital because dehydration can also contribute to fatigue, especially with regard to endurance. It is important to drink an adequate amount, usually a *diluted* fruit juice or sport drink before the match and at half-time. In hot weather, it is also advisable to drink something during the breaks in play, just as the players do. We used to be amazed during our active referee days to hear certain persons in high positions in the refereeing hierarchy tell referees not to drink fluids during the match, because it "looked bad." Thankfully, such outdated notions have gone the way of the dinosaurs, and it is now common to see referees in top games sensibly avail themselves of a drink when there is a stoppage for injury treatment to a player. The exhausted or dehydrated referee is of no use to anyone.

A good diet should be well-balanced with protein and fat, and it also should include an adequate supply of vitamins. Vitamin deficiencies can result in impaired performance, and although a balanced diet with plenty of fresh fruits, vegetables etc., will provide a good vitamin supply, the importance of this cannot be overstated. Therefore a daily multivitamin tablet can be very valuable.

Being in good physical condition includes maintaining the proper weight, and avoiding junk food, and getting an adequate amount of sleep. Smoking is totally incompatible with good performance and good health. Quite simply put, if you are a smoker, you should quit if you wish to become a top referee. Alcohol consumption in excess is harmful, although moderate consumption has been shown to have some beneficial effects (not before the game!) Alcohol impairs brain functioning and should be avoided 24 hours before refereeing a match. Use of artificial stimulants or drugs used to increase strength and performance (so-called doping) should be avoided, period. Although they can provide short term benefits, the long term effects can be dangerous. Caffeine does improve alertness, and for some people may prove useful in moderation.

The human body operates on a natural daily cycle, known as the circadian rhythm. This can provide difficulties for scheduling training. Most games are in the afternoons or evenings. Therefore it is better to schedule your training for those times, so that your body gets used to exercise at that time of the day. If you train in the mornings but referee in the afternoons or evenings, you will not be at your best, because you are asking your body to perform at a time when normally it is at rest. Likewise, it is important to recognize the effects of time-zone shifts that can occur when you are scheduled to referee away from home. This can occur when going to tournaments, or other states or countries for single matches in the case of professional and international referees. A game scheduled for 8:00 PM in Los Angeles will not end until after midnight Eastern time. For a referee who is from the East coast involved in such a game, this would mean that he would be up and running around, supposedly alert, when his body is expecting to be in bed asleep!! Traveling the day before, or adjusting your routine in the days leading up the game are ways to deal with this problem.

Several years ago the idea of biorhythms was popular. In this there were supposed to be peak days and low days in three different cycles.

When all three peaks coincided, that was a good day, but if all three lows coincided, that was a bad day. Activities that demand concentration such as refereeing were supposed to be avoided on the low days. There are no adequate scientific data on this concept, and as far as refereeing is concerned, it can be dismissed. (That's a polite way of saying that it's nonsense.)

Are you fit to make decisions?

As well as making it harder to run about the pitch, fatigue also has a negative effect on decision-making. Studies have shown that *people make more mistakes on simple tests of logic and mathematics immediately following exercise than they do when rested.* The reasons for this are not fully understood and are likely to be complex, since stress causes the release of a variety of substances into the bloodstream, some of which may effect mental processing in some way. An essential element in our body fluids, sodium, is directly involved in the transmission of messages along the nervous system. Deplete sodium from your system, as you will do if you sweat profusely and don't replace the fluids and salts, and your nervous system won't function as well as normal. Hence for referees the more you can avoid fatigue, the better will be your decision-making. And since fatigue occurs at the end of the game, when the players are also tired, poor decisions at that time can and do have severe consequences. *The way to stave off fatigue is by training.* That's worth saying again: *The way to stave off fatigue and become a better referee is by systematic physical training.*

Where did we find all that scientific stuff?

Numbers in parentheses in the text refer to these articles:

1. C. Catterall, T. Reilly, G. Atkinson and A. Coldwells. 1993 *"Analysis of the work rates and heart rates of Association Football Referees."* British Journal of Sports Medicine, Vol. 27, p193-196.
2. T. Asami, H. Togari and J. Ohashi. 1987 *"Analysis of movement patterns of referees during soccer matches."* In "Science and Football", T.Reilly *et al* (Eds). E & F.N. Spon, London. p. 341-345.

3. L. Johnston and L. McNaughton. 1994 *"The physiological requirements of soccer refereeing."* The Australian Journal of Science and Medicine in Sport. Vol. 26, p67-72.

4. T. Reilly. 1997. *"Energetics of high-intensity exercise (soccer) with particular reference to fatigue."* Journal of Sports Sciences, Vol 15, p257-263.

5. P. Leatt and I Jacobs. 1989. *"Effects of glucose polymer ingestion on glycogen depletion during a soccer match."* Canadian Journal of Sports Sciences, Vol. 14, p112-116.

6. D.T. Kirkendall. 1993. *"Effects of nutrition on performance in soccer."* Medicine and Science in Sport and Exercise. Vol. 25, p1370-1374.

17

EMOTIONS, EGO, AMBITION AND OTHER MENTAL FACTORS

If you can keep your head when all about you
are losing theirs and blaming it on you;
If you can trust yourself when all men doubt you,
But make allowance for their doubting too;

Rudyard Kipling
English writer

Emotions in the game.

The game was tough, very tough. Heavy fouls seemed to be the order of battle, and even after issuing several cautions, the referee didn't seem to be slowing down the contact. What made it worse was the fact that this was the referee's first experience at a new level of competition. He was unfamiliar with the players, most of whom were openly scornful of his decisions. He could hear both coaches when they shouted unpleasant comments about the job he was doing. The man with the whistle was struggling to maintain his composure; he kept looking at his watch, as though by looking at it he would cause it to accelerate. The referee wanted this game to be over.

Then the captain of one of the teams committed a terrible foul after losing the ball to an opponent. Should it be a yellow card or a red? As the referee reached for his pocket,

IN THIS CHAPTER:

- *Refereeing is an emotional experience*
- *The power of the position is seductive*
- *The game is not for you, but for the players*
- *Become a "compleat referee"*
- *There's not much room at the top*
- *Don't forget who helped you succeed*

several players crowded around him, making their appeals, some asking for the player to be sent off, others appealing that it was an accident, that he didn't mean it, that it wasn't worth a red. Still trying to make up his mind, the referee separated the captain from the other players. What seemed to matter most to him was the potential reaction from players on both sides. If I send him off, I'm going to get a mouthful from the captain, and hear more opinions and abuse from his teammates. If I don't send him off, the other team will call me a coward and I'll have to live with their opinions for the rest of the game. What am I going to do?

Holding the book in his left hand, the referee asked the player his name. Back came a sneering reply: "Smith, Bobby Smith. Can you spell it, ref? You can't do much else!" Holding his pencil as tightly as he could, the referee started to write the name down, but the pencil wouldn't respond properly in his hand, which was shaking uncontrollably. Anxiety had taken over, the automatic bodily responses to danger had sent a surge of adrenaline into his system, making his muscles twitch and his heart race in preparation for rapid physical action that under other circumstances, might save his life. But this was only a soccer match. What was going on?

Does this bring back memories of an unpleasant match? It should, because most referees we know have gone through this at one time or another. What we have attempted to do is to describe a normal response to extreme stress on the soccer field, stress that can destroy the referee's ability to make sound decisions. The question is: Why is there stress? After all, it's only a game....

For any referee, a game can be a stressful experience because his own emotions become involved, his own wishes and desires. He wants to succeed and be chosen for more important matches. He wants the participants to like him and then thank him at the end of the game. He wants the assistant referee, who is more senior than he, to tell him he did a good job. And he doesn't want to make a mistake in front of one of the coaches, a retired professional player who knows

INSULT? — OR HARMLESS BANTER?

We have mentioned the soccer-playing humorist Rodney Marsh several times in these pages, because we believe that study of players is an essential part of effective refereeing. Players like Rodney have much to teach us; witness the following true tale of an encounter with him in an NASL match between Tampa Bay and Minnesota.

It is customary in professional matches for a defender to introduce himself to a skilful opponent by hammering him early in the game. Call it the intimidatory welcome that signifies respect. The Minnesota defender Alan Merrick greeted Rodney Marsh this way in the first few minutes of the game by fouling him from behind. The referee (RE) gave a free-kick and administered a chewing to Merrick, who loudly proclaimed that Marsh was a cissy and hadn't been touched.

Several minutes later Merrick repeated the welcome, and got a yellow card for his pains. As the referee was administering the caution and letting Merrick know in no uncertain terms what was going to happen with another foul like that, Marsh was standing with his foot on the ball a few yards away from where the referee and Merrick were engaged in conversation.

"C'mon, Bob, I never touched him. He falls over if you breathe on him!"

"Ah, shut up, Merrick," says Rodney, "if we'd had a real referee, he'd have sent you off for that!"

Now, there's no doubt that Marsh's remark could be taken as dissent. It could also be taken as an insult, so what should the referee do? Perhaps more important is to ask yourself how you would feel if a top-class player said something like that to you. Many referees, we have no doubt, would react to the remark by pulling out a card on Marsh. The cheeky remark might touch a sensitive little spot for a referee who has a certain amount of insecurity, a certain lack of complete confidence in himself. Feeling hurt by the insult, and perhaps a little angry, the referee would respond with a card to soothe his own bruised ego. But would it be wise?

Marsh was testing the referee by trying to see his reaction to a humorous comment. Could he tolerate some give-and-take during the game? In this particular match, the referee simply turned his head, looked Marsh right in the eye and grinned at his cheekiness. Marsh smiled back and said nothing, for nothing more was needed. Was any great harm done? No.

The moral of this tale is this: sometimes we take action against players, not because of the laws, but simply because our own ego has been touched. We are offended and so we retaliate. Five years prior to this incident, this referee might have done just that, but by the time this match came around, he was more than capable of handling some insults, and engaging in banter. The day after the match—Why is it that the best repartee comes too late?—he thought of the perfect response to Marsh: "No, Rodney, only real players get real referees!

more about the game than he ever will. Most of the little psychological foibles we all have are out in the open when we expose ourselves to twenty-two competitive athletes determined to win, and free to express their opinion about what the referee is doing. Experienced players will try to find the weak spots in a referee's psyche, and then exploit it for their own benefit. But mostly, we know our own weak spots and try to protect them. And when we feel that our protection is failing us, *that's* when we feel the stress.

But, we have to say that neither of us is qualified to write a discourse on the psychology of intense personal interaction, which is what refereeing really is. All we can do is express what we have learned from our own life-experiences, and what we understand of the motivations that are at play among many referees. Furthermore, since this is a book about *technique*, we will describe what we were able to do to overcome the stress of refereeing. Notice that we are not saying "what we did to eliminate stress"; we learned—as you can learn—that you can't eliminate it, but you can finds ways to live with it, and to use it in your favor.

Let's say that you are anxious not to make a mistake, because you know that players will climb all over you and involve you in an unpleasant scene. Some referees are so concerned about this that they do nothing, preferring the apparent safety of inaction to the commitment that comes with blowing the whistle. The best way to live with the anxiety is to make sure that you don't make a mistake, or at least make as few as possible. You do that by learning everything you can about the job you are supposed to do. You study tape, you talk to players, you talk to coaches, you learn from other referees, you do all the things we have been preaching throughout this book. The more you know and understand, the less likely you are to be in error. Here's a reality to live by: *If you are constantly getting complaints and criticism from other participants in the game, you are probably doing something wrong. So find out what it is and fix it!*

Now let's go one step deeper into the psyche. Ask yourself why you don't like criticism, whether it be from players and coaches, or from assessors and other referees. Does it raise old feelings of "not being good enough", or of being "worthless"? Does it remind you of those days when parents or teachers criticized but never praised you? Does it make you depressed to the point that you want to withdraw into yourself? Or does it produce the opposite effect, making you angry that your efforts are not being acknowledged? Try and figure out what these feelings mean, because when you understand them, you have a way to manage them. Here's how.

Once you become familiar with your response to a stressful situation, and once you understand where that response comes from, you can prepare yourself for it. You give a penalty-kick. Once you blow the whistle and point to the spot, you know there will be dissent and criticism. But with your self-understanding, you also know how you would normally react. You know what to expect. Instead of succumbing to the familiar feelings, you tell yourself internally that this was a good decision, that you are doing the right thing, that there is nothing inadequate about you at this moment. In other words, you contradict an old behavior by superimposing a new one. You replace a saboteur with an ally. And once you have done this often enough, you will find that your personal level of stress diminishes to the point that it will not affect your performance.

You can lower your level of stress by striving to become the best referee you can be, and by using that effort and knowledge to remind yourself of your value to the players and the game.

The sly seductress: Power.

The referee can be the most powerful influence on a game. Once he or she shows up at the field or the stadium, the referee is in charge of just about everything connected with the match to be played. He can send players off, or let them stay. He can remove people from the bench, insisting that they have no further connection with the team. The most famous player or coach in the world is under the command of the person with the whistle. And therein lies a problem....

For some people *enjoy* the use of power, and do everything they can to exercise it. Once they taste the sweet intoxicant, they become addicted. Henry Kissinger called it the great aphrodisiac, and almost everyone is familiar with Lord Acton's dictum: "Power tends to corrupt and absolute power corrupts absolutely," a statement as true today as it was in the nineteenth century, when it was written. How does this affect referees?

Be aware of unpleasant use of insensitive power when you referee. Do you react immediately and forcefully at the first hint of disagreement from anyone? Do you insist upon having the last word when you get into a discussion with a player? When you put the ball down on the penalty-spot, do you absolutely refuse to let the kicker touch it or move it? Do you do everything "by the book"? Have you ever disliked a particular player—who may have made a smart remark at your expense—and then wished that he would do something wrong so that you could take action and show him who's boss? Have you ever cautioned a 12-year-old for dissent?

All these are signs that you may like the power of the position too much and that it is affecting your handling of the game (and at the same time spoiling the pleasure of the players). Ken Aston, quoted several times in these pages, once remarked that "he who has all the power doesn't need to be aggressive". And yet we see referees treat 12-year-olds as though they were deserving of humiliation. Our advice is to encourage you ask yourself why you behave this way. Is it a protection of your fragile psyche? Is it your way of compensating for how you feel about yourself? Whatever the cause, find out what it is and correct it, because you are damaging the sport, which needs statesmen not dictators. *The most successful referees are those who are aware of the power of the position, but who temper it by applying it with wisdom and discretion.*

Whose game is it, anyway?

We are not going to belabor this point here, because we have dealt with it thoroughly in previous chapters, but we are going to remind our readers again: *The referee is a servant of the game, not its master. Your ultimate goal should be to provide pleasure for the players and the spectators. And believe us, you can have a great time doing it!*

"The Compleat Referee."

In the years when we were learning the basics of this profession, we attended clinic after clinic, determined to absorb all we could from experienced referees and instructors. While doing all that, we were struck by the different attributes that each of these sources recommended. Some instructors and referees stressed the Laws of the Game, and all the minutiae thereof—including players lighting cigarettes, dogs on the pitch, balls that burst against the crossbar and so on. (Incidentally, never in our more than 50 years of combined refereeing experience did a player light a cigarette during a match; we never once saw the ball burst, and only one time for each of us did a dog run onto the pitch.) Other instructors stressed the application of the Laws, that they should be enforced with unbending, uncompromising authority: Players *will be cautioned if...*; players *must be sent off if...*and so on. Still others stressed a more reasonable approach, advocating a need for "man-management", or being the players' referee and speaking their language. Many of these well-intentioned instructors stressed the need for uniformity and consistency—the cry of the unhappy coach. We all must do the same, week in week out! (They never told us how to do that, mind you!) And finally there were the fitness gurus. Run six miles a day uphill and on the beach through the waves, and you can referee anywhere just like me.

While watching other referees, we saw the same differences of opinion and attitude. Some were quick to eliminate dissent by cautioning offenders, but in the same match allowed horrendous fouls to go unpunished. Some were the opposite, being nonchalant about discussions but enforcing the law on unfair challenges. Others would be strict on encroachment and time-wasting, but would allow players to argue with them and belittle them. When the subject of mobility came up—and we advocated maintaining a high level of fitness—some senior referees would argue that if you emphasized running, then all you would get would be greyhounds who couldn't referee a game properly. (We noticed incidentally that it was only the unfit referees who downplayed the importance of mobility....) They were at home in the center-circle.

It appeared to us as though many referees were treating each of these matters as alternatives, that you either do one or the other but not both. Then we heard the reasoning that "I cannot do it all at one time, so I will concentrate on this and not so much on that." Neither of us was happy with that, because it occurred to us that it should be possible to be a complete referee, to be able to control *all* aspects of the game, and with the same intensity or fervor. Surely, we thought, a referee can use a reasonable approach without letting things get out of control. Does he have to be overbearing before the players would accept his authority? In order to allow spectators who paid for a ticket to enjoy the game, without it getting too out of control, surely the referee could do his job without being too much a part of the game. As for fitness, we asked, why was it not possible for a "greyhound" to be a very good referee, or for an otherwise good referee to train to a higher level of fitness? Could not a referee be and do everything?

We were able to answer our own questions, because we found that it is possible to do it all. You *can* control a game by dealing with bad fouls *and* dissent *and* encroachment *and* persistent infringement. You can insist on free-kicks and throw-ins being taken from the correct place, and yet allow advantage or ignore trifling and dubious offenses. It is possible to converse with players, to establish a reasonable relationship with them, to admire their skills, yet not fall into the trap of trying to be their "friend." And it is most definitely possible to be very fit *and* make correct decisions. As the years went by, we learned more about being a "compleat referee" (with acknowledgements to the great seventeenth-century writer, Isaak Walton, author of "The Compleat Angler")

How many have heard the following lament. "I am a good referee, but a lousy linesman", or vice-versa. Sometimes it may not *be* a lament, but a boast. Why should this be so? Why does being one exclude being the other? Even as members of the FIFA list, we prided ourselves on our lining ability, and could not give an answer as to which activity we were better at. As a matter of pride and professionalism, we strove to be excellent at both, as well as at fourth official if that duty came our way. In recent years FIFA has recognized that many referees do not run line well, and after a series of disasters due to poor linesmanship in World Cups—the Maradona "hand of god" goal and some questionable offside decisions—they instituted separate categories of referees and assistant referees, with non-overlapping responsibilities. Although we fully understand the motivation of FIFA, the decision reinforces our opinions about the training of match officials (Chapter 18). Now the sad state of affairs has arisen where referees appointed to World Cup finals complain that they have nothing to do if they do not referee, whereas previously an official could be active at several games as either referee or linesman. The upshot of this is that now referees wishing to progress with their careers are faced with a choice: Do I wait for an appointment to the International Panel as a referee, or should I choose to be an international Referee's Assistant?

We are adamant that you can be a good referee *and* a good linesman, and we admit that we would have disliked choosing one or the other, especially in view of the fact that we both had excellent experiences and recognition in each duty at both domestic and international levels. We can put it succinctly: *If either of us were appointed to an important match, and had the privilege of selecting our own linesmen, our first choice would be each other. Yes, you can be a "compleat referee".*

There's not much room at the top.

A word or two about ambition and reality are in order. If you start at the right age—say, your early twenties—and have the right attitude, temperament and knowledge for the task, you have the prospect of reaching the international panel of officials. In this country, with more than one hundred thousand registered referees, only ten of whom are on the list in any given year, you have a 1 in 10,000 chance of making it in a particular year. The higher up the ladder you go, the better your chances are, but even so, don't bet on it. Don't rely upon the thought of that particular success to give you motivation. *If you don't enjoy the act of refereeing, if you do it only to satisfy your ambitions, give it up!* The probability is that you will become frustrated, even bitter, and it will show whenever you take the field. So, don't inflict your ambitions upon the players. But if you get a great deal of pleasure from mingling in the game and providing an atmosphere for players to succeed in and have fun, then by all means keep doing it. You are the kind of person the players and the game need.

What about progress up the refereeing ladder? How can you manage that? The most important thing you can take care of is to do games. Each one can be a learning experience, and the more you do, the more likely you are to encounter every conceivable situation, every weird occurrence, every activity that can bedevil a referee. There is just no substitute for getting games under your belt.

Most referees spend most of their time refereeing in a league of some sort, and given that almost everywhere there is a shortage of officials, most can get almost all the appointments they want. But the ambitious referee must start to get the "plum" games, the important games: top-of-the-table clashes, playoff games, championship games. Thus it is important to know how to survive in these competitions. You have to be careful not to get "unwanted" by league officers and coaches. They certainly will not want incompetent officials, but they also do not want those who perhaps might be intolerant or too strict. Some coaches would like the games to be a little "loose" so that their players can cheat and win. So it is an unpleasant reality that there are people out there who don't like referees to be too good!

We have both been victims of such tactics but were fortunate to have strong individuals making the appointments who were not influenced by such. In one notorious case, a certain coach asked for one of us to be taken off a professional game only one hour before it started! This happened because there had been a conflict with this coach in another league, and he was subjected to disciplinary action, and soon realized that he could not bully nor intimidate the referee. When he recognized who was about to do his game he was not happy. The Director of Officials was at the match and stood firm, despite the additional protests from the team president. As it happened his team won by a very wide margin. But this is not always the case.

So a referee must learn to be tactful, diplomatic, sometimes accommodating and always pleasant to coaches and officials, no matter what you may think of them, or what you know they think of you. If you have to take action against one of their players, you had better do it using such a style that you don't offend unnecessarily. You certainly don't cheat on their behalf, but you can and must be circumspect before taking drastic action against them or their players. For example, take the case of a coach who is yelling at you from the touchline. In most cases, you would give one warning—perhaps by a hand signal—and then take action without any further hesitation. In other cases, where you know the individual can do you damage, you might give him the opportunity to talk to you, so that you can appeal to his better nature or explain the necessity of doing what you are doing. You will try to control the situation in a more diplomatic way than simply getting rid of him at the first protest. Be aware that this kind of approach will necessary as you progress from one league to the next, and is a continual happening. So keep your wits about you!

By way of contrast, in many tournaments there are teams from other areas of the country, or even from overseas, with officials you are not likely to encounter again, and whose negative opinions off the field will not have any effect on your local progress. In these games, you can referee more 'purely', and apply the laws the way they are supposed—theoretically—to be applied. And when you finally reach that pinnacle of your career, a national or international championship final, then you can absolutely "Do it your Way!" It is a wonderful feeling, knowing that all you have to do is referee the way you know is right!

Your progress as a referee.

Many factors go into determining how well you will advance and develop as a referee. It would seem that if you have the ability and are fit enough, then you should be able to climb the ladder all the way to the top. It is certain that without these qualities, you will not progress very far, but what else is important?

First, you have to get assignments. As mentioned above, regular league assignments are not difficult to find. But getting the top appointments is what will count. These are handed out based on several criteria, ability being only one of them. Others include personal factors, political factors and just plain favoritism. It is important to keep on good terms with people in positions to advance or derail your refereeing career, and many of these people you might find you do not like. Make it a point not to alienate people as you climb the ladder. You can quite often find that these people may decide to become administrators in soccer, and could get in a position to influence your career at a later date.

A very important point that is often overlooked in discussions of referee advancement is what kind of occupation a referee has. Being available to take assignments, especially those involving tournaments, that may take several days is a significant factor in a referee's development. If you are in an occupation where getting away several times a year is impossible, then you will find it difficult to advance no matter how good a referee you are. It is for this reason that many referees have changed careers, or gone into business for themselves.

Finally, consider your family situation. A single referee with no children has no obligations other than to himself, but a married person with children must take the family into consideration. It can be difficult at times to juggle career, family and active refereeing. Usually something has to give somewhere. A successful referee always has a very understanding spouse and a considerate boss, or none of the above.

Other referees.

You will not get very far in refereeing circles without the friendship and respect of your fellow referees. You should endeavor to build close personal friendships with these other officials, especially because you are likely to come to rely on them to help you in future games. Take time to help other referees, congratulate them on their successes, thank them for their efforts when they work with you. In the days of the NASL, we both used to send small "thank you" cards to the linesmen who had worked with us, and when we saw they had been promoted to referee, we sent them our congratulations. It's such an easy thing to do, but it does create goodwill.

Unfortunately, some referees can be very jealous of others' success. They quite often feel that they are equally as good as the guy who was selected for the big game, and want to know why did they not get it. This can lead to unpleasant behind-the-scenes gossip and backbiting, both of which can severely damage healthy referee relations. Good competition is fine, as long as that all it is, but sometimes this gets taken to extremes. At one national referee fitness testing session, a very senior referee beat a younger up-and-coming rival in one of the runs, and loudly exclaimed "F__k you _____!" as he crossed the finish line. The younger referee concerned had not done anything to the senior referee to justify this, except to be in a position to possibly take away his prestige. That was enough. Needless to say, all this did was to lower the senior man's standing in the eyes of all the other referees who were watching.

And finally, you have to be prepared to be fairly lonely in the soccer community of which you may have been an important part. A close friend of ours once remarked that when he became a referee, he lost all his friends from his playing and coaching days. And then as he began to be successful as a referee, he gradually lost most of his friends in refereeing circles too. It was a sad fact that many of the players and coaches came to regard him as "the enemy", and many of the referees envied him for his success at taking "their" spot.

Other mental factors.

We have spent several chapters telling you how to prepare yourself for a game. Some things, however, you cannot prepare for, except that you do need to know what you are getting into. Some of the mental factors that affect the referee came under scrutiny during the 1986 World Cup.

During 16 games in the last round, referees made a total of 2167 decisions. This means that on average there were 1.6 decisions per minute or about 1 decision every 40 seconds! In other words, there is no time to relax, for you must concentrate all the time and not be distracted from your main task. You are on a hectic ride and you can't get off! As for the decisions, 57% were for fouls and offside, 42% were for ball-in-and-out of play, and the other 1% were for misconduct. You will be pleased to learn that after subsequent video analysis by qualified experienced observers, it was concluded that the correct decision was made in 98.8% of the decisions for a direct free-kick, but only 87% in the case of offside decisions.

Physiological factors that affect referees' decisions.

The typical human being takes two-tenths of a second to react by muscle movement to a visual or audible stimulus. Let us think about what that means to soccer referees and assistant referees. A player running at a quick pace can travel 15-20 feet per second, so that in two-tenths of a second he would travel 3-5 feet, and a player running in the opposite direction would also travel about the same distance, making anywhere between 6 and 10 feet the effective motion in the time between an assistant referee seeing the position of players and then raising his flag. Thus if a forward were in an offside position by one or two feet when the ball was played, by the time the assistant referee reacts he could appear to be *onside* by up to 8 feet, and the crowd would go wild when the flag goes up. Can you take the heat when you make such a decision?

Let's do the same kind of calculations for penalty kicks. A well-struck ball moves at 100 kilometers per hour (60 mph). The time it takes to travel to the goal line is four-tenths of a second. Thus for a goalkeeper to save the shot he must move 12-14 feet in two-tenths of a second (four-tenths of a second minus two-tenths for reaction time). This computes to 72 feet per second or 49 mph, which is clearly impossible. Now you know why the goalkeepers have to guess and move early in order to save a penalty kick. Before the recent change in the law, this would mean that the referee *should* have ordered the kick re-taken almost every time one was saved. Most referees know that if they did this, there would usually be major protests and dissent, likely resulting in cautions and perhaps sendings-off. Few had the courage to take that kind of heat at every penalty kick, so retakes were rare. The recent change in the laws that allows the goalkeeper to anticipate and move sideways on the goal line before the ball is kicked is a sensible improvement and beneficial to referees. But the goalkeeper is NOT allowed to advance forward off the line to make the save, as was done by the goalkeeper for the USA team more than once in the kicks-from-the-penalty-mark in the 1999 Women's World Cup Final.

Home advantage.

We have all heard the shout at matches "Referee, you are a f_____g homer!" In fact during our refereeing days it became quite apparent that players expected referees to give the home teams a bit of a break., and we used this to our advantage to get out of some difficult situations (see Chapter 12). Perhaps by doing so we contributed to the myth of hometown referees. But is it entirely a myth?

It seems to be a well-known phenomenon, and it is for this reason that the semi-final and final matches in the F.A. Cup are always played at a neutral stadium, as are similar contests in other sports. For further confirmation of home advantage, we only have to look at the results of the World Cup, which the home country won six times, and was runner-up twice. In addition, other winners have been from a country in close proximity to the host country six times. This is more than coincidence. Is the referee one of the factors contributing to home advantage?

In a study of home advantage in the English and Scottish professional leagues, the home team won 60% of the games. But

A FAR-REACHING DECISION?

Towards the close of the 1998-99 English Premier League season, Manchester United, attempting to become the first English team to win the treble of League Championship, FA Cup, and European Champions Cup, were playing a match at Anfield, the home of their hated rivals Liverpool. Never wishing to lose to United, Liverpool were playing only for pride as they had no chance to win the league, and only an outside chance of a place in the UEFA Cup. But United needed the win to keep up their challenge

Continued on next page

for the championship. In any event, these Liverpool-United matches at Anfield are always highly-charged affairs, played in front of a stadium full of passionate die-hard supporters, the vast majority supporting Liverpool. And as anyone who has ever been to Anfield will tell you, the atmosphere is electric under normal times, but for the visit of their hated rivals, and a chance to derail their ambitions . . . Well, you can imagine what it was like!

The Premier League sent one of its most experienced officials to referee this match. The referee had kept his usual tight control of the game, and had cautioned several players. With about 10 minutes to play, and the score 2-1 in favor of United, Liverpool were pressing hard for the equalizer. Denis Irwin, the United left-back, ran after a loose ball along the touchline, going away from the United goal, but was unable to reach it before it rolled over the line for what would be a Liverpool throw. The ball then curved back into the field of play and it appeared as though a Liverpool player would get it first and perhaps take a quick throw-in, catching Irwin out of position. So he did what many an experienced defender would do, and instantly after the whistle blew following the linesman's flag, he kept running and tapped the ball further upfield to buy time for him to get back into position. A cautionable offense for timewasting, delaying a restart? Probably so. But Irwin had already received a yellow card. Another would mean he would be sent off. The referee produced the yellow and red cards, and Irwin went off.

Was this decision correct as far as the Laws are concerned? Yes it was. A tough one to make, perhaps, but correct. In Chapter 3 we used this incident to make a point about prevention. But now let's ask an additional question about home advantage: Would the referee have made the same decision at Old Trafford, the home of Manchester United? Or would he have made the same decision if a Liverpool player had committed the same offence here at Anfield?

We will never know, but the referee was widely pilloried for this decision. Not only did Liverpool go on to score and tie the game, thus taking 2 valuable points from United, but Irwin was also suspended from playing in the FA Cup Final a few weeks later as a result of his sending-off. Therefore this referee's one decision could possibly have cost United both the League and the Cup. Understandably, the club was very annoyed and made their opinion clear in the press. But happily for them, they did win both the league and cup, and went on to win the European Champions League to boot. The Manchester United officials duly apologized for their public criticism of the referee, and the their manager, Alex Ferguson, received a knighthood from the Queen of England for his achievements.

And to think one referee's decision might have prevented all of this—power indeed!!

where the size of the crowd was small, home advantage was greatly reduced. The researchers looked further into this finding and decided to examine penalty kicks awarded and sendings-off (red cards), reasoning that these decisions may play an important role in the outcome of matches. Once again the data showed that the home team benefited more, and the extent of the difference was correlated with the size of the crowds. For example, in Premier League games, average attendance 22,000, the home team were given 71% of penalties; whereas in the Scottish First Division, attendance 2000, the home team had only 47%. For red cards, Premier League away teams had 67%, compared to 54% in the Vauxhall League (semi-pro feeder league), attendance 1000, and 46% in the Scottish Second Division, attendance 500. What does it mean?

As a follow-up to their original study, the researchers attempted to study the effect of crowd noise on decisions. They used videotape recordings of matches, and had experienced observers examine possible fouls, and decide whether they would penalize or not. And they made the observer make the decision with no crowd noise, and with crowd noise playing. For most incidents, there was no difference, but for contentious or doubtful incidents they observed a slight preference for giving the free-kick to the home side if the sound were on. The conclusion was that the observers relied on or were swayed by the crowd reaction in those tight incidents. How can referees use this information, and attempt to remove the referee from the equation of home advantage?

Now that you know about the possibility of the referee being a factor in home advantage, you have to be harshly honest with yourself. Will you admit that you have been, or can be influenced by crowds? Will you admit that in order to correct for that tendency, you sometimes go too far in the other direction, overpenalizing the home team? Every time you make one of these tough decisions, be prepared to ask yourself: "Would I make this decision if it were in favor of the other team?"

18

EDUCATION AND DEVELOPMENT OF REFEREES

By education most have been misled;

John Dryden,
English poet

The basic education.

Most would-be referees in any country in the world start their careers in a series of training sessions in the classroom, where they receive instruction on the Laws of the Game, get some rudimentary advice on positioning and mechanics, and take a standardized exam of some sort. These training sessions are usually instructed by other referees, perhaps retired, who have been through a course of training for instructors. The instructor may or may not have been a top class referee, but at this stage that is not important. He or she will have done more than the students in the classroom, and can guide them through all that they need to know....in the beginning. After the instruction, the new referee is then sent out to his first match, which in this country is almost certain to be a youth match with very young players.

In countries where soccer is well-established,

> **IN THIS CHAPTER:**
> - *The basic education, and then what?*
> - *Who should be the instructors?*
> - *Immerse yourself in the game*
> - *Find a mentor*
> - *Assessors must be instructors not detractors*
> - *The best of advice from assessors*
> - *It's time to change the way we prepare referees*

the rookie referee may have been a player, and may already have a sound knowledge and understanding of the game, or he may have been a keen spectator, and would therefore have some idea about what referees do. However, in countries where soccer is a developing sport—and despite more than thirty years of professional soccer in the U.S., we are still lacking a widespread understanding of the sport—people *without* a playing or watching background are frequently encouraged or even required by youth leagues to become referees. In many cases, new referees are assigned as assistant referees for a few matches to get the feel of things, but in many cases such a luxury is impossible and our victim is appointed to referee a match of low skill level, where fortunately, he cannot do much harm.

But as the referee progresses, he quickly finds that there is not much else in the way of further useful instruction to help him improve. He can go to the occasional seminar, in which famous referees come to give advice but often spend their time telling personal war stories, or even worse, just telling everyone how fantastic they are and how they were cheated out of the World Cup finals. There are usually compulsory annual clinics for continuing education, and perhaps a few special clinics for those wishing to be promoted to a higher grade. But largely, these are re-hashes of the original training clinic, with discussions thrown in of any new Laws, and instructions on how to enforce them. Referees are reminded of their responsibilities, but few of these intermediate clinics get down to the real substance of refereeing: the interaction of players and officials, or the influence—both tactical and psychological—that the referee has on the game. The law is taught, but not technique.

Who are the instructors?

At the national level, we have had a similar problem, exacerbated by the use of instructors—albeit very skilled teachers—who themselves had no top-class game experience, or any experience at all. The most notorious case was that of one individual brought in to be a consultant on physical fitness for the referees in the North American Soccer League. A big, friendly man, full of humor and good cheer, and supposedly with a Ph.D. in Exercise Physiology, he seemed ideal for the job.... until you dug a little deeper. We were skeptical right from the start, because this fitness expert was at least fifty pounds heavier than he ought to be as an example to us. Then it became clear that his knowledge of exercise physiology was superficial at best, and downright wrong in substance. (For the right stuff, see Chapter 16). His degree (not completed at the time) was to be from a small southern college with no scientific reputation, and the ideas that the man tried to foist off on us were old-fashioned and inaccurate recommendations about training. The last straw for us was when he tried to do "research" on use and loss of body fluids of the officials in a big match. After a few minutes' discussion it became clear to both of us that he didn't have a clue about how to set up an experiment to measure anything. But he had persuaded enough people—who ought to have checked him out—that he should be hired as a consultant to advise the best referees in the country! We have also had various administrators lecture on the referee's responsibilities in the professional game—when none of them had ever been in one.

Perhaps this is the place to state our philosophy about the preparation of referees:

Referees should be taught by trained instructors who themselves have had experience at the level of the play they are talking about.

The may seem like a statement of the obvious, but it is puzzling to us that it is not always practiced. Before we embarked on our professional lives, our education and training followed the principle we just described. During our graduate student days, we were taught and trained by professors who themselves held the Ph.D. degree, and who had research experience in the fields that we wished to investigate. It is unthinkable, if not impossible, for a person with only bachelor's or master's degree to supervise and examine a candidate for the Ph.D. The same is true in other professions.

Medical students are trained initially by people who already are MD's, and if they decide to go into a specialty, such as surgery or ophthalmology, they are trained and supervised by doctors well qualified in those areas. Legal training, accountant training, architect training, and many other professions operate in similar fashion. But in referee training, for some reason, people think they can train referees without any experience themselves at the level they are teaching. Is it any wonder that there are continually complaints about poor referees? Many of these complaints are justified, and in our opinion they reflect more on the training than on the referee.

In our years in the NASL, we noticed that few of the assessors had been professional referees themselves, although most had refereed at some level. Several of them were 'big-wigs' in the state or region where the NASL teams were located, and because of their influence they were able to get themselves appointed to those positions. (To be fair, we have to admit that there were not many people around with professional refereeing experience in those days, so there is some excuse; but that is not true nowadays, and yet the problem persists.) We found a similar situation after we were promoted to the International scene. The main person in charge of referees for over 20 years in Central and North America and the Caribbean, the man responsible for referee training, preparing seminars for very advanced referees, not to mention appointing referees for important matches and prestigious FIFA tournaments, had never stepped onto the field with a whistle. He's gone now, and his position has been held for the past few years by individuals with refereeing experience at the highest possible level. It is a harsh reality for the aspiring referee in any country of the world, that referee training is not very sophisticated. A little further on in this chapter we will show you the evidence. We believe that for the good of the game, referee training must change.

Our advice: Immerse yourself in the game.

So what can the aspiring referee do? Well, we can tell you what we did, and what worked for several other referees. We decided that since the advanced training provided by the various organizations was not going to do the job, we had to fend for ourselves. What did this mean? Quite simply, it meant total immersion in the game.

We refereed and ran line as often as possible. We watched as many matches as possible, live or on TV. This included local youth games, amateur games, college games as well as professional games. We were fortunate in that our scientific careers we travelled to foreign countries, where we could attend professional matches of high caliber: in England, Nigeria, Germany, Russia, Argentina, Brazil, Mexico. We studied the differences in play from one country to the next; what fouls caused anger in one country yet hardly caused a murmur in others. We watched the reactions of players to incidents, and stored the information away for future use. But besides watching all those games, we helped each other.

If one of us was refereeing, the other tried to be there. Then over a beer after the match, or by phone later we dissected each match in detail to see where we could have done better, where we might have been completely wrong—and where we did things correctly! We also did this with our other professional colleague, Manuel Ortiz, Sr., a very successful referee in the NASL. For many televised matches we taped the game, and went over the tapes—in slow motion if necessary—to improve our analysis of the incident, our recognition of the foul, and to get a much better understanding of each situation. We committed all this information into memory to be used during games we later officiated. You can learn something from every referee you watch, whether what you learn is positive or negative, in youth games or international matches.

We also recommend that the ambitious referee read as much as possible about the game. Autobiographical accounts of careers can be fascinating, and give us great insight into what made the individuals tick, and how they thought. In Chapter 6 we describe a penalty-kick in a pre-season NASL match, where the referee was fooled by deceptive play by Rodney Marsh, a clever, experienced professional player. In his autobiography written in the 1970s, Gordon Hill, a former Football League and NASL referee, described an identical piece of deception by the same player in a Football League match in England. Had the NASL referee read Gordon Hill's book, he would have been forewarned about the deception, as we were.

Autobiographies also provided information on critical events that occurred in referees' lives, both on and off the pitch, and how they were able to manage work, family and soccer. The memoirs explain how to fit in a rigorous training schedule, and describe the problems of travel to other areas of the country as well as overseas. They also tell about the things that go on at major tournaments, what leads to certain referees being given plum assignments, how everything is noticed, down to what you eat and drink, not to mention one's personal habits such as wearing pajamas in bed! (For some weird reason in certain quarters, this was considered important in the overall evaluation of a referee.)

Also many other types of soccer books have been written: memoirs of famous players or famous coaches, books written by journalists, and books written by psychologists, anthropologists, historians, and by ordinary fans. All of these are 'must' reading for ambitious referees, because they provide additional insights into the game, insights you won't get in normal referee training courses or law books. It is also useful to take a look at some coaching guides, or even better, take a coaching course. Nowhere else will you get a better understanding of the game from the coach's and the players' perspective. From these you learn how referees are viewed and what it is that referees do that really upsets coaches and players. It comes down to this: *Gather all the information you can about this game.*

Find a mentor.

What we were really doing by talking about all those games was mentoring each other as we went along. We had to, because there was no-one close by to help us. As is the case with other professions, a real mentor can be of great help to a developing referee. So here's some advice:

If you can find someone with experience, or who knows what refereeing is all about, ask him or her to help you regularly. There is much you can learn from that person.

Furthermore, if that mentor of yours has any influence with assignors and referee committees, he can quite often be in a position to help you advance your career by recommending you—when you are ready—for certain key matches or tournaments. In the memoir of his career, Jack Taylor, probably best-known as the referee of the World Cup Final in 1974 between Holland and West Germany, ascribes his success to just such a mentor. This person, a much older retired referee, accompanied Taylor to as many of his games as possible throughout his career, especially his early career, and after the games would point out the good and the bad points. Even more valuable was his technique of asking Jack how he *felt* when he made this or that decision. He probed Jack's emotions to let him become aware of how emotions affected decision-making (see Chapter 17). With Jim Lock's help, Jack was able to modify and improve his technique continually. We admit that it was from reading Jack Taylor's book that we got the idea to do what we did, even though we didn't have the permanent mentor nearby and available to us.

Assessors as instructors, not detractors.

A referee must be evaluated in order to advance. The helpful people who do this are known as assessors, the subject of much wicked humor from referees. "Those who can, do. Those who can't, instruct. Those who can't instruct, assess," goes the old joke. Like most humor, that aphorism has a pith of truth within it, for many officials have encountered individuals who had no great distinction as referees, yet seemed to assume in their new career as an assessor a mysterious wisdom—and power—that never was evident when they were on the field. This we will get to in a moment. But referees should realize that there is more to assessing than advancement, for evaluation is always part of any educational process.

A good and sensitive assessor can be—and should be—as valuable as the most erudite and skilled instructor. He or she can see whether the referee puts into practice what was taught in the classroom, and can observe the interactions among one team and their opponents, as well as those between players and officials, interactions of which the referee may not be aware. Furthermore, the assessor can reinforce behavior and techniques that the referee uses successfully.

The sad fact of the refereeing life, however, is that many assessors regard their job as one of finding fault, rather than one of finding what is good. Perhaps it is no more than another expression of our culture, which in the raising of its children seems to prefer punishment over praise. Whatever its root cause, it does the budding referee no good, for too many of the people

THE ASSESSOR AND HIS SON

This never-to-be-forgotten incident—and true story—occurred in a game in the NASL, when less than fifteen minutes into the match, the referee had to leave the field because of an injury to his hamstring. The senior linesman took his place, and the fourth official went on the line.

After the game, the assessor inquired of the referee the nature of the incident early in the game when the changes took place. Evidently he had not noticed the referee leaving the field, nor the substitution of the other officials!

Since the officials were strangers to him, perhaps he could be forgiven for not noticing. (The referee was about five-ten, one-seventy; the linesman six-two, two-thirty!) But the acuteness of the assessor's observation skills did come into question we reveal that the original fourth official, who had now been the second linesman for 75 minutes was actually his own son!

doing assessment are either not qualified for the level they are examining, or are not aware of their primary responsibility—that of teaching.

Be that as it may, they still march to the field, clipboard in hand, binoculars over one shoulder, prepared to spend much of the match duly scribbling notes on pre-printed forms. Determined to find fault with what they see, they have a profound effect upon referees, many of whom are influenced in their decision-making by "What will the assessor think ?" In other words, they referee in order to impress the assessor, or at least, not to displease him. The result is a man or woman who becomes—at least for that one game—a referee-by-the-book, and not a referee-for-the-good-of-the-game. And woe betide the referee who challenges an assessor who a few years before had been the type of referee we so lovingly described in Chapter 2! A man besotted with power relinquishes it very reluctantly, even it means damaging a fellow referee's career.

True assessing should be more like the mentoring we have described earlier—a learning experience, not a test or examination. Inevitably it has a high degree of subjectivity thrown in, subjectivity determined by the experience of the assessor, and by his view of the particular game he is watching. But the personal bias is one of judgement, not mere condemnation of an individual based upon whether the assessor *liked* the official. Lest we seem especially negative about the assessment process, let us emphasize that we personally benefited from the wisdom of assessors whose opinions we trusted.

All that having been said, this book is intended as a volume of advice, so here's our advice about living with a flawed system. The most important thing is for you to get information that you may be able to use. If the information does not come out spontaneously from the assessor, you have to squeeze it out of him (figuratively, of course!)

Rule number one: Never argue with an assessor. We promise you that it does no good, and in fact can do you great harm. Remember, you want information, and you want him to give you a good score. If you expose his deficiencies you are not likely to get it.

Rule number two: Never forget rule number 1.

Rule number three: Get some information from him.

If he says something like: "You missed three offside flags," ask him if he noticed where you were and in which direction you were looking on each of those occasions. He may not know, in which case you have taught him something about his job, but if he did notice, he may tell you that each time it was on an occasion when you were far behind play and you were not expecting an offside decision after a long clearance from the defenders. *That is useful information!*

He might say that you didn't have good control of the ten yards at free kicks. Follow it up by asking where the free kicks were on the field, and what he would recommend. By asking you are probing his depth of knowledge, and forcing him to be constructive not merely critical. Then if his comments are sensible, use them.

Rule number four: Thank the assessor for his comments, whatever they are—insightful or obvious, brilliant or dumb, nonsensical or wise. Do *not* get defensive and try to justify your actions and decisions. Hear what the man says, then go away and analyze it later. Decide what part of the advice was useful, and then act on it. Discard the rest. Sometimes you will find a jewel in the dross left by even the worst observer, and if you pay attention, it may help your refereeing.

Additional Ways of Interacting with Assessors:

If you are fit, make sure the assessor notices it. One technique that is sure to work, is to be seen to be just as mobile in the last 10 minutes of the match as you were in the first half. Therefore, towards the end of the game, take a glance at your watch and if you are in the last ten minutes, make a point of doing a couple of good 50-60 yards long sprints. If possible, sprint past a couple of tired midfield players who are trying to get up with play. Of course, you cannot actually do this if you are not really fit enough, but if you follow the procedures and techniques in Chapter 16, you will be able to do it. And we guarantee that the first thing the assessor will say to you at the end of the game will be: "You were running as hard at the end of the game as you were at the beginning! That's great!" He has watched you for two hours, and you have given him something positive at the end of the match. Then, following rule number four, you bow your head modestly, thank him for his observation, and tell him you are pleased that he noticed.

If you know you have an assessor you don't trust, or who is out of his depth, distract him with tasks and observations you are familiar with already. If the assessor comes to see you before the match, you can ask him if he wouldn't mind watching out for something new you have been trying, and to let you know how it works out. This could be something like a special position at free-kicks, or your mechanics of issuing a caution, or turning your back on a situation that might produce mild dissent. Then after the match, ask him for his opinions on what you did, how it seemed to work. Of course, you weren't trying out anything new, but by getting him to focus on something he may not have thought of, you know what to expect at the end of the match, and no harm is done. And, it stops him looking for trivialities.

Relax! If you have a lot of confidence, and you want to have a bit of fun with the assessor, without seeming to challenge what he's saying, you can use phrases like these, with what you really mean in parentheses:

"That's a surprising observation. I've never thought of it that way." (And no one else has, either!)

"Thanks for that advice. I'll pass it on to other referees." (Especially the ones I don't like!)

"That's wonderful! Who taught you that?" (I'll make sure I stay away from him!)

The best of advice from assessors.

The following is a list of statements made by various assessors to us and to other referees. We gathered them over the years to illustrate the dangers of unqualified people being asked to evaluate referees. Now we use them to advise our readers to be careful about using opinions from assessors who may not have had the right education or experience. Take it from two referees who throughout their careers used a fundamental dictum of the science that was their profession: Question everything! (But we remind you: Don't do it after the match. Wait until later, when you have an opportunity to ask someone you trust.) All of the statements below are nonsense, and deserve no further comment, and we are sure that you have your own collection!

Never step off the field of play—it looks very bad.

Don't overrule your linesman—it lowers the credibility of the officiating team.

Never go more than a few yards off your diagonal.

Don't ever get ahead of the play, because you'll have too far to go to catch up when possession changes.

Never turn your back to the ball.

Don't get too familiar with the players by using their first names.

Stay aloof from the players before a match—they might try to manipulate you.

At corner-kicks, stay near the top of the penalty-area so that you can recover quickly when the ball is cleared.

Don't allow a free kick to be taken until you are ready.

Don't let a player take a free-kick until you've blown your whistle.

Always show the card first when giving a caution.

Always show the card last when giving a caution.

Refereeing is serious business—don't laugh when you're on the field.

It's time to change the way we prepare referees.

It should be apparent that we have firmly-held opinions about this profession of refereeing, and the way that the training of officials goes on. But neither of us believes that negative comments serve any purpose unless they are supported by suggestions for improvement of whatever it is we are complaining about. So, herewith, our suggestions for change, bearing in mind a principle we have stated several times: *The sport of soccer is changing, and we the referees must change with it.*

A few years ago, before the first season of the Major League Soccer, all the referee hopefuls gathered in California to undergo a weekend of education and preparation for the return of professional soccer to the U.S. Two or three days is not enough to prepare officials for what they were about to face, but the session was a good start. One of us (RE) was invited to the meeting as an instructor, and what he found was revealing and frightening.

The group gathered to consider free-kicks, and all the varieties thereof. After a few minutes of questions to the group about what they would do at this free-kick or that, it became apparent that no one in the room was aware of the idea that not all free-kicks are the same, that encroachment does not need to be enforced on each and every one. The idea that you could have prior knowledge of what teams were going to do, or that the previous game between the teams might influence a decision was also an alien concept. Most of the ideas that we talk about in Chapter 3 were new to this group, presumably the best and brightest, the most experienced referees in the country. This is an observation that should spur us to action. But the U.S. is not alone in suffering from this deficiency.

Look at matches from around the world, and you can see the same lack of preparation. Referees have not collected information that is essential for the conduct of the game. Referees adopt one position— always—at various set-pieces, and the press wonders why things go wrong. Interactions between referee and player are most often formal and authoritative, rarely collegial and amicable. *What is clear is that referee training is out-of-date, and that instructors concentrate on the laws, the responsibilities, on principles and generalities, but not on technique.*

That session before the inaugural season of the MLS convinced us that something needs to be done, and provided us with part of the impetus for writing this book. So herewith, our suggestions for adding some things to the way that we prepare referees:

> Insist that assessors attend the same training sessions as referees, so that as officiating improves and concepts change, the assessors become aware of the changes and pass them on to the officials they watch. In fact assessing and instructing should not be separate activities with separate registration and training. All assessors should be instructors.

> By the time a referee begins to work games in which the players have a measure of skill, and the coaches are reasonably sophisticated, he or she must be taught the subtleties of preparing properly for a game, of varying his or her position to suit the occasion, of developing a level of fitness that can match the speed of the game, of what the old International Board Decision number 8 means to the game, and so on. When properly coached, fourteen-year-old players take quick free kicks, learn how to delay the proceedings when their opponents get a free kick, and know how to put pressure on a referee. They also respond to the approach we have been preaching about in these pages.

Professional management of a match should be taught long before a referee ever steps onto the professional field. No one should have to go to a session before a pro season and hear the instructor say—as those earnest young men heard in the meeting we have mentioned—"Gentlemen, based upon what you have told me today, I have to say that you are not ready for what you are about to face in a few weeks."

Once referees have been taught the law, training sessions should focus on technique, not on repetition of familiar material.

Assessors at any level should have some experience of it, or should have extensive training by referees and instructors who have been in the thick of that level of competition.

Abandon lecturing on general subjects like: "Working as a team," or "Becoming a professional," or "Calling the perfect game." Those topics may be inspirational for a moment, but the effect doesn't last. The referees have nothing to take away with them except vague generalities.

What referees need is a systematic education in the sophisticated techniques of successful officiating at all levels of the game. The game is changing and we must change with it.

By the way, what we are saying here is not totally new. Gordon Hill made similar observations in his autobiography published in 1975! It seems unlikely that things will change institutionally as a result of our recommendations, so therefore referees will continue to be left to their own devices. And of course, we would recommend this book as a text, but we will leave it to our readers to decide whether they have learned anything from these pages.....

But now let's defend our position that something is fundamentally wrong with the way we prepare referees.

How do we know this?

When members of the International Board of FIFA change any law, they do so because of something that is going on in the game at the highest level—professional and international soccer. The International Board does not change the laws because of something that happens in youth soccer or in Sunday afternoon pub league matches. No, it is the top-level game that gets the attention of lawmakers.

What that means is that the games in which things are going wrong, the games that cause the law to be changed, are matches refereed by the most experienced and capable referees on the planet. Invariably, these men are FIFA referees, nominated by their country and confirmed by the authorities in Switzerland. But here is the frightening thought, the one that convinces us that referee training is inadequate....everywhere.

If you look at the most recent changes in the Laws of the Game, almost all of them have come about because *the referees were not doing their job*, or were not aware of techniques that some other referees were using to prevent problems and enforce the law. And as we said in the paragraph above, the officials whose deficiencies caused the laws to be changed were the best and brightest in the world.

The obvious conclusion from this is that *if the top referees are deficient, then something is wrong with the way we train all referees.*

Law changes caused by referees' failings.

Law 1: The Field of Play

Decision 6 of the International F. A. Board specifies that a mark may be made 10 yards from the corner arc to show when the ten-yard requirement is being observed. This came about because referees and linesmen were not enforcing the law, and because some linesmen were not being instructed in the *technique* of stepping in to deal with the encroachment.

Law 5: The Referee

The change in the advantage clause came about because many referees were not trained in the *technique* of using it, and because others were waiting a second or two before making a decision. The law now states what many referees were doing anyway.

Worst of all, in our opinion, is that FIFA is authorizing experiments with two referees because too many referees are not covering the field well and are not aware of where to look to see things happening. This is a deficiency in referee training and promotion, not a signal that the game is too fast for one official, as some will claim. Our chapters on fitness and tactics expose the weaknesses of referee training in these two important aspects of the officials' *technique.*

Law 6: The Assistant Referees

Recent experimentation with electronic notification to the referee when the flag is raised is a statement that referees and linesmen didn't know the *techniques* of three-person communication. Properly trained officials don't miss flags! (See the Guide to Procedures for Referees and Linesmen, published by the United States Soccer Federation.)

Law 7: The Duration of the Match

The reasons for adding time at the half or at the end of the game are described because many referees didn't know how to time a game. They hadn't been taught the *technique.*

Law 11: Offside

The most significant change in recent years, that of specifying that a player shall be penalized only when he gains an advantage, tells us that too many referees were punishing *position, not involvement.* The new drawings showing how the law is to be applied became necessary for the same reason....except of course, here in the U.S., where the correct application of the law has been taught since the mid-seventies.

Law 12: Fouls and Misconduct

The list of recent changes in this law should be a source of embarrassment to referees worldwide, for the changes show how weak we have been in enforcing a law that gave us discretion to stop these abuses. Who would send off a player for chopping a forward with a goal-scoring opportunity? Who would even caution—let alone send off—a defender who handled to save a goal with his goalkeeper already beaten? And who would dismiss a goalkeeper for preventing a goal by handling outside his area? We are also required to send off a player who endangers an opponent in a foul tackle from behind, but even now, this change is not being enforced uniformly.

Why have there been all the recent experiments with the goalkeepers' steps and the goalkeepers' holding of the ball? Because referees had not been trained in *techniques* of enforcing the laws that were already there for them to use!

Law 13: Free Kicks

The law now states that the signal for an indirect free kick must be maintained until the ball has touched another player or has passed out of bounds. Why wasn't this simple technique taught worldwide in the beginning courses? Why did it take some embarrassing incidents in very public matches for the authorities to realize that referees weren't doing their job?

Even now, after years and years of exhortation for referees to deal with encroachment, there is talk about moving a free kick forward in order to punish players who don't respect the 10-yard distance. Why aren't referees doing what they are supposed to do? (And as we advocate very clearly in Chapters 7 and 14.)

Law 14: The Penalty Kick

Movement by the goalkeeper—albeit only from side to side—is now allowed in recognition that almost no referees in the world enforced the law about movement. What's next—allowing movement forward, because referees do not enforce that? (Remember the kicks from the penalty-mark in the 1999 Women's World Cup final!)

Law 15: The Throw-In

It was the simplest thing in the world for a referee—one who knew the *technique*—to prevent a player from taking a throw from the wrong place, and not to let that encroachment down the line use up any time. But everywhere, the referee wasn't doing it, even at the top matches, and so the law had to be changed to prevent the cheating. Now the throw goes the other way.

Law 16: The Goal Kick

Not too long ago the law was changed to allow placement of the ball anywhere in the goal area, irrespective of where the ball crossed the goal line. Part of the reason was to attempt to speed up play, but part of it was the fact that players would make a game out of delaying the kick by pretending not to know where to place the ball. Referees who did not know the *techniques* needed to prevent this, were the players' accomplices in time-wasting.

Can we argue too, that the granting to coaches the privilege of giving instructions from the sidelines is a consequence of too many referees who lacked the courage or the knowledge of *techniques* to prevent it, as the laws used to require?

Notice how frequently we have used the word "technique" in explaining how referees' deficiencies have provoked changes in the laws. This was a calculated strategy on our part, to emphasize our belief that techniques are what should be taught in referee courses throughout the world, yet regrettably, are often omitted.

Note that we are not saying that *all* the recent changes in the Laws of the Game are the consequence of poor refereeing, for some are ideas to speed up the game and to prevent negative play, such as no longer allowing passing the ball back to the goalkeeper for him to hold (and delay). But as we were writing this list, we couldn't help but cringe at the thought of so many changes being the indirect result of inadequate referee training. But this book may stimulate the powers-that-be to do something about it.

Bibliography:

The details of the two books we specifically mention in this chapter are provided below.

Titles of the numerous other books available on soccer can be most easily obtained from various soccer suppliers, and of course from on-line bookstores.

"Jack Taylor, World Soccer Referee" by Jack Taylor. Pelham Press, London, 1976.

"Give a Little Whistle" by Gordon Hill & Jason Tomas. Souvenir Press, London 1975.

EPILOGUE

Let us begin at the beginning...

Dylan Thomas,
Welsh poet

In this, the final section we write for the book, there are no more words of wisdom, no lectures, no exhortations. There's enough of all those things in the hundreds of previous pages you have been reading. No, all we do here is try to give you some idea of why two research scientists immersed in trying to understand complex biochemistry, and in trying to describe and understand movement of the Earth's crust, chose to spend a great amount of their time running around a field with players who were running around a field chasing a ball that was running around a field. Refereeing would seem to be the very antithesis of our "normal" life.

So our purpose in the next paragraphs is to try to answer—briefly, we're pleased to say—two questions: Why did we start refereeing, and what kept us in it? We are sure that every referee has his or her own story about taking up officiating. Some of the stories will be the usual ones: a parent trying to help out the local youth league; a player forced to retire early because of injury; an irate parent determined to fix the officiating he sees every week. Others will be unique. Whatever *your* reason, we thought that since you have spent many hours with us as we tried to explain our attitude to this wonderful game, you might be interested in ours. And we should add that the details of what happened in between our blowing the whistle for the first time and the last are perhaps the subject of other books.

Ed:

My brother-in-law, Mick, not unlike many males of his generation from Liverpool, is a keen soccer fan. He has been an avid supporter of a certain team—whose name I am unable to write or speak—in that city all his life, attending games both home and away. Whenever our families gather, we inevitably find time to attend a game or watch games on TV together. He frequently comments that watching a game with me is a totally different experience from the one he normally encounters with his other pals. This is because he and his friends are watching the ball, and admiring the skills of the players with the ball, and the sheer beauty of the goals that are scored. By contrast, I am *also* commenting on all kinds of other things that are going on, what the referee is doing, how the players are interacting with the referee, and predicting what is about to happen between two players, usually with a fair degree of accuracy. In our many discussions about the game, he tells me he cannot understand why anyone would even think about becoming a referee, because of all the criticism they come in for. He has frequently made the observation "They cannot win, whatever they do!" So on the one hand he seems to recognize the special insights that refereeing has given me, but on the other wonders why I did it.

I think that this is typical of many people with interests in soccer. They simply do not understand what referees really do and how they get any satisfaction from it. In my sojourn through the referee life-cycle, I was somewhat dismayed to be viewed by players and coaches as *merely* a referee. This is because I never considered myself as *just* a referee. That may have been what I did at the time, but it was only part of my participation in the game.

Prior to becoming a referee, I was a player for many years, playing for enjoyment. I realized during my high school years that although I possessed some of the physical attributes for soccer: size, speed, strength and understanding of the game, I did not have ball skills good enough to make it as a professional player. Furthermore, at home and at school, it was made clear to me that a better guarantee of escaping a working-class existence was to take advantage of the post-WWII opportunities in further education—based on academic ability rather than on wealth and privilege—that were available for the first time to children in England. So I became a recreational player, and concentrated most of my effort on my academic studies. I was fortunate, I suppose, because some of my friends who were extremely good players, but not quite as academically gifted, actually attempted to make soccer their career, but were unable to do so.

I had never really given any thought to refereeing. One of my father's friends from his wartime days in the Coldstream Guards, Malcolm Dixon, had become a Football League referee, and it was always a treat when he came to referee at Liverpool. We would get his complimentary tickets to the best seats in the stadium, (otherwise we normally stood behind one of the goals) and after the match could go into the dressing room area and meet the players. For a 10-year old boy, this was nirvana! I surmise that these events may have had an effect on me subconsciously, but I did not have time to act upon them, being too busy playing and studying. I continued to play throughout high school and University, and even after I actually got a real job. I also kept my interest in the as a spectator and fan. As a player—and this is probably true for most players—I never paid much attention to the referee. I was there to have a good time, and although we played to win it wasn't such a big deal if we didn't. We just shook it off and came back next week.

When I came to Texas, I was initially disappointed to find that as a faculty member, I was ineligible to play on the team at the University. But, the players said, we do need a coach, and so I began my non-playing involvement. I coached the team for six years, with a fair degree of success, and even took a coaching course under famed coach Dettmar Cramer and qualified with a "C" badge! But I was also still playing with local men's amateur teams, one of which, with (although he would say because of) Bob Evans between the posts, won the State Championship. During this time, it became evident, as it does to us all, that time was taking its toll, and I could no longer compete successfully at that level. There were younger players who were faster and fitter than I, which was a new and astonishing experience to me. Also, my academic and research career was reaching a point where I was not able to schedule fixed times for practices and games. Not wanting to give up entirely my involvement in the game, I decided to take up the whistle. Fortunately, there was an NASL club in Dallas, and the League needed local officials, so as well as there being the opportunity to observe professional referees, there was something for me to aim for, which I needed as I have never been one to settle for mere mediocrity.

I took the beginning referee clinic (given by Bob Evans), bought the kit, and went out to referee. I found that, as expected, I immediately enjoyed it, and found a deep satisfaction at being able to help these young boys enjoy a game. I soon progressed through the leagues and referee ranks, and people began to give me compliments about the way I handled the games. But more significantly, I was getting far more out of the process than I had ever imagined. The chance to work as a team with colleagues, to analyze a different aspect of various games, and in general to see others benefit as a result of my efforts were very gratifying.

Runners, mountain climbers, bungee jumpers and other such active people, all report a sense of achieving a mental "high" during their activities, which then spurs them on more and more. I had the same experience during the process of refereeing, particularly in a challenging match. We now know that this pleasurable feeling is caused by production of substances known as endorphins in the brain. These compounds induce a feeling of well-being and happiness, not unlike those of certain recreational drugs (so I am told). Indeed, a dedication to refereeing has often been compared to an addiction, and perhaps this is why those who are not addicted can't understand why people choose to be referees.

I experienced a greater sense of pride after getting into the professional game, and even more when I reached the international level. Interacting with brilliant, world-famous players, with ex-players who were now coaches, earning their respect (even if given begrudgingly) was a delight beyond compare for a man who is still a boy at heart when it comes to soccer. One of my most vivid recollections is that of travelling slowly in a car towards the central stadium in Guatemala City on a Sunday morning, with throngs of people all around us, blocking traffic, walking excitedly in the same direction. We were on our way to officiate at a World Cup preliminary round match, and for these people, it might just as well have been the Final. Three hours before kick off the stadium was full and closed, and fans had climbed into trees and onto the stadium rooftops in order to watch the game. The passion could be felt, providing me with a feeling of anticipation that is difficult to describe.

Many referees have a hard time knowing when to retire, and all too many continue on well past their prime, becoming subjects of derision. And when forced to quit due to age requirements or simply because of not getting any more assignments, they become angry and disaffected. Determined not to let that happen, and wanting to be in control of my own destiny, I prepared myself for the eventuality of retirement, and chose my own date for withdrawing from international soccer. Just as with the sudden withdrawal of the professional league, I missed it terribly at first. But I continued for several more seasons at the local level, before finally retiring completely in 1997. I retired knowing that I had given my best, had travelled the world, met many fascinating characters and made untold numbers of new friends in the extended soccer family. I would not have traded that for anything. My life has definitely been far richer because of refereeing.

And now, thanks to satellite TV and the internet, I still make it a point to follow the progress of my favorite team and to take a keen interest in other competitions such as Champions' League, World Cup and Olympics. And I imagine I will until I draw my last breath!

Bob:

It began with a broken leg, and ended with a worn-out knee, did my career as a referee. Those twenty-eight years started and ended with pain, but Oh! what pleasures and wonderful experiences occupied the time in between.....

In 1964 in Halifax, Nova Scotia, while playing for Keith's Brewery, I ran out to scoop up a ball, but stepped in a hole I didn't see. It held my foot fast while the rest of me went hurtling forward to the ground. All the players and spectators heard a loud crack, and I felt a sharp, momentary pain in my right ankle. As I rolled over—with the ball firmly clutched to my chest, I'm happy to say—I could see my right foot flopping freely off to the side of my leg, with the end of my tibia in the position normally occupied by my heel. The ankle was completely dislocated, and the fibula was broken. Stitches, stainless steel and plaster held it all together for the healing, and crutches kept me upright for months.

It was a year before I could play again, and in the meantime I watched many a match in that same league. One day while venting the usual comments that frustrated and disgruntled players make about officiating, I heard a gentleman beside me ask if I had ever thought about refereeing. No, says I, why would a healthy young bloke do something silly like that when he still has the legs to play? Well, he replied smoothly, with your knowledge of the game and your temperament you might just think about it, and in the meantime here's a set of the Laws you can look at. If you would like to take the test, let me know.

Seduced by the man's obvious insight into my knowledge and character, I took the booklet home and gave it a good read. What a revelation it was! I didn't know half the stuff that was in there, and I have to admit that a lot of it made sense. So, with nothing else to do, I studied the laws, called the man up, and asked to take the test. I passed the exam with flying colors, and so, without training of any sort, without a single piece of advice, I became a qualified referee. Qualified or not, I didn't have a clue!

A few years later, after games here and there, including some college games in Kansas, where I went to graduate school, I moved to Dallas believing that my soccer career—playing, coaching and refereeing—was over. Little did I know that it was only beginning...

The game was rapidly expanding there, and while refereeing in the youth and senior leagues in north Texas, I learned quickly. When I saw another referee make a hash of something, I vowed never to make that same mistake myself. I read everything I could about the business, and then when the opportunity for refereeing a higher brand of soccer came via the need for NASL officials, I knew that this is what I wanted to do. I kept on playing, but after I received my first professional refereeing assignment in 1972, I gave it up to concentrate on officiating. One of my best decisions, that, because a few years later I was on the international panel!

Countries passed by as I travelled with the game: Canada, Bermuda, England, Mexico, Costa Rica, Guatemala, Panama, Honduras, Cayman Islands, Turkey, Japan, Korea, Malaysia. So too did national teams: Peru, Argentina, Australia, Egypt, Morocco, East Germany, Peoples' Republic of China, Canada, Mexico, Nigeria, Panama, Guatemala, Honduras, Costa Rica, Korea, West Germany, Pakistan, North Korea and tiny Nepal. And the best part of all was the great players I got to see up close.

They were wonderful to watch: the elegant Franz Beckenbauer, never caught in possession, knocking the ball forty yards to the foot of a moving teammate; the rock-solid Bobby Moore, always cool and reliable; the mercurial George Best, twisting and turning with the ball at the same time as he gave the referee fits; Johann Cruyff, he of the amazing acceleration and touch, scoring from fifty yards when he caught a goalkeeper at the top of the penalty-area hamming it up for the crowd. I doubt that there will ever be a better shoot-out expert than Cruyff, lifting the ball and then hammering it with top-spin over the top of the goalkeeper. There was one-footed Diego Maradona, but what a left foot! And the incomparable Pele, teasing opponents just with his presence, such was his reputation.

Despite all the great players, I have to say that the most wonderful moment of all was in a stadium in Monterrey, Mexico, with my friends Angelo Bratsis and Ed Bellion—the referee—when Argentina played Mexico in front of a sellout crowd of more than 65,000. The spectators got what they wanted: a fine and entertaining match, for on that day the three of us refereed and ran line as well as any three officials in the world could have done. It was a demonstration that despite our adopted country's reputation as a lesser football nation, we could produce the best.

And our best was given to all the players in all the other games we refereed. For the truth is that for every international match you do, you will do fifty other ones. For me, there was infinite pleasure in walking onto a field with twenty-two strangers all set to play a game, studying them before the match, learning as much about them as I could once the game started, and then coming off at the end with everybody content, and one or two saying: "Thanks, ref!" It is a great feeling.

And since the day I did my last international—this one in the Olympic Stadium in Seoul, Korea—and my last-ever match, an under-12 game in the Dallas Cup, I have only one thing to say: Oh! How I miss it!

INDEX

NOTES

NOTES

For additional resources for the referee, coach or
league administrator contact your local retailer or:

Youth Sports Publishing
7349 Canoga Avenue, Canoga Park, CA 91303
(800) 297-6386